D1558180

DALTON'S GOLD RUSH TRAIL

DALTON'S
GOLD RUSH TRAIL

EXPLORING THE ROUTE OF THE KLONDIKE CATTLE DRIVES

Michael Gates

Copyright © 2012 by Michael Gates

2 3 4 5 6 — 17 16 15 14

All rights reserved. No part of this publication may be reproduced, stored in a retrieval system or transmitted, in any form or by any means, without prior permission of the publisher or, in the case of photocopying or other reprographic copying, a licence from Access Copyright, www.accesscopyright.ca, 1-800-893-5777, info@accesscopyright.ca.

Harbour Publishing Co. Ltd.
P.O. Box 219, Madeira Park, BC, V0N 2H0
www.harbourpublishing.com
Lost Moose is an imprint of Harbour Publishing

Cover collage photographs: Overlooking the Dezadeash River near where it joins the Kaskawulsh River, 1891 / Edward James Glave Collection, 77-32-096, Archives, University of Alaska Fairbank; Jack Dalton, 1898 / MacBride Museum of Yukon History collection 1989-30-132
Maps by S. Daniel, Starshell Maps, 2011
Edited by Elaine Park
Cover design by Teresa Karbashewski
Text design by Mary White
Printed and bound in Canada

 Canada Council for the Arts Conseil des Arts du Canada  BRITISH COLUMBIA ARTS COUNCIL An agency of the Province of British Columbia

Harbour Publishing acknowledges financial support from the Government of Canada through the Canada Book Fund and the Canada Council for the Arts, and from the Province of British Columbia through the BC Arts Council and the Book Publishing Tax Credit.

Library and Archives Canada Cataloguing in Publication

Gates, Michael, 1949–
    Dalton's gold rush trail : exploring the route of the Klondike cattle drives / Michael Gates.

Includes index.
ISBN 978-1-55017-570-7

    1. Dalton Trail (Alaska and Yukon)—History. 2. Alaska—History—1867–1959. 3. Yukon—History—1895–1918. 4. Dalton, Jack, 1856–1944. I. Title.

F909.G38 2012   979.8'03   C2012-900328-X

In memory of Alan Innes-Taylor, who introduced me to the Dalton Trail, opened my eyes to a new way of seeing the world and influenced greatly my decision to make the Yukon my home.

Contents

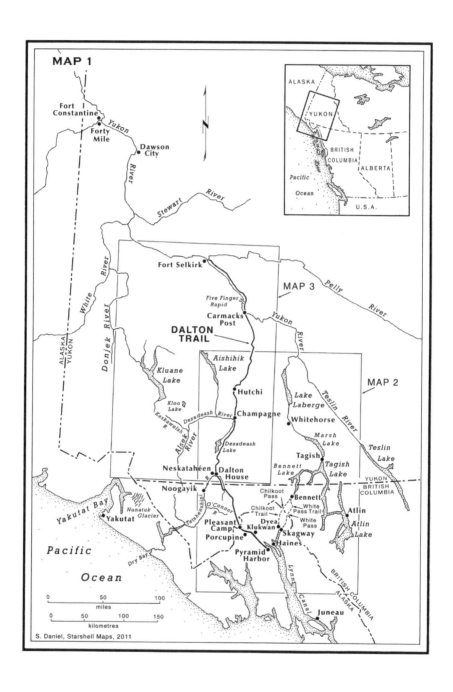

MAP 1

Fort
Constantine
Forty
Mile
Dawson
City

Yukon

River

Stewart *River*

ALASKA
YUKON

BRITISH
COLUMBIA

ALBERTA

Pacific

Ocean

U.S.A.

White *River*

Donjek River

ALASKA
YUKON

Fort Selkirk

MAP 3

Pelly *River*

Five Finger
Rapid
Carmacks
Post

**DALTON
TRAIL**

Yukon *River*

Aishihik
Lake

Kluane
Lake

Hutchi

Lake
Laberge

Teslin River

MAP 2

Kloo
Lake

Kaskawulsh
R.

Dezadeash *River*

Champagne

Whitehorse

Marsh
Lake

Teslin
Lake

Alsek *River*

Dezadeash
Lake

Tagish

Tagish
Lake

Bennett
Lake

YUKON
BRITISH
COLUMBIA

Neskatahéen

Dalton
House

Noogayik

R.

Tatshenshini *R.*

O'Connor

Chilkoot
Pass

Chilkoot
Trail

White
Pass Trail

Bennett

Atlin

Yakutat Bay

Nunatuk
Glacier

Yakutat

Pleasant
Camp
Porcupine

Dyea
Klukwan

White
Pass

Skagway
Haines

Atlin
Lake

Pacific

Ocean

Dry Bay

Pyramid
Harbor

Lynn *Canal*

BRITISH
COLUMBIA
ALASKA

Juneau

0   50   100
miles

0   50   100   150
kilometres

S. Daniel, Starshell Maps, 2011

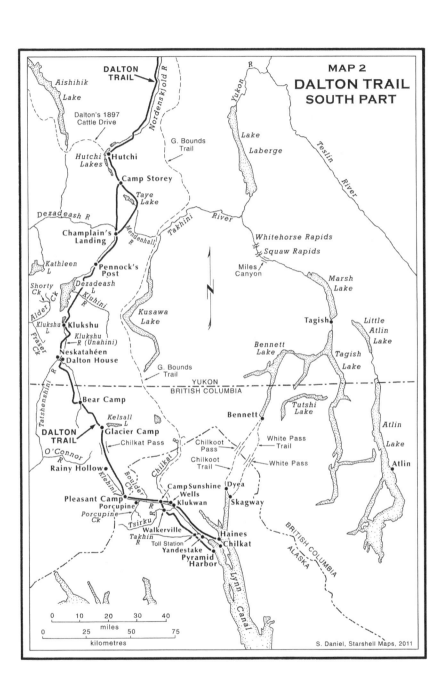

MAP 2
DALTON TRAIL
SOUTH PART

DALTON TRAIL

Aishihik Lake

Dalton's 1897 Cattle Drive

Nordenskjold R

Yukon R

Lake Laberge

Teslin River

G. Bounds Trail

Hutchi Lakes ● Hutchi

Camp Storey

Taye Lake

Dezadeash R

Mendenhall R

Takhini River

Whitehorse Rapids

Squaw Rapids

Champlain's Landing

Kathleen L

Pennock's Post

Miles Canyon

Marsh Lake

Shorty Ck

Dezadeash L

Alder Ck

Kluhini R

Kusawa Lake

Tagish ●

Little Atlin Lake

Klukshu L ● Klukshu

Klukshu R (Unahini)

Fraser Ck

Neskatahéen ● Dalton House

Bennett Lake

Tagish Lake

G. Bounds Trail

YUKON

BRITISH COLUMBIA

Tatshenshini R

● Bear Camp

Kelsall L

Tutshi Lake

Bennett ●

DALTON TRAIL → ● Glacier Camp

Chilkat Pass

Chilkoot Pass

Atlin Lake

O'Connor R

Chilkat R

Chilkoot Trail

White Pass Trail

White Pass

● Atlin

Rainy Hollow ●

Boulder Ck

Klehini R

Camp Sunshine Wells

Dyea

Pleasant Camp ●

Porcupine ●

Porcupine Ck

Tsirku R

● Klukwan

Skagway

BRITISH COLUMBIA

ALASKA

Takhin R

Walkerville

Toll Station

● Haines

Yandestake

Pyramid Harbor

● Chilkat

Lynn Canal

| 0 | 10 | 20 | 30 | 40 |
miles
| 0 | 25 | | 50 | | 75 |
kilometres

S. Daniel, Starshell Maps, 2011

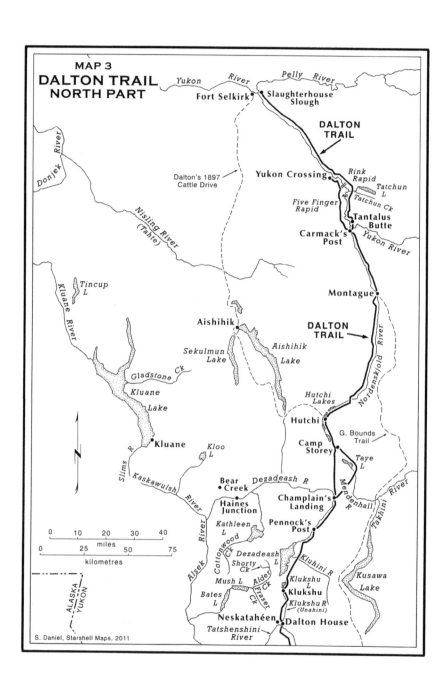

MAP 3
**DALTON TRAIL
NORTH PART**

Yukon River
Pelly River
Fort Selkirk • Slaughterhouse
Slough

**DALTON
TRAIL**

Donjek River

Dalton's 1897
Cattle Drive

Yukon Crossing Rink
Rapid
Tatchun
L
Tatchun Ck
Five Finger
Rapid
**Tantalus
Butte**
**Carmack's
Post**
Yukon River

Nisling River
(Tahte)

Tincup
L

Montague

Kluane River

Aishihik
Aishihik
Lake
**DALTON
TRAIL**
Sekulmun
Lake

Nordenskjold River

Gladstone Ck
**Kluane
Lake**
Hutchi
Lakes
Hutchi
G. Bounds
Trail
Slims R
Kloo
L
•**Kluane**
**Camp
Storey**
Taye
L
Kaskawulsh River
Bear
• Creek
Dezadeash R
Mendenhall R
Takhini River
**Haines
Junction**
**Champlain's
Landing**
Kathleen
L
**Pennock's
Post**

0 10 20 30 40
miles
0   25   50   75
kilometres

Alsek River
Cottonwood Ck
Dezadeash
L
Shorty
Ck
Kluhini R
Kusawa
Lake
Mush L
Alder Ck
**Klukshu
L**
Klukshu
Bates
L
Fraser Ck
Klukshu R
(Unahini)
Neskatahéen•**Dalton House**
ALASKA
YUKON
Tatshenshini
River

S. Daniel, Starshell Maps, 2011

Introduction

For most of the forty years I've lived in the Yukon, I've been looking for a lost path through the wilderness known as the Dalton Trail. I made my first connection with Jack Dalton unknowingly in the summer of 1971 when I went into the North with my newly minted degree in archeology and assisted on an archeological project in the southwest Yukon. One night I camped near the place, as I learned later, where the great pathfinder had slept in 1891. A year later I stayed at and recorded the buildings in the small settlement beside the Tatshenshini River named for him. I learned things that made me want to know more about the man and the trail he borrowed.

In the years that followed I would come across references to Dalton and his trail, but the traces of their story were fragmented and few. I began to wonder who Dalton was; I wondered where his trail went, and what happened along its length. Eventually I became a historical detective. This book is the report of my investigations so far.

"Who has ever heard of the Dalton Trail?" asked one publisher when I suggested the topic. His skepticism was understandable because little has been written about this important part of the Klondike gold rush—and that's the point. For centuries the Native peoples had an important trade route that ran three hundred miles from the Lynn Canal over the Chilkat Pass to the Yukon River. In the last years of the nineteenth century, the frontiersman Jack Dalton—an extraordinary opportunist—usurped control of this trail from its traditional owners and operated it as a toll road during the Klondike gold rush. In the dramatic decade between 1895 and 1905, hundreds of gold-obsessed travellers and entrepreneurs chasing a quick fortune passed over it. Thousands of cattle were herded over what became the longest cattle trail the West has ever seen. Then, after the gold rush, the trail fell into disuse and obscurity.

Now only the old-timers of the Yukon are familiar with the story, although some people who grew up in the area know about the trail, too. Why has the Dalton Trail been neglected for so long? It could be because other places in the Yukon and Alaska linked with the Klondike have had their champions who have kept their stories alive while the Dalton Trail has not been so fortunate. You have to look hard to find it in the official histories. The US National Park Service in Skagway does not include this important trail in its brochures. Its version of the gold rush addresses the Chilkoot and the White Pass Trails—both undeniably important gold rush routes—but ignores the Dalton Trail. Parks Canada does little better with its presentation of the gold rush history in Canada where its mandate is the Chilkoot Trail.

With the exception of the Sheldon Museum in Haines, Alaska, the museums that I have visited in Alaska and the Yukon say little, if anything, about the Dalton Trail. It is overlooked in maps and addressed only superficially in the literature on the gold rush. Pierre Berton, the celebrated author and champion of the Klondike, gives it virtually no mention, even omitting it from his maps of routes to the Klondike. With few exceptions, other historians give it little attention.

The fact that the trail has been ignored was what attracted me first to the subject. Then, as I discovered more about it, I saw a story begging to be told that has as much adventure and pathos as any to come out of the Klondike gold rush. From its early use for aboriginal trade to its prominence during the great stampede, the story of the Dalton Trail was full of enterprise, conflict, survival, hope and disappointment.

Over the years I have been drawn back to the trail many times in both body and spirit. I have hiked over the parts that are still passable, I have boated along it and I have flown over it. My physical rediscovery of the old trail has made it easier for me to recognize and understand the traces of it I found as I trawled through old newspapers, books, maps, police records and Klondike memoirs. Everywhere I looked, on the land and in the libraries and museums, the trail told me a story of cruelty and courage.

I owe much to two other history hunters who have a passionate interest in the Dalton Trail. They are Mark Kirchhoff and Cynthia (CJ) Jones. Both of them have an intense curiosity about the man and his trail. Whenever we get together it seems as though we can talk forever on the topic of the man and the pathway to the interior. They shared with me their knowledge and experiences in their own quests to uncover the Dalton story. My wife, Kathy, who supported me with her patience, was my sounding board for many discussions, and she listened without complaint whenever I enthusiastically reported upon my latest historical find or field trip

In this account I have combined the two dimensions of my search for the Dalton Trail—the personal and the historical. For me, they make one big story and I hope my readers appreciate it that way, too.

Trail Hunting on the Dezadeash River

On a cool May morning in 2008, I woke up to a chorus of bird songs. I was in a tent on the beach at the lower end of Dezadeash (pronounced *Dez-dee-ash*)Lake where in places a shelf of ice still lined the shore. The previous night, taking advantage of a favourable wind, I had crossed the turbulent north end of the lake with my guide, Ron Chambers.

The haunting call of a loon echoed across the waters that now lay calm under the rising sun. I could see an eagle nesting in the top of a tree no more than fifty feet from our tent. It screeched loudly and suddenly a magpie cawed raucously from a nearby tree and a trumpeter swan, swimming upon the glassy lake surface, uttered a low honk. A green-winged teal paddled in front of our camp site, apparently undisturbed by our appearance. We were the only humans in a pristine wilderness. But we knew that once there had been others here, and we were about to hunt for their traces.

Ron and I planned to travel down the Dezadeash River for two days, searching for physical evidence of the fabled Dalton Trail. We also hoped to locate other historical remains along the way. I was looking particularly for signs of the gold seekers known as "the Mysterious Thirty-Six," who had prospected along the Dezadeash valley in 1898. When hiking north of Champagne on the Dalton Trail some years before, I had found a derelict cabin erected by members of this secretive party at a spot they had called Camp Storey, and I wondered if the cabin was still standing. This time I hoped to locate another cabin known as Pennock's Post.

With any luck we would also find remnants of the old trail and determine its current condition. I had heard that the path had been cleared some years ago, but I knew no one who could confirm it was still passable. If we found the trail to be well defined we would return to hike over it later in the summer.

Ron Chambers was an ideal partner for a Yukon history-hunting expedition. Years previously, he had been on the team of the eminent archeologist Richard MacNeish of the National Museum of Canada when MacNeish established the cultural timeline for the southwest Yukon. Ron had worked as a warden for Parks Canada for more than twenty years, and during that time he had travelled the width and breadth of Kluane (pronounced *Kloo-aw-nee*) National Park, whose tall peaks were now casting morning shadows around us.

Ron lived and breathed archeology. He seemed unable to take a step without scanning the ground for signs of past human presence. As we travelled along Dezadeash Lake and explored its shore, Ron began finding small flakes of chert and obsidian, obvious clues to prehistoric tool manufacture, as well as fire-cracked rock and fragments of bone.

The water levels were low and the shallow waters of Six Mile Lake, below Dezadeash Lake, were difficult to navigate. The propeller on our fourteen-foot inflatable boat kept hitting bottom, so we had to row. It was slow going, but calm and quiet. Across the smooth waters in the distance, trumpeter swans floated majestically, treating us to a memorable aural performance. Their sporadic honks reverberated across the lake. When they took flight they were like jumbo jets, slow and lumbering at first, but then gaining speed and elevation. As they sought the air their wing tips would slap the water, leaving a trail of widening circles in the water behind them.

As if to show that they had no fear of us intruding in their domain, they glided gracefully past our awkward little craft, flaunting their freedom. I could almost reach out and touch them as they winged past.

I carried fishing gear—an inexpensive but functional telescoping rod and a small pocket-sized tackle box filled with an assortment of flies and lures. Travellers on the Dalton Trail during the gold rush had reported an abundance of fish in the region's waters, and now I, too, reeled in enough grayling for lunch and dinner. I experienced what they experienced: I took the fish when they offered themselves and enjoyed the bounty at our next meal.

Over our campfire Ron told of being born and raised in the Yukon. He had a curious connection to the trail I was trying to find: one of his grandfathers was Harold "Shorty" Chambers, who once drove livestock along the trail for Jack Dalton. Ron told me that before Shorty came north he had been a horse rustler, living one step ahead of the law on the Canadian prairies. Ironically, Ron's other grandfather, Tom Dickson, was a tall, proud Mountie who had been stationed on the prairies before being sent to patrol the Yukon. Not only were Ron's two grandfathers physical opposites; Tom had patrolled the prairies while Shorty was rustling horses there. Ron said they used to kid each other about this fact.

Not all the artifacts we discovered were ancient. At one location a few hundred yards up a tributary of the Dezadeash River, we spotted the remains of an old truck rusting in the swampy ground and overgrown by the thick vegetation. The truck could have made it to that place only during the winter when the marshy ground was frozen hard. Its reason for being there was an enigma.

A short distance farther downstream from the old truck we located the remains of Pennock's Post. The Mysterious Thirty-Six had constructed this cabin as a temporary cache and rally point, and I knew its approximate location from a description of the cabin I found in a book of the era and from old photographs and a map. It was Ron who spotted the well-concealed remnants.

All that remained of the cabin were a few rotting logs lying on the ground, but by comparing the written descriptions of its location and my photographs from the earlier trip with those taken of the site in 1898, I knew that we had found the right place. I looked at the dry, beetle-killed spruce standing around the site, and I speculated that soon a forest fire would destroy any physical evidence that this place ever existed.

Later we passed the remains of a trapping cabin once used by the well-known Native elder, the late Johnny Fraser, who served as a special constable for the Mounted Police in the early days. Fraser's cabin was collapsing from decades of disuse and riverbank erosion. In order to reach our destination in time for pick-up we had to keep going, so we viewed the cabin only in passing. With sadness I realized that here was another piece of Yukon about to disappear.

At one point as we paddled along the Dezadeash River we went ashore and struck out across the valley in hopes of intercepting a portion of the historic trail, but we found no sign of it. In other areas we could see that the land on either side of the river was low and marshy and not suitable for traversing. If the trail was there, we would have to make another trip to find it.

I went home to Whitehorse frustrated. My lost trail was still lost.

Later that summer I flew over this area in hopes of locating from the air the vestiges of the trail we could not find on the ground. As Ray Wilch, pilot for Alkan Air, circled the region, criss-crossing the valley, I was able to spot a small segment of trail on an exposed treeless hillside for a hundred yards or so. I saw another section of trail along a creek, but it seemed to be running in the wrong direction. If I was going to locate the Dalton Trail, I would have to return to the Dezadeash at ground level.

Over the winter I talked about my plan to try again to find the pathway with a friend and neighbour, Mark Iceton. Mark, who works for the city of Whitehorse, is a volunteer fireman, an avid outdoorsman and hunter. We made plans and agreed that if the weather forecast was favourable, we would take the trip the weekend of May 23, 2009.

At the mouth of the Dezadeash River where Ron Chambers and I had stopped the year before, Mark and I would undertake a more thorough investigation of the terrain. All the old maps showed that the trail passed between the mountains and the Dezadeash River at this point. It had to be there somewhere. I reasoned that if we walked all the way from the bank of the Dezadeash River to the mountain, a mile or more distant, we would have to intersect the trail at some point.

We went up the river from Champagne and set up camp at the chosen spot. The following morning we hiked off toward the distant mountains. At first we encountered terrain typical of the Dezadeash shoreline: low-lying marshy ground consisting of swamp, filled with grassy tussocks. We cross-cut the east side of the valley, hiking in marsh, up and down hills, stumbling through dense willow, over fire-killed deadfall and across beaver-dammed creeks.

The gold rush accounts of the trail refer to fires all along the route. Were the rotting charcoal-coated stumps that we saw everywhere the remains from these old fires? If so, then the forest had grown in again over the past 110 years.

Our progress was frustratingly slow because of the terrain and many obstacles that we had to circumvent. We wondered if, after 110 years, the trail would be visible at all. We discussed the behaviour of cattle along the trail. Would the animals walk across an open landscape in single file, or would they spread out and walk in a large fan? If they fanned out, would they leave any lasting mark on the landscape at all? During the gold rush, cattle fared well on the trail, but horses did not. Perhaps we would know we had found the historic track if we found the remains of one of these dead horses.

Several hours later we returned to the shore of the Six-Mile Lake, some distance above our camp. There we found the signs of a trail. Back in camp, I referred to the study notes I had compiled and sure enough, a government surveyor had commented that the trail skirted the lake at this point.

The trail had not survived over the years in this marshy and overgrown area. In more elevated and drier terrain it was incised and easy to see, but in the low-lying sections, the imprint disappeared in the moss, willows and muskeg.

Having found the trail, we knew our luck was improving. We followed the track back to our camp and then continued north down the river, where it was still well marked and visible after more than a century. The path would disappear into swamp and then reappear where we reached the higher ground beyond.

Downstream, at Pennock's Post, we walked away from the Dezadeash River in a straight line. At a distance of several hundred yards we again found a well-defined trail leading in both directions. We followed it for a mile to make sure it wasn't just a game trail.

Now more confident, we travelled back down the Dezadeash to the boat launch just above Champagne. There we found the trail again and followed it south toward the cleft through which we had just floated on the river. We moved first along an exposed sunny hillside, but then the trail took us down into the forested valley bottom. The trail was well defined, but obstructed by deadfalls and new growth. Though not used actively in recent times, it obviously had been a well-used trail in the past.

About a mile along the trail we found a horse skull lying by the path. Nearby lay a bleaching pelvis. I had found my dead horse. And I felt that I had completed one part of my quest for the Dalton Trail.

I got back to Whitehorse to find that a collection of photos had arrived from the Bancroft Library at Berkeley, California. They depicted a cattle drive along the Dalton Trail in 1898. Some of the images seemed to answer the questions that Mark and I had posed to each other about the movement of cattle along the trail. In one photo the beasts are moving across a treeless landscape, fanned out, but it is easy to see a pathway incised into the earth in the foreground. In another photo they are walking down a tree-covered hillside, single file, along a path. In the foreground it is clear that trees have been cut down and laid across the trail.

The trail visible in these photographs is likely the one whose imprint we followed along the Dezadeash River. Today in my mind's eye I still see the trail as I found it in 2009, overgrown and unused. In some places it is clear and easy to follow; in others, it is hidden in the moss and wetlands. Perhaps, with a little effort, it could be made passable again, and other seekers could find and follow it.

I could almost reach out and touch the swans as they winged past. MICHAEL GATES COLLECTION

CHAPTER 1

The Ancient Trail

This is the story of two lands, and the trail that runs through them. One land is coastal Alaska, bordered by the waters of the Pacific Ocean but sheltered from most of its violence by a buffer zone of coastal islands. The Tlingit people who have lived on the coast for millennia enjoy a mild moist climate and the productivity of this littoral region where an abundant off-shore fishery is complemented by the rich upstream migrations of eulachon and salmon. Before the coming of Europeans, Tlingit villages dotted the coastline. Behind them, the coastal mountains created a formidable barrier to the winds and weather, as well as to anyone contemplating an exploration beyond them. The St. Elias Mountains that march north from present-day Haines, Alaska, contain several of the tallest peaks in North America. Their summits are shrouded in permanent snow and huge glaciers and they encompass the largest non-polar icefield anywhere in the world, a place so emblematic of endless winter that it has been designated a World Heritage Site by UNESCO. The icefields are not an easy place to live in or even pass through. The only breach in the wall of mountains opens where the Alsek River drains through a gash in the rocky wall into Dry Bay, near Yakutat, Alaska. In either direction from the river gorge there is nothing but ice or small rivers draining off the flank of the coastal mountains into the ocean.

Beyond the mountains in the interior of the continent is the present-day Yukon, home of the Southern Tutchone, who are a branch of the Athapascan people. Their traditions tie them to the area from time immemorial; archeologists can trace human occupation in the region twelve thousand years or more into the past. Life in the interior is more challenging than on the coast. Shielded by the St. Elias Mountains, the Yukon interior is a drier, less abundant land, yet it is rich with moose and caribou and the salmon that run up the Alsek and Tatshenshini rivers to their headwaters. Dozens of lakes, large and small, spread out between low ranges of mountains and hills. In some places the vistas are breathtaking. Unlike the coast, the interior is a place of climatic extremes: hot summers with weeks of continuous daylight give way quickly to long winters, the coldest temperatures on the continent and an unrelieved twilight.

Both landscapes offer resources to nourish and support the people who live there, but their resources have always been different. It was only natural that exchanges between them would enrich the lives of those living on both sides of the mountains. It is difficult to pinpoint the time when the people of the coast first made contact with the people of the interior, but they both have stories that describe the first meeting. According to Tlingit accounts, the first coast-dweller to encounter the interior people was a man named Qakē'q!utê from Hoonah on Chichagof Island on the Alaskan panhandle.[1] A survivor of an epidemic that had devastated his entire village, Qakē'q!utê fled inland, climbing cliffs and crossing glaciers for ten days before arriving at the Alsek River. He travelled upriver to the country of the Alsek headwaters where he encountered people whose ways and speech were strange to him. From a hidden vantage point in the riverside bushes, he observed the inefficient manner in which they were catching fish. He waited until they went away then went down to the river with two nets, which he soon filled with fish. He piled his catch on the shore and hid again. When the Athapascans returned and found the fish, they were perplexed. They sought advice from a shaman who performed his rituals and eventually advised them to hang ". . . all kinds of food around there." When Qakē'q!utê did not eat the food, they left a copper spear. This he accepted. Thus Tlingit and Athapascans established contact, and the fisherman from the coast taught the inland people how to fish using nets or traps. When the salmon started to run, he showed the Athapascans how to spear them efficiently and how to make salmon traps. He taught them to prepare the salmon by smoking it so that they had enough to last them through the winter and he showed them how to preserve berries, as well. He demonstrated how to cook hemlock bark in skunk cabbage and how to prepare certain roots. In exchange, the Athapascans gave him a wife, or wives (depending upon the account), two copper spears and the skins of moose, marten and beaver. This was the beginning of trade between the peoples of the coast and the interior.

After a lengthy stay in the interior, the Tlingit refugee returned home, taking some of the interior people with him, loaded with coppers (and presumably other items to trade), to meet his own people. However, his home village sent them away, so the travellers went on to the village of L!ūk!nAxAdî. According to one account,

> The L!ūk!nAxAdî saw that they had coppers, and took them away. Then the L!ūk!nAxAdî said, "You are going to be our people." Each man took a man [Athapascan] out of the canoe and said: "You will be my friend." That was the way they used to do. They would take away a person's goods and give them just what they wanted to. The Athapascans were foolish enough to allow it.[2]

Southern Tutchone people at Champlain's Landing (Champagne), 1898. ALASKA STATE LIBRARY, FRED HOVEY PHOTOGRAPH COLLECTION, P352-70

The story adds that the people from the first village realized later what they had lost by sending the Athapascans away, and it concludes with a lesson about the value of trade: "Therefore, when a person is unlucky nowadays, they say of him, 'He sent the Athapascans away.'"[3]

An Athapascan myth recounts the first meeting differently. In the Southern Tutchone version, at a point in the distant past the Tlingit came up the Tatshenshini River to the village of Noogaayík (now long abandoned), where they noticed wood chips floating down the river. Curious about their origin, the Tlingit went farther upriver and encountered the interior people for the first time.[4] To the Southern Tutchone, the Tlingit looked impoverished. According to the story as told by Southern Tutchone elder Annie Ned, "They've got nothing, those Tlingit people, just cloth clothes, groundhog clothes. Nothing! Goat and groundhog, that's all."[5] The two peoples established a trade in which the Southern Tutchone provided the Tlingit with moccasins, parkas and mittens made from soft, finely tanned skins, as well as babiche (leather lacing) and sinew for sewing. In return the Tlingit brought in trade items from the coast, which after European contact included knives, axes, needles, sugar, tea, tobacco, cloth and guns. The price the Tlingit put on a rifle was a stack of Tutchone furs as high as the top of the barrel when stood on end.

The coastal Tlingit also exchanged goods with other Tlingit who lived along the Lynn Canal and the Chilkat Inlet. Although the Tlingit of Dry Bay and Yakutat could reach the Tlingit of Chilkat Inlet by a long boat journey around the coast, the tribes developed an alternate route overland that stretched from Dry Bay into the mountains, up the Alsek and Tatshenshini rivers, then up the O'Connor River and over the continental divide to the Klehini River and Chilkat Inlet. By this route, the Chilkat Tlingit exchanged furs for copper from the Tlingit people of Yakutat, eventually establishing trading settlements at places such as Noogaayík on the Tatshenshini River, then later at Neskatahéen, farther upstream.[6] Located just east of the divide along this trail, the Chilkat Tlingit village of Klukwan was positioned perfectly to benefit by trade, and its people flourished. Once trade was established between the two peoples, lasting partnerships between individuals often were cemented by intermarriage. Some Tlingit moved permanently to the interior. The Chilkat Tlingit regarded the area in the interior as far as the

Pelly and White rivers as a kind of trading hinterland within their sphere of influence, and they held sway over it with complex trading relationships, regulated trading itineraries and well-established rendezvous locations. Their extensive network of trails in the interior of the Yukon provided opportunity for the exchange of goods, access to various resources during the seasonal round, social contact and interchange between small, highly mobile family units. The Chilkat trade network was widespread by the mid-nineteenth century, although it became more centralized at Neskatahéen toward the end of the century. By then, the Southern Tutchone were acting as the middlemen for Chilkat trade farther into the interior.

The Chilkat were aggressive traders who were able to assume a dominant position in the trade network of the Pacific Northwest because of their advantageously located home villages. Certain clans controlled specific passes to the interior; for instance, the Ganaxtedi'h, a raven moiety clan, and the Dåklåwedi'h, an eagle moiety clan from Klukwan, assumed ownership of the trail to the interior via Kusuwa Lake.[7] They were fiercely protective of their monopoly, and while they might invite trading partners to accompany them to the coast, they would not allow these trading partners to exchange goods directly with European traders. Similarly, Europeans were barred from any access to the interior (although this control started to weaken and collapse toward the end of the nineteenth century.)

The extent and force of the Chilkat monopoly in the early nineteenth century is illustrated by the Chilkats' destruction of the Hudson's Bay Company trading post at Fort Selkirk. The fort stood on the banks of the Yukon River opposite the confluence with the Pelly, more than three hundred miles from the Chilkat trading centre at Klukwan. Fort Selkirk was one of the most isolated trading posts of the entire HBC network and its supply line was stretched thin. It never had the rich abundance of trade goods that were available at other posts more centrally located, yet it offered the inland Southern Tutchone an alternative to trading with the Chilkat Tlingit from the coast.

The Chilkat were aware of this fact, and uncomfortable with the competition, so they decided to act. In July of 1852, the Chilkat warrior Kohklux, also known as (X)ša.txíčx (a name sometimes anglicized to Shotridge or Shotrich) departed from Klukwan with a party of raiders led by his father.

They canoed up the Chilkat River, portaged over the summit to Kusawa Lake and crossed to the Takhini River, which flows from Kusawa, eventually joining the Yukon a few miles below the Whitehorse Rapid. From there they skirted the shore of Lake Laberge and entered the Yukon River, down which they floated until they reached Fort Selkirk.

Robert Campbell, the head trader at Fort Selkirk, had only a handful of men at the Hudson's Bay trading post and he knew that there was going to be trouble from the moment twenty-seven Chilkat warriors landed below the fort on August 20. The Chilkats outnumbered and outgunned Campbell's party and it quickly became apparent that the lives of the European occupants of the settlement were at risk. Soon Campbell was staring down the barrel of a loaded musket, and as he struggled against several of the Chilkat he narrowly avoided being stabbed. All the company traders could do was watch helplessly as the intruders pillaged the post and threatened the lives of its inhabitants. Campbell deployed his staff in several key buildings that evening in the hope of protecting their supplies, but marauders wandered around the site all night, boldly getting into mischief. Campbell didn't get much sleep, and the following day things got worse.

On August 22 Campbell and his party fled the post by canoe and put ashore a few miles below. When they returned on foot a day later they found the trading post abandoned. What supplies had not been taken away lay strewn about, destroyed. The buildings had been vandalized and the post was now unlivable. Campbell contemplated pursuing the raiding party, but when he sought assistance from the local Athapascans, they decided not to antagonize their traditional trading partners. With the trading post destroyed, the Athapascans could see they would be dependent once again upon the Chilkat for their trade goods.

Campbell left Fort Selkirk shortly after the Chilkat raid, making his way back over the Hudson's Bay Company trade route to his headquarters thousands of miles away, expecting that the company would give him the support to re-provision the post, but this was denied. The great trading company did not return to Fort Selkirk until well into the twentieth century. Thirty years after the raid, all that remained of the post were the decaying ruins of the stone fireplaces. The Chilkat were thus able to extend their control over trade in the southern Yukon for another forty years.

Not much remained of Fort Selkirk when it was visited by George Dawson in 1887. G.M. DAWSON / LIBRARY AND ARCHIVES CANADA / C-000006

After the raid of 1852, the reputation of Kohklux became formidable among both Native people and Europeans. Tall and broad-chested, he was universally acknowledged as the greatest warrior and diplomat of all the tribes of the Pacific Northwest. One European observer described him as

> a chief of advanced and liberal notions, a high-strung, imperious old fellow, . . . [with]a fine countenance, marred only by the wound on his cheek, which was received at the hands of one of his own tribe during some internecine troubles. His assailant held a revolver to . . . [his] head and when the chief looked scornfully at it, the trigger was snapped. Weak powder prevented the ball from inflicting any more serious injuries than to enter his cheek and tear away a few teeth. Kloh-kutz [Kohklux] swallowed his teeth and handed the bullet back to his assailant with a fine gesture, saying: 'You cannot hurt me. See!'[8]

Apparently undeterred by the fact that three Chilkat men had been shot in recent months, Kohklux paid a visit to Sitka in 1869. While there, he was put into jail by Sitka's commander, General Jefferson C. Davis. During his incarceration he had an eventful meeting with an American scientist, George Davidson, who negotiated the chief's freedom. In return for the release of Kohklux, the chief agreed to provide safe passage and accommodation for Davidson and his party at Klukwan to make observations of a solar eclipse.

According to the Sitka *Alaskan* newspaper:

> At the village the principal Chief Kohklux had his large house prepared for the party and furnished fish and food gratuitously during their stay. Their reception by the Indians was friendly.... On the 7th of August, the weather was cloudy but the different phases of the eclipse were observed and the time of the beginning of totality well determined. The rose-coloured flames were splendid and distinctly visible to the unassisted eye.... The Indians were intensely scared and shut themselves in their houses as the darkness increased, and at totality not a word could be heard in the great village. As the light reappeared they came out, and by degrees approached the observatory but looked upon the coast survey party as the men who made the sun 'hiyou sick.'[9]

Kohklux and Davidson, two men from strikingly different cultures, reached a level of mutual respect. Of Kohklux, Davidson reported: "In our future relations we found him truthful and absolutely honest. With all the instruments, tools, camp equipage, stores, carried and handled by his people, we never lost a single article during our stay at his strong village."[10] Having impressed Kohklux as a powerful "medicine man" who had made the sun grow dark, Davidson shared the secret of the eclipse, writing some details of it on a board covered by black and red designs. Kohklux valued this gesture highly. To reciprocate, the great chief shared with Davidson certain knowledge of the overland route that he and the other Chilkats had taken to get to and from Fort Selkirk seventeen years before. This was the same trail that would one day approximate the Dalton Trail.

Kohklux drew two maps. The second, larger one, drawn in pencil on the back of a large navigational chart measuring forty-three by twenty-seven inches, took Kohklux and his two wives two or three days to create. This was the first time he had ever used pencil and paper. Upon this map Davidson, at their direction, wrote over one hundred place names in his crude phonic rendering of the Tlingit terms. The map showed how, after the destruction of the trading post at Fort Selkirk, the raiding party had gone back up the Yukon River to the mouth of the Nordenskjold River that they followed south until they reached the village of Hutchi. From there they paralleled the Dezadeash River, proceeding to Klukshu. Beyond this point they followed Klukshu Creek to its junction, at Neskatahéen, with the Tatshenshini River, then went over the upland, across the Chilkat Pass and down the Klehini River back to Klukwan.

By the end of the century this route had become the Dalton Trail, a major thoroughfare for European transport to the Klondike, but the Kohklux map itself served no useful purpose for gold rush travellers as its secrets were not revealed to the world until 1901, by which time the route was well known and the great gold stampede had already subsided.[11] At the time of its creation in 1869, however, Kohklux was sharing his closely guarded knowledge of this trail with the man whose control over the sun had impressed him so.[12] Despite his revelation to Davidson of the Chilkat overland route into the interior and the Yukon River, it remained a secret unknown to other Europeans, and no white man set foot on it for another two decades.

By then the incessant push of colonial exploration was exposing inexorably the mysteries of the northwest corner of the continent. In 1880 white travellers gained access to the Yukon interior via the Chilkoot Pass to the east of Klukwan at the head of the Lynn Canal,[13] but the European intrusion into the fiercely guarded Chilkat region to the west did not occur until 1882. The first white man to gaze into the interior Yukon plateau from the Chilkat Pass was a scientist. In 1881 the Geographical Society of Bremen, Germany, appointed two teachers of natural science, Aurel and Arthur Krause, to undertake a study of the natural history of the Chukchi Peninsula of Siberia and the northwest coast of Alaska.[14] They arrived at Haines Mission, site of present-day Haines, in late December of 1881. Over the next several months they gathered natural history specimens and studied the Tlingit people who lived there. Aurel returned to Germany after four months and compiled the notes they had taken into an authoritative text on the Tlingit culture.

Arthur stayed on until the fall of 1882, collecting more specimens and making more observations. During the summer he made excursions over the Chilkoot and Chilkat passes. To tackle the latter route he engaged the services of one of the younger sons of Kohklux as well as a Tlingit man, named Jelchtelch, to guide him over the Chilkat Pass to the interior of the Yukon. The three men departed Klukwan June 20, proceeding northwest up the Klehini River. Within a week they had ascended the summit of the Chilkat Pass and made some progress into the interior. Arthur Krause was busy making observations and collecting specimens as they moved along. A short distance north of Kelsall Lake the three men turned east and ascended another pass from which they could look west toward the Tatshenshini Valley; they then descended to a small lake called Danaaku from which the Kusawa River drains north to Kusawa Lake. From a hill near Danaaku Lake, Krause looked north and saw the southern end of Kusawa Lake in the distance. Jelchtelch told him that he was the first "gutzgakon" (stranger from far away) who had ever laid eyes on this body of water.

Because they were acting counter to the strong proprietary traditions of the Chilkat, the guides may have felt some discomfort at this moment, perhaps suspecting that it presaged the inevitable surrender of Chilkat control of access to this remote country. Kohklux's son suddenly became ill and the party was forced to stop. The delay seemed to please Jelchtelch, who had become increasingly reluctant to advance as they travelled farther along the trail to Kusawa Lake. The following day Krause left the others in camp and explored the vicinity on his own. When he returned at day's end he found the two guides had retreated to another camp a short distance back up the trail, and closer to their home at Klukwan. Krause surrendered any intention of going farther into the interior. The young boy's condition seemed remarkably improved at this camp, so they returned to Klukwan, reaching the village July 2, and Krause arrived back at the Haines Mission later in the day.

Krause's accomplishment was significant because this small party had reached the interior Yukon using one of the traditional Chilkat routes of access. It is important to note that there are alternate routes that lead to the interior from Klukwan: one proceeds up the Chilkat River and across a glacier to the east side of Kusawa Lake. Another proceeds north from Kelsall Lake to Neskatahéen while a third reaches the Tatshenshini River below Neskatahéen via the O'Connor River. By virtue of their position in the Chilkat Valley, the people of Klukwan controlled all of them. While their control over these routes and their trade to the interior was secure for the moment, Krause's trip was the harbinger of change. The ancient trade trail to the Yukon River would soon take on a different role and a new name.

Crossing Paths

I came into the North for the first time early in the summer of 1971. I was twenty-two years old, a recent graduate of the archeology program at the University of Calgary and I had left a well-paying job in a brewery for a chance of wilderness adventure. Jim Bennett, an archeology graduate student, had hired me as an assistant to, among other things, help him in his hunt for a source of obsidian in the Alsek River area in the Yukon. Jim knew from geological reports and maps that the glass-like volcanic rock was present in the region. What he hoped to find at the obsidian source was a prehistoric quarry nearby. Obsidian was highly prized by early peoples for the manufacture of tools and weapons, and old quarries in other regions had proved to be rich archeological sites.

Our initial attempt to get to the target area was a failure. We inflated our Zodiac boat and launched it into the Dezadeash River near the bridge at Haines Junction. We made quick progress in the rapidly rushing water, but several miles downstream Jim was inspired to turn the boat around and see what the return trip would be like. In order to make headway against the strong current he had to operate the motor at full throttle. The stern dug into the water under the power of the motor and the propeller caught on the gravel bottom, breaking a shear pin. We stopped to replace the broken pin and tried again, with a similar result.

"This isn't going to work, Mike," he told me. "If we go down river where

I would like to be, we won't have enough shear pins or enough fuel to get us back to the Junction."

We limped back into Haines Junction under low throttle and put the Zodiac away, realizing we would have to walk to the target area. A few days later we shouldered our heavy backpacks and left the Alaska Highway near the MacIntosh Lodge at Bear Creek, heading south toward the Alsek River. A stray white dog adopted us and tagged along. We were glad of his company, reasoning that he could fend for himself and he might alert us to the presence of bears. As it turned out, the country was for the most part open rocky ground with scattered sparse vegetation. We could see for a considerable distance in all directions as we moved toward the gap between the tall mountains that confined the Dezadeash River. When we glimpsed grizzlies, all we saw of them was their vanishing posteriors.

The weather was cool, dry and windy, ideal for hiking. As we entered the broad pass to the Alsek River we could look far up on the mountainside and see successive windrows of rock clinging to the slopes. They were old beach lines, some dating back thousands of years, clear proof that the sporadic advances and retreats of the Lowell Glacier occasionally have created lakes in this valley. Along the way on our first day of walking we found a derelict boat decaying on an old beach line some distance above the present channel. Its design appeared to belong to the early twentieth century, and its stranded location away from the modern water line suggested to us that a damming of the Alsek River had occurred not long after 1900.

On the first night of our hike Jim and I camped beside the water. Years later I learned that the campsite was not far from the spot where the English explorer, Edward Glave, and the Alaskan pathfinder, Jack Dalton, slept after their perilous crossing of the Dezadeash River in 1891.

On the second day Jim and I arrived at a point from which we could overlook the Kaskawulsh River coming in from the west to join the Dezadeash. Here before us was the beginning of the Alsek River. Below, we could see where the Kaskawulsh spread out into a wide valley bottom and split into a dozen meandering channels. Beyond were the peaks that we wanted to explore. We realized that even if we were able to make our way across the muddy flat straddling the valley bottom, we would not have enough food to carry us to our destination and back. After discussing the matter and exploring various options, which we rejected one by one, we turned back in disappointment.

A few days later we took another exploratory trip, this time up Sheep Creek, one of the tributaries feeding the Slims River not far from its mouth. Just before making this trip I had climbed to the top of Sheep Mountain (which is known in the Southern Tutchone language as Tachäl Dhäl). The view from the top was spectacular, with the Kaskawulsh glacier twisting and turning between the mountains in the distance, but the following day my muscles paid the price of my climb. I was not yet in condition for this kind of exertion. Progress up Sheep Creek carrying a full pack was not easy. My legs were so stiffened that I could walk only if I locked my knee, swayed slightly and swung my leg forward, then repeated the action with the opposite limb.

Other archeologists proved later that the mountains that beckoned us from across the Kaskawulsh River did contain important obsidian quarries for early hunters as Jim Bennett had predicted, and the trail that we followed

One of the Gladstone Lakes, north of Kluane Lake. Tools 8,000 years old were found preserved in snow banks not far from where this photograph was taken.
MICHAEL GATES COLLECTION

up Sheep Creek was identified subsequently as a route traditionally used by the First Nation people of this region

Another trip took us into the mountains north of Kluane Lake. We were able to hitch a ride on a helicopter taking supplies to a mining camp in the hills just beyond where we wanted to go. After the chopper receded in the distance, we were left alone to set up a camp and explore the mountains and valleys nearby, looking for evidence of ancient hunters. When we completed our reconnaissance in this area we hiked out of the mountains and returned to our base camp at the south end of Kluane Lake.

To reach these various locations we travelled routes that had been used for centuries by people of the First Nations, and at many points we crossed the path taken at the end of the nineteenth century by Glave and Dalton, the first non-Native explorers to record their travels in the Yukon interior. In the Slims River area we had chosen a camp site near the spot where Glave and Dalton had rested. From the top of Sheep Mountain I had overlooked the scene of the near-fatal sinking on Kluane Lake of Edward Glave and Jack Dalton in their borrowed canoe. Somewhere near the end of the lake as we returned from our Gladstone expedition, we crossed the southward route that Glave and Dalton followed after leaving Nanchay's camp in 1891.

In 2006 I came back into this region while working for Parks Canada. With a party of First Nation workers and Parks Canada employees, I examined a cluster of brush shelters that had been found a few miles up the Slims River valley. Here again I crossed paths with the explorers Glave and Dalton. When travelling through this country more than a hundred years earlier, Glave reported seeing numerous "rude huts of tamarack boughs used as winter camps by hunters and trappers."[15] His words described exactly what I found on my excursion.

The memories of these trips, as well as my Tatshenshini pack horse adventure of 1972, were vital to me as I assembled the story of the Dalton Trail. My visits to the places where Glave and Dalton passed through gave a vivid reality to the story Glave told. They made the narrative rise from the pages and assume for me a tangible three-dimensional form.

CHAPTER 2

1890–1891: Glave and Dalton—
A Tale of Two Explorers

Native people maintained their control of the trade routes through the southern Yukon interior and northwest British Columbia until 1888, when foreign adventurers began an inexorable penetration of the area. The discovery of coal on the Alaskan coast at Yakutat drew the attention of speculators to the Alsek and Tatshenshini rivers, while gold seekers, encouraged by the productivity of the fields along the Fortymile River in the Yukon interior, began to wonder about the mineral potential of the country to the south. For the next sixteen years, speculative interest in the Yukon interior would become intense.

Europeans first penetrated the interior of British Columbia and Tatshenshini River from Klukwan in 1888; then in the winter of 1889–90, three men in search of gold travelled inland and explored the Tatshenshini River together.[16] William Meehan and two Norwegian companions, Thomas Johnson and Lewis Lund, crossed a pass in the coastal mountains and dragged their sled down the Tatshenshini River to the confluence with a river called Kla-tsa-kult, possibly the Alsek, which joins the Tatshenshini from the north. They worked there through the winter but found no sign of their longed-for bonanza. When the snow melted in the spring they abandoned most of their equipment and headed back to the coast, packing their remaining supplies on their backs. Meehan chose to carry a lighter pack and moved quickly, outdistancing the Norwegians and arriving first at the Klehini River.

On the Klehini he encountered a small party of three men, including British explorer Heywood Seton-Karr, who were slowly making their way up the river. Seton-Karr, who already had made three trips into Alaska, was intrigued by the uncharted interior from which Meehan was emerging. On one of his previous trips Seton-Karr had joined Lieutenant Frederick Schwatka (US Army) and Professor Libbey from Princeton College in an unsuccessful attempt to climb Mount St. Elias. On this new expedition he was hoping to ascend the Chilkat Pass and explore the valleys beyond.

Meehan indicated he had been over this route and told the Englishman of a small Chilkat trading village "just over the pass." He may have been referring to the native village of Neskatahéen or one of the other villages farther down the Tatshenshini River. Listening to Meehan, Seton-Karr reconsidered the difficulties of the route when he realized he could not afford to pay Chilkat packers to haul his supplies, and he decided to go back to the coast.[17] Meehan joined him on the return journey, unaware that behind him his fellow gold seekers would come to grief. Thomas Johnson drowned in the Klehini. Lund survived and then struggled on alone to the coast.

Seton-Karr was not alone in the attempt to breach the Coast Mountains from Klukwan in the spring of 1890. Another party had been sponsored by *Frank Leslie's Illustrated Newspaper* in New York City. They were better financed than Seton-Karr and had engaged a Chilkat guide and thirty Chilkat packers to haul their equipment

Edward Glave had several years experience in the Congo and had written a book about the experience before he came to Alaska in 1890.
EDWARD JAMES GLAVE COLLECTION, ARCHIVES, UNIVERSITY OF ALASKA FAIRBANKS

over the mountains. The two parties knew about each other and by mutual consent agreed that if Seton-Karr went up the Klehini River, the other group would choose an alternate route, up the Chilkat River. E. Hazard Wells, the leader of the newspaper-sponsored group, was a journalist from Cincinnati. Alfred Schanz, an astronomer, was the party's scientist. Edward Glave, an Englishman, had spent several years in equatorial Africa, some of them working for famed British explorer Henry Morton Stanley, before being recruited to join this expedition. Three other members of the party were hired because of their previous Alaskan experience. One was the Chilkat guide Indiank, who had accompanied Frederick Schwatka on a widely publicized expedition down the Yukon River in 1883. The other knowledgeable Alaska hands, hired in San Francisco, were Frank Price and Jack Dalton. Dalton was the man destined to open up one of the great trails into the Klondike gold fields.

Dalton was an ideal choice to accompany the Leslie party into the unmapped regions of Alaska and the Yukon. He was a consummate outdoorsman who had acquired numerous skills in his three and a half decades. Though short and stocky, he was powerfully built and had great stamina. Born the third child of sixteen in an Irish Catholic immigrant family, he had been a railway labourer and a muleskinner, worked with cattle and horses most of his life and had travelled widely throughout the western United States. He had come to Alaska in 1885 on the run from the law after what he vaguely referred to as "shooting scrapes" in Oregon. In 1886 Dalton was one of a number of local guides hired by Frederick Schwatka to accompany him on the Mount St. Elias expedition. In 1888 Dalton had prospected successfully for coal deposits at the head of Yakutat Bay. By the time he was recruited to the newspaper party, Dalton had a reputation as a man who got things done and did not wilt under the challenges of working in uncharted reaches of Alaska. He did not draw attention to himself, but exuded an easily discernible charisma, according to his friends and associates.

The Chilkat Trail

The group of six adventurers departed Klukwan on May 12 and within a couple of days got a taste of what it was like to hire Chilkat packers. At the first opportunity the packers discarded undesirable weight along the trail.

Glave and Dalton picked up behind them, with comical results. In his narrative of the expedition, Edward Glave described what happened:

> The Indians perceiving our considerate attention immediately took advantage of it and left out from their loads little articles which were cumbersome and awkward to carry. Upon gathering these relics together, we found we had to bring up the rear loaded with a queer combination of miscellaneous property. Dalton carried three pairs of snow-shoes, one large gold pan, one bread pan, and four large saucepans slung around his waist, all about the same size, so that they could not be placed one within the other. These culinary implements, combined with his blanket and rubber sheet, rifle, revolver, and ammunition, formed a goodly load. A large pail, a big saucepan, a teapot, blanket and rubber sheet, small camera, books, heavy overcoat and a canvas-back duck formed my share. We had three miles to travel with this assortment, and a clattering of pans and kettles attending our every step sounded like a band of the Salvation Army.[18]

After they ascended the Chilkat Valley and crossed a large ice field, the men were trapped in a storm on the side of a mountain for three days. When it abated, they crossed the summit and, probably by way of the Takhini River, reached Kusawa Lake. Wells, the expedition leader, assumed naming privileges and called it Lake Arkell in honour of W. J Arkell, proprietor of the *Illustrated News*. (The name did not stick. Today the lake is still known as Kusawa.) On the shore of Kusawa Lake Dalton constructed a sizeable raft, complete with sweeps and a square-rigged sail, and on this contraption the party started down the lake toward its outlet.

The group stopped midway down the lake, however, and after a discussion that concluded in mutual agreement they divided into two smaller parties. Wells chose to continue down the lake with the other members of the party, but Glave and Dalton wanted to strike out in a southwesterly direction in search of the headwaters of the Tatshenshini River. They believed the Tatshenshini River would lead them through the mountains to the Pacific Ocean. They had the motivation of discovery to propel them on this quest, as Glave said in his diary:

Our attempt to cover so much ground with such small resources seemed foolhardy; but there is a keen fascination in traveling through unknown lands; to be the first white men to erase from the map the hypothetical and fill up the blank area with the mountains, lakes, and rivers which belong to it. It is a great consolation to have some such comforting reflection, and with such an incentive, discomfort can be suffered and hardship and privation endured. There are few men with whom I would have undertaken the trip under such conditions, but I knew that Dalton, my companion, was a man of undoubted pluck and energy.[19]

The men departed with Indiank accompanying them for the first day to point them in the right direction. They carried with them only the bare essentials: some food, an axe, a hatchet, gold pan, utensils, blankets and rubber sheets, Kodak camera, sketch and notebooks, rifles and ammunition, as well as a selection of small items suitable for trade along the way. They had neither enough food nor any notion of the path ahead. As Glave reported, Indiank had sketched a frightful picture of the Tatshenshini River, "painting its dangers in blood-curdling tints, and enumerating the number of friends he had lost in their attempts to battle against its angry waters." Glave's own description of the landscape was contradictory: he spoke of a land wild and unpeopled, yet he sprinkled frequent references to the presence of Native people everywhere they went.

After hiking for twelve miles they reached a lake several miles long that Glave named after his deceased brother, Frederick. At its lower end, having parted company with Indiank, they met a Gunena (Southern Tutchone Native) family consisting of Koona Ack Saï, an aged native man, Koon Tcha, his wife, and three young sons, with whom they traded some tobacco for fish. After three days of rest on the shore of the lake they broke camp. Glave and Dalton followed Koona Ack Saï and his family south past Dezadeash Lake to Klukshu Lake where the remains of decaying buildings indicated there had once been a substantial stopping place. They spent a day at Klukshu, then travelled another twenty miles to the village of Neskatahéen, which consisted of a dozen impressive log houses on the banks of the Tatshenshini River, similar in design to the Chilkat long houses of the distant coast.[20]

According to Glave's description, "They are built of heavy planks, hewed into shape with the native adze, the roofs either covered with rough, heavy shingles or thatched with hemlock bark. They are all fitted with a large opening in the centre of the roof as an escape for the smoke."[21]

Across a small stream from this village, a cemetery held a few brightly coloured burial structures housing the cremated remains of the village ancestors. The most numerous inhabitants of the village were the mosquitoes that swarmed everywhere in dense clouds and plagued anybody who dared to venture out of doors. At the time of their visit there was only one house occupied and it held a party of Chilkat traders, travellers like themselves; the remainder of the community had gone down the Tatshenshini River to take advantage of the salmon run.

A few days later, still in the company of Koona Ack Saï and his family, the Englishman and his American sidekick ventured down the valley of the Tatshenshini, a route that did lead them, as they had hoped, to the Pacific Ocean. Glave described the nature of the valley through which they were travelling:

> A few patches of forest dotted here and there amidst the vast area of meadow land; the rich green grass delicately tinted in streaks and patches with the varied colors of the wild flowers, among which were the wild sun-flower, violet, daisy, buttercup, cowslip, and innumerable other tiny herbs. In some places the ground was whitened with wild strawberry blossoms; a cool clear stream flowed in a winding course over the surface of the valley. There can be no finer grazing land in the whole world: the pastures are composed of the very richest grasses, red top, blue top, buffalo, bunch-grass, and wild Timothy. The keen southern and northern winds are barred out from here by the barrier of mountains which rise to mighty walls around.[22]

They travelled for several days in a southwesterly direction, stopping to feast whenever they chanced upon game along the way. At one point they encountered another party of Chilkat traders coming up the valley laden with skins and furs. These Chilkats were not pleased to see the two white men, and chastised Koona Ack Saï for acting as their guide. Their hostility to this intrusion into their territory was just the beginning of a long history of animosity between Dalton and the Tlingit traders. Eventually the travelling party found a small dugout on the bank of the Tatshenshini, and while the Natives continued on foot, the explorers and their guide let the strong, turbulent waters of the Tatshenshini carry them downstream until they reached the Gunena summer encampment of Noogaayík.[23]

According to Glave:

> The fishing-camps are pitched at intervals of three and four hundred yards along the western bank of the river, extending for about a mile and a half. The settlement is known as Alseck and is a well-selected position. The keen southwest wind which prevails here is broken by a big rugged bluff, behind which the rude dwellings nestle amid a sparse growth of willow and small shrub of sufficient density to ward off the violence of the wind, but at the same time permitting circulation enough to keep the settlement clear of mosquitoes.... Each little camp was composed of a log hut or two roofed with hemlock bark, while some of the Indian families preferred to live under their old cotton shelters about eight feet square. At the back of this a heap of small branches was thrown to add to its effectiveness as a barrier against the wind storms. Their stock of cooking vessels, skins, furs, moccasins, blankets, guns, and other miscellaneous items of property were stowed away under this cover. Rude platforms of stout poles, six feet from the ground, were attached to each dwelling, on which they were drying their salmon.[24]

In this settlement along the river they met War Saine, one of the Gunena chiefs, who extended the hospitality of a tent, firewood, water and a salmon. The warmth of their reception by War Saine was due in part to the impression he had gained that Glave and Dalton were representatives of the American government, and the two visitors, who were enjoying the benefits of the chief's benevolence, were not about to set the record straight. Glave's general impression of the character of his guides and hosts during his travels through the interior was positive:

They are without exception the most peaceful people I have ever met in my life. They are never armed, and never an angry word is exchanged; they appear to be living on the best of terms together. They are lively and genial and full of fun; one does not see that sullen countenance and manner which is a peculiar characteristic of the other tribes, besides which they display more affection and consideration for their wives and families. The quiet and orderly conduct existing throughout the whole line of camps is remarkable.[25]

The two white men were treated well during their stay at this remote encampment, but their provisions were running low and they did not wish to abuse the hospitality that they had received. Shank, the village shaman, found a twenty-foot dugout canoe that was suitable for their trip downriver, and agreed to guide them to the coast. Dalton evaluated the river craft and judged that it was too shallow for their requirements. Shank, aided by War Saine, obliged Dalton by lashing four-inch sideboards to the gunwhales with moosehide thongs.

Finally, the little boat, containing Dalton, Glave, Shank and a Gunena healer who was accompanying them to the coast, pushed off into the nine-knot current, powered by the deft paddle strokes of Dalton and Shank. The sharp prow of the dugout cut through the rough waters of the Tatshenshini, drenching the men, but the Gunena healer, gripping the bow in terror, served as a form of watershed, reducing the amount of water that came in over the forward end of the craft. The current quickly carried them through the vale that was encircled by snow-capped peaks and encased in glaciers. Glave described this section of the river:

This stream is the wildest I have ever seen; there is scarcely a one-hundred-yard stretch of fair water anywhere along its course. Running with an eight to ten knot current, and aggravated by rocky points, sharp bends, and immense boulders, the stream is also rendered dangerous by the innumerable rapids and eddies which disturb its surface.[26]

Delayed by bad weather, they camped at the confluence of the Tatshenshini and the Alsek, and then proceeded down the Alsek into what would be the most treacherous part of their journey. The river, swollen with the water from both tributaries, flowed through a constricting passage. A glacier on the bank to their left extended for more than a mile and a half and towered more than a hundred feet above them. The wash from any chunks calving off this ice face could have swamped their delicate little craft easily. They passed a second glacier, and through this section the river narrowed into a single channel with rapids spreading across the entire width of the water. Dalton and Shank nimbly guided the little dugout between two massive boulders into violent foaming water from which it and its passengers emerged sodden. If the little craft had capsized at this place, everyone on board would have perished in the icy grey, glacier-fed waters. For Glave, the experience was terrifying:

> Just ahead of us is the dreaded cañon. Shank remains silent as death, grimly scanning the points of danger, and guiding the little craft as she leaps along with the whirling current toward the narrow pass ahead, and the paddlers, who have been reserving their strength for the final effort, now pull with all their might, and we dart along at a bewildering pace between the treacherous walls. Large blocks from the wall of ice toppled over in the water, lashing the already wild torrent into a veritable chaos. On the opposite shore the resistless flood swept and carried in its waters huge boulders from the rocky bank. The din of rolling rocks, the roar of surging stream, and the loud crackling and splashing of the falling ice continue in a thundering uproar. For a few minutes only we ride among the waves and are buffeted about among the fragments of ice which are borne along with the stream; then gradually the river widens and we pass along in safety.[27]

Finally they emerged from the terrifying passage through the glaciers into Dry Bay, a shallow, calm catch basin. Early in the evening they reached a small native village at the mouth of the Alsek where they were welcomed into the hut of the medicine-man, Shata. That night, bathed by the flickering firelight in the little structure, the entire village, some thirty souls in all, crowded into the tiny space and listened to Shank eloquently relate in their native tongue the narrative of this voyage. Now out of supplies, Glave and Dalton negotiated with two Yakutat Natives to take their outfit ninety miles up the coast while the two explorers, tired of being in a boat, walked to the white settlement in Yakutat Bay, where they arrived three days later. Shank and the Gunena healer stayed behind with the villagers in Dry Bay.

The two men had completed their remarkable voyage over the Chilkat Pass and into the interior of what was to become the Yukon. They had found the Tatshenshini River, the only river to cut through the coastal mountains for hundreds of miles, and followed it to the Pacific Ocean. In total, the two men had traversed more than three hundred miles of uncharted country with almost no supplies by living off the land and relying upon the generosity of the Native residents they met along the way. In fact, Glave admitted: "Had we not been able to avail ourselves of their local knowledge and valuable guidance, we should have had great difficulty in covering the stretch of rough country." [28]

Glave published his account of the expedition in a series of articles in *Frank Leslie's Illustrated Newspaper* between August 1890 and January 1891. In describing the country through which they travelled, he used the Native names for the places that they passed. Unlike most of his contemporaries, he recognized the importance of these places to the people who lived there:

> I have retained the native names of geographical points wherever I could learn them. In my opinion this should always be studied. The Indian names of mountains, lakes, and rivers are natural landmarks for the traveller, whoever he may be; to destroy these by substituting words of a foreign tongue is to destroy the natural guides. You ask for some point and mention its native name; your Indian guide will take you there. Ask for the same place in your substituted English word and you will not be understood. Traveling in Alaska has already sufficient difficulties, and they ought not to be increased by changing all the picturesque Indian names. Another very good reason why these native names should be preserved is that some tradition of tribal importance is always connected with them. These

people have no written language, but the retention of their native names is an excellent medium through which to learn their history.[29]

Glave took pains to describe in detail the people, their clothing, food, lifestyle and customs, and he noted where he and Dalton encountered signs of old or present camps. The high number of abandoned and derelict camps and villages mentioned by Glave pointed to a larger population of native people who had dwelled in the region before disease and other factors swept through the land ahead of the incursions of the white man. The journey of Dalton and Glave opened a previously unknown piece of the continent to European eyes, but the two men had succeeded in their quest for a crossing to the Pacific only because they were able to rely upon the knowledge and assistance of the people who already lived in the interior. Similar cooperation from native people would shape the course of events for Dalton and Glave when they continued their exploration of the Yukon the following year.

Pioneer Packhorses in the Yukon

In 1891 Glave returned to Alaska. Lacking sponsorship, he came at his own expense; the project would eventually cost him four thousand dollars.[30] The expedition of the previous year had cost triple its original estimate; W.J. Arkell, proprietor of *Frank Leslie's Illustrated Newspaper*, complained heartily that by the time all of the bills had been paid on the 1890 expedition, the cost had ballooned from five thousand to sixteen thousand dollars.[31] He was not willing to stick his neck out for another expedition to the north, nor was Glave able to get financial or logistical support from the American government, even for the loan of navigation instruments for mapping the country. Again, Glave engaged Dalton as his outfitter and companion. His main objectives for this summer's exploration were to find rich mineral deposits, to map the interior region of the Yukon and to prove that packhorses were a viable alternative to the use of native packers and guides. In Glave's view

> The Indian carrier was the only means of transportation; he controlled the situation and commanded exorbitant pay. Moreover, his arrogance, inconsistency, cunning, and general unreliability are

ever on the alert to thwart the white man. No matter how important your mission, your Indian carriers, though they have duly contracted to accompany you, will delay your departure till it suits their
convenience, and any exhibition of impatience on your part, will
only remind them of your utter dependence upon them; and then
intrigue for increase of pay will at once begin. Often the Indians
will carry their loads some part of the way agreed upon, then demand an extravagant increase of pay or a goodly share of the white
man's stores, and failing to get either, will fling down their packs
and return to their village, leaving their white employer helplessly
stranded.[32]

Native packers, Glave noted, generally charged a minimum of two dollars a
day.

Even larger than the expense of pack hire was the cost of food for the
packers. A man carrying ninety to one hundred pounds of supplies could eat
more than three pounds of food a day, so that within a month he theoretical-
ly could consume everything he was carrying on his back. Packhorses, Glave
felt, should prove to be a suitable alternative to the unpredictable Chilkat
packers. He expected to find fodder for the animals along the way, and it
was therefore his intention to explore the interior region of the Yukon with
packhorses.

Glave hoped that he and Dalton might discover mineral deposits that
would make them wealthy. Rumours of rich copper deposits in the White
River area were constantly on their minds. Glave was also aware that a successful expedition might open the door to further funding and a chance to
return to Africa. In March of 1891 Glave travelled from New York to Seattle
by train, leaving behind an unnamed love interest. Privately, he hoped that
he could get something out of his venture that would establish his reputation
and allow him to settle down in comfort. He saw discovering rich mineral
deposits and exploring unknown regions as a means of achieving this dream,
but he knew it would not be realized without some hardship and suffering
on his part.

Dalton joined him in Seattle where they purchased four compact ponies, pack saddles and other equipment. From Seattle they sailed up the

coast to Pyramid Harbor. Though ready to proceed, they could not start until the snow had receded in the high country. In preparation, they moved up the Chilkat Inlet just beyond Klukwan, where they found a suitable pasture for their horses. There they also engaged the services of three Chilkat men to accompany them to the interior. Shank, the man who had guided them the previous year, acted as interpreter, while two others served as guides.

The season advanced quickly. Toward the end of May they started moving up the Klehini River toward the Chilkat Pass with their horses, using a different approach to the mountains than they had the year before. They crossed the Klehini by boat with the horses swimming in tow behind them in the flat gravelly channels. Although they floundered temporarily in quicksand, they were able to proceed another twenty miles before they had to stop again because snow was still deep on the ground.

Here, while tormented by hordes of mosquitoes, Dalton set about demonstrating why he became known as one of the best outdoorsmen in Alaska. In order to move ahead into the snow-cloaked pass, he constructed snowshoes for the horses. He looped spruce saplings into hoops fourteen inches

Dalton fashioned snowshoes for the horses to wear. "When first experimenting with these, a horse would snort and . . . he would savagely paw the air, then quickly tumble on to his fore-legs and kick, frantically." EDWARD JAMES GLAVE COLLECTION, 77-32-097, ARCHIVES, UNIVERSITY OF ALASKA FAIRBANKS

in diameter and filled the enclosed space with plaited rope. He then lashed these to the horses' hooves by a series of loops drawn up tight around their fetlocks. The horses did not like these strange devices strapped to their feet. According to Glave, "When first experimenting with these, a horse would snort and tremble upon lifting his feet. Then he would make the most vigorous efforts to shake them off. Standing on his hind-legs, he would savagely paw the air, then quickly tumble on to his fore-legs and kick, frantically."[33] But after a few days of rehearsal, the animals became accustomed to the strange footwear.

Meanwhile, the two adventurers made several reconnaissance trips and found the best route to the top of the 3,500-foot summit. The weather improved and the snow continued to melt. They found they were able to coax their horses, without snowshoes, across the hard frozen crust. While crossing one snow-filled gully, Glave and his horse broke through the frozen shell and tumbled into a stream flowing below. The mare remained stoically calm and quiet until he was able to coax her out of the hole.

The scenery at the summit was spectacular. The air was cold and crisp and all around them the mountain peaks were cloaked in snow that, when the sun shone upon it, could be so intense as to cause painful temporary blindness. Glave and Dalton led their small cavalcade through this sparkling landscape. They had been travelling due north; now for two days they tracked west across a treeless countryside. Over fields of glacial till they scrambled; through quaking bogs they floundered, sometimes sinking almost out of view. Finally they found themselves on a tree-covered bluff overlooking the Tarjansini [Tatshenshini] River. On the opposite side, nestled in the valley plain below a tree-covered terrace, a cluster of remarkable buildings spread out along the river bank. It was the village of Neskatahéen, which had been virtually empty when they stopped there the year before, but now they could see many villagers busy with their tasks.

Their volley of rifle fire attracted the attention of the inhabitants and in a matter of minutes Glave, Dalton and their supplies were ferried across the swift-flowing river, with the horses swimming behind. The arrival of this unusual entourage on the shore in front of the village caused a remarkable stir. The inhabitants of the village had never seen horses before. Women and children ran for cover in their houses or hid in the surrounding forest.

One woman, thinking these new arrivals were some form of big dog, started removing her meat from the drying racks so that these strange creatures wouldn't consume it.

Here the service of their guides ended, and Glave took the opportunity to pen a letter for them to carry back to the coast which was received in Seattle on July 21 and published in the *New York Times* the following day. He wrote:

> We have been entirely successful with our venture of taking a pack horse into the heart of Alaska. The attempt was considered by many quite quixotic, but I am writing this from one of the most central inner parts of inner Alaska . . . with all our horses in as good condition as in Seattle. They have carried their 250 pounds with ease and are enjoying timothy, blue top and bunch grass, growing thickly everywhere . . . [and]now that we have proved that transportation by pack horses is practicable, nothing is to prevent Alaska at once assuming an important position as a mineral producing region . . .[34]

They were confident that by following the Native trails wherever possible a fully loaded pack train could make the trip from the coast to Neskatahéen in seven days, while bypassing the obstructive and extortionate Chilkat packers. "The bolted gate hitherto guarded by them, to the exclusion of enterprise and progress, has swung back at the approach of the packhorse,"[35] Glave asserted.

War Saine, the local chief whom they had met the previous summer, invited them into his hut and offered them a corner to occupy during their stay. If they were troubled by insects or close quarters, their troubles were nothing compared to those of their hardy pack animals. The horses were shrouded by clouds of mosquitoes so thick that it was hard to make out their outlines. Thus plagued, they could neither eat nor rest and their condition declined.

The two men were eager to move farther into the interior, but they could not convince anyone to act as their guide. They learned that since arriving at Neskatahéen, Shank had been conspiring with the inhabitants of the village to undermine Glave's hopes of exploring the region. A local chief and medicine man named Shah Shah had intimidated the local Natives into refusing to help. Even with the promise of food and money, Dalton and Glave were unable to recruit guides. They suspected Shah Shah was plotting to get the lucrative assignment for himself, so they decided to foil his plan and proceed on their own.

In the meantime, Glave played the amateur anthropologist, recording and reporting details of the lives of the residents. Whiling away his time, he spoke with many of the men, and making liberal use of pencil and paper, and with generous offerings of tobacco, he was able to induce some of them to draw crude maps showing important landmarks in the region that could guide them to the reputed copper deposits of the White River. Nobody was willing to take them there; old hostilities between the villagers and the people of the White and Copper rivers had led to bloodshed, and they were not disposed to tempt fate by any close encounters. "They begged us to change our plans," Glave reported, ". . . and to make a journey through some safer part of the land, and to avail ourselves of their considerate guidance at two dollars a day and board."[36]

Glave and Dalton resolved to follow the trail north on their own. Each leading two of their pack animals, they struck out in a northwesterly direction and settled into a routine of back-breaking work that included striking camp in the morning, loading the pack bags and mounting on the horses, searching for the trail and following it where they could and cutting their own when they couldn't. At day's end they unpacked the loads, set up a camp, prepared meals and constantly watched the horses, which, despite being hobbled, were prone to wander off.

The terrain over which they travelled was variable. The landscape was filled with grassy meadows, dotted with spruce and tamarack. They followed the local trails where they were visible, but despite Dalton's skills as a woodsman, they were often delayed for hours as they searched for any sign of a path, a campfire or a footprint that confirmed they were headed in the right direction. The trails could seem to be deceptively easy, but then they would encounter grassy meadows that proved to be treacherous bogs overlain by a thin skin of sod that sagged beneath their weight and set up "slimy grassy waves." Two of their horses sank into one of these bogs and it took them two hours to extract the struggling beasts.

In this fashion they covered seventy miles before they were compelled to admit that while not lost, they had no idea where to go. They agreed that

Dalton would return to Neskatahéen under the guise of picking up supplies, and attempt to hire a guide, if necessary for $2.50 a day. There Dalton found a robust man who agreed to guide him, but insisted on riding while Dalton walked. This guide complained constantly and disappeared a day after Dalton and Glave were reunited. Fortunately for them, a couple of days later they encountered a pair of men from Hutchi: an old Southern Tutchone man named Nanchay, and Tsook, his son. In exchange for having their loads carried by the horses, Nanchay agreed to take the two explorers along, and it cost them nothing. The two white men weren't heading to the White River as planned, but at least they were no longer wandering about directionless.

The route they eventually followed from Neskatahéen took them northwest up Fraser Creek, skirting the northern shore of Mush Lake and along Cottonwood Creek. They followed a series of small lakes and soon entered the valley of the Alsek River, coming to a point above where the Kaskawush and the Dezadeash met in a broad, braided river channel. The stream coming in from the north was fed by Dezadeash Lake, while the other came from the melt waters of the Kaskawulsh glacier. On the shore of the river they fashioned a crude raft on which Glave, Nanchay and Tsook poled across with their supplies heaped on top, while Dalton, mounted on one of the ponies, swam across.

For three days they hiked to the north beyond Kloo Lake, finding signs of human occupation such as occasional animal traps, brush shelters and winter-cut stumps. Eventually they spied a wisp of smoke in the distance. It was the camp of Nanchay's family, and he was soon reunited with them. For the family members it was a momentous event: the arrival of the first white men they had ever seen, with their strange animals. Many years later elder Jimmie Johnson described his first encounter with Dalton and Glave: Johnson's party was camped near the south end of Kluane Lake when they heard strange sounds coming nearer. "Large animals of some kind were coming towards them along the trail, but their footsteps had no familiar rhythm to them." Everyone stopped what they were doing; the dogs stood at full alert: "the animals themselves came in sight down the trail. There were four of them, strange beasts with no antlers at all, though it seemed almost impossible, there was no doubt about it, men were riding on the backs of three of them, while they led the other by a rope tied in some way about his head."[37]

The strangers were so pale, they looked dead! Could they be the cloud people talked about in stories?[38] The newcomers also brought strange things with them. They controlled these strange animals, spoke a strange language and could only communicate with gestures and a few words. They wore strange clothing, started fires with little slivers of wood and ate little cakes made from what looked like volcanic ash. Nobody would eat ash, it was useless! When Jimmie Johnson and his people were offered these cakes, they didn't like them and spat them out.

The pale men looked at the native bows and arrows and laughed at them, so the natives set up a target and shot repeated bull's-eyes. The strangers' attitude toward the weapons seemed to change somewhat, but still the white men laughed at them. To make a point, one of the strangers strode off about thirty paces and turned his back toward them and bent over, presenting his butt to them with gestures that made his meaning obvious. The incredulous natives obliged him by selecting a blunt-tipped bird point, and one of them took careful aim and hit his target dead-centre! That stranger was Jack Dalton; after that, as Jimmie Johnson's story goes, Dalton never laughed at their bows again.[39]

What the explorers had found was a temporary seasonal hunting camp. The local people moved constantly over a landscape well known to them, exploiting various resources and gathering a supply of food to carry them through the winter. They would cache meat at various locations during the summer and then transport it to more permanent winter camps once the weather changed and snow cover made it possible to use dogs to transport large loads.

The people in Nanchay's camp showed Dalton and Glave tantalizing specimens of native copper from the White River area and regaled them with accounts of boulders of solid copper, but they wouldn't reveal the precise origin of these samples.[40] These specimens and other stories of copper far away in the interior would lure Dalton back some day, but now the two companions turned away from the path to White River and travelled along the shores of Kluane Lake.

Then, in early August, they encountered evidence at a small lake of what they thought was another white man's camp that had been vacated recently. Glave surmised it could be the camp of Frederick Schwatka, the American explorer reported to be making his second expedition into the Yukon. Eight years earlier Schwatka had accomplished a well-publicized reconnaissance trip over the Chilkoot Pass and down the Yukon River for the American army, naming landmarks as he went while assessing the military threat posed by the indigenous people. The first half of Schwatka's earlier journey from the coast had been through Canadian territory, but the American had disregarded the niceties of anyone else's claim to sovereignty. [41] Now, eight years later, Schwatka's reputation was waning and he was making this new venture into the Yukon to revive his career. Accompanying him was C. Willard Hayes, a rookie geologist from the US Geological Survey, and they were seeking the legendary source of native copper along the White River.

Glave acknowledged the unpleasant possibility that Schwatka was preceding them through this country of majestic mountains, but he reasoned that he and Dalton were making the more significant contribution to northern exploration: "Even if Schwatka has explored the sheet of water before us," he rationalized, "our having made a shortcut overland is a far more important journey as we can give information concerning the feasible development and the nature of the land."[42] In fact, though Schwatka had passed through this region a few weeks earlier and farther to the north, the paths of the two explorers never actually crossed. Schwatka died shortly after completing his voyage, and his account of the journey was buried in the pages of a short-lived New York newspaper, and thus lost to the public for a century.[43]

The Terror of Kluane

The season was progressing so the two intrepid explorers turned back toward the coast. They accompanied a party of Southern Tutchone hunters headed to Kluane Lake to hunt sheep. When Glave could not convince them to take them in the direction of the Kaskawulsh Glacier, they decided instead to explore the shores of the big lake, and the decision almost killed them.

They appropriated a canoe belonging to the Natives and put it to use to carry them along the lakeshore. Dalton used his remarkable skills of improvisation to construct oarlocks, hew a pair of oars and rig a mast. When they started out, on August 17, the lake was gentle and calm, but the icy water of

Kluane soon revealed its fickle temperament. Glave and Dalton found themselves battling high, rolling waves. They could not bail fast enough to keep up with the water flooding the dugout and their little craft eventually capsized. Most of their belongings went to the bottom of the lake as they battled for their lives—rifles, ammunition, cooking utensils, food and scientific instruments; only their blankets, Glave's camera and his notebooks, which were lashed to the canoe in a water-proof oilskin sack, made it safely to shore.

Glave realized that their lives were in serious peril:

> We swam toward the shore. Angry waves rolled over our heads, flinging us about as if trying to wrench away from us the upturned dugout, which alone could save us. The wind blowing along the shore denied us aid, and the icy waters had chilled us till we were almost speechless; but we doggedly fought our way, and at last were nearing the shore. The prospect of saving ourselves was still a feeble one. On shore a bare wall of stone caving in at the water-line bordered the lake. We were rapidly carried on to this by the rolling breakers, which flung us against the rocky wall, or carried us in a surging foam into the hideous cave beneath. Each time we struck we propelled ourselves violently along the wall. Soon we found an opening, and when abreast of this, a big sea with a hissing crest swept us ashore, where, paralyzed with cold and battered almost senseless, we lay in a heap piled on the rocks with a splintered canoe.[44]

They had survived—but just barely, dragging themselves ashore shivering and with teeth chattering so badly it was some time before they regained their strength and were able to speak again. They recovered their dangerous little craft when it blew ashore and after the wind died down they paddled back across the water to where they had left their horses. They were now short of essential supplies. Their cooking pots were gone, as well as their drinking cups; for the remainder of the trip they drank from a baking powder tin and a soup plate, and baked their bread in their gold pan.[45] Glave reflected upon this episode:

> I have had the contents of a flint-lock musket emptied at me at short

range, and have experienced the comforting sensation as the bullet missed its mark; I have felt the satisfaction of stopping a charging buffalo; but I don't think I ever felt such heartfelt thankfulness as when I was out of reach of the angry waves on the rocky shores of Lake Tloo Arny.[46]

Now lacking some of their instruments, with some essential supplies and equipment gone, they realized their progress and effectiveness would be hampered. Each day their travelling time was shrinking as August brought fewer daylight hours and tinges of autumn colour started to fleck the landscape. Another demoralizing factor was the possibility that Schwatka and geologist Hayes had travelled through the country before them. Though they didn't know it at the time, the Schwatka party had indeed reached the river of copper that eluded them. The two explorers decided it was time to turn south for the coast. In his notebook, as though trying to convince himself of the value of his little expedition, Glave repeatedly rationalized that their trip had value because he and Dalton had opened up a new "road" into the interior from coastal Alaska.

After their brush with death on the treacherous waters of the great lake, it was as though they made a new start at this point in their journey. From their camp at the upper end of Kluane Lake, which Glave called camp number one, he chronicled their return to the coast. The weather was influenced by the nearby icefields of Mount St. Elias from which a continuous cold and often dust-laden wind assaulted them. The terrain was rugged and variable. Some days they made good progress, but on other days they struggled to cover a short distance. They camped wherever they found a good supply of feed and water for the horses.

They proceeded up the east side of the Slims River Valley toward the Kaskawulsh glacier, at the foot of which they camped on the third day of their retreat. At this point they noted that the water from the massive churning wall of ice fed two different drainage systems. To the west the water drained through a short, meandering course into Kluane Lake, then escaped north toward the White River, which eventually joined the Yukon. In the other direction, spread out before them was a broad flat valley below the foot of the glacier where the streams led off to the east to mingle with another river

Overlooking the Dezadeash River near where it joins the Kaskawulsh River, 1891. EDWARD JAMES GLAVE COLLECTION, 77-32-096, ARCHIVES, UNIVERSITY OF ALASKA FAIRBANKS

draining from Dezadeash Lake. That water flowed south through the mountains, eventually joining the river that passed the village of Neskatahéen. Glave had these connections figured out because he had talked to the men at Neskatahéen and captured much of this information on the crudely sketched maps that they had drawn. Although hampered by the loss of some of his instruments and uncertain of the correct time (his chronometer had stopped for a day and a half after the dunking in Kluane Lake), he continued to take readings and record the conditions as they moved along. Glave assumed that when he returned to Pyramid Harbor he would be able to recalibrate all of his readings once he could establish the correct time.

On August 26, the sixth day after leaving Kluane Lake, the two weathered explorers reached the point where they had crossed the Alsek River before on the inward-bound journey. Here, again, Dalton nearly drowned. After they had found and rehabilitated their previously abandoned raft, Glave poled across to the opposite shore. Dalton took the animals across. In mid-stream the horse he was riding started to flounder. Dalton hung on for dear life as the horse sank and rose three times. Turning its head for shore, he managed to steer the exhausted horse back to the riverbank. After a second attempt to cross the river failed, he let the animal loose to swim across on its own, where it rejoined the other horses. Dalton was marooned on the opposite bank but he didn't lack ingenuity. Using the horse's lead rope, he lashed a number of logs together and poled across the stream on this improvised raft.

The Englishman and the American retraced their inbound route for the next few days, enduring cold, cloudy days filled with rain as they plodded toward the tiny village of Neskatahéen. The conditions of their return journey were decidedly different from those they had encountered on the way in. The countryside was showing the signs of the rapid transition to autumn: frost at night, snow on the surrounding mountains and chilly mornings. One day they climbed the mountain behind their camp to scan the surrounding country, and could see distant tantalizing places that they regretted they would not be able to visit. Despite their frustration Glave emphasized the positive in his journal, reciting their exploits and contemplating the significance of their accomplishments: he told himself that they had "proved the practicability of overland travelling in this country—we were the first to discover the . . . best road to the Interior of Alaska—we have demonstrated the feasibility of our journey this year."

He contemplated the article he was going to write and continued to take photographs as they moved forward. On August 30 they passed a large lake to the southwest, probably Mush Lake, and the next day, having spent eight hours in steady travel, they arrived at the practically deserted village of Neskatahéen. Though eager to return to the coast, the duo was delayed by weather and logistical requirements. They established their temporary headquarters in the vacated house belonging to War Saine. Dalton tended to his animals. A couple of days after arriving in the little cluster of timber buildings, he again demonstrated his resourcefulness under frontier conditions. He replaced some missing horseshoes by crafting his own. Using a cast-off English flint-lock rifle as his stock, a boulder as an anvil and the back of his hatchet as a hammer, he fashioned the footwear necessary to protect the horses' vulnerable hooves.[47] One day a large grizzly roamed through the village as the two white men, without rifles, watched helplessly.

The Natives in residence persuaded Glave and Dalton to delay their departure from Neskatahéen by showing them a sample of mineralized quartz and offering to guide them, for a price, to the source of the ore. To their dismay, the Natives led them on what seemed to be a deliberately inconvenient trek to nowhere, and they found no trace of gold or copper. On September 11 Dalton loaded up two of his horses and headed off down the valley by himself, looking for the will-o'-the-wisp outcrop from which the quartz allegedly came. Glave endured five solitary, monotonous days while the American searched the hills for promising mineral exposures without result.

In his journal Glave reported day after day of unpleasant rainy weather and the advance of the changing season, but he used an opportune moment to take more readings with his remaining instruments and made notes of his observations of the practices of the local inhabitants. Although Glave mused on what he and Dalton had accomplished, his journal entries show that at times he was verging on despair. The Englishman had spent a great deal of his

Using a cast-off English flint-lock rifle as his stock, a boulder as an anvil and the back of his hatchet as a hammer, Dalton fashioned horseshoes to protect the horses' vulnerable hooves. EDWARD JAMES GLAVE COLLECTION, 77-32-032, ARCHIVES, UNIVERSITY OF ALASKA FAIRBANKS

own money but had not reached the tantalizing copper mines of the White River. His scientific instruments had been lost or had malfunctioned. He and Dalton had almost drowned in Kluane Lake, and in saving themselves had lost many of their provisions. Finally, they had learned that another explorer might have taken away the glory they had hoped to win by being the first to "discover" this land.

On September 20 after a three-week stay in the tiny village, and fearing that any further delay might prevent them from escaping the interior before the onset of winter, the two men left Neskatahéen. In gratitude for having the use of War Saine's house and his tools during their stay, they left anything they did not need for their absentee host. It was bitterly cold the morning they departed and conditions got steadily worse. A frigid wind assaulted them as they made their dash for the coast. Ice sealed the ponds and the drifting snow and sleet peppered them for two hours as they slipped and skidded over the icy terrain. In some places the drifts were four feet deep. That night they camped below the summit on barren, hostile, treeless terrain, without food for their horses. They could not put up their tent, so instead they slept under a large tarpaulin. In the morning they woke up buried beneath a foot of snow. Without food or water for their horses, the two men moved on quickly, struggling through thick brush, swamp and loose rock on a steep, treacherous downhill trail until they reached a point on the Klehini River where they had camped on their inward journey.

They were exhausted. In two days, perched precariously atop their pack saddles, they had travelled fifty miles in a mad dash for the coast through the storm-blasted Chilkat Pass. They camped for a day to rest and recuperate. The weather was more temperate here, but the mosquitoes were back with a vengeance. As if in compensation, the low water in the adjacent river was filled with one of nature's wonders—thousands of spawning salmon. They carried on to Pyramid Harbor, passing along the way a party of five prospectors, who, fired by rumours that the two trail-worn travellers had been working a rich deposit of placer gold in the interior, were foolishly attempting to breach the mountainous palisade to find them.

The two explorers left Pyramid Harbor on the steamer *Mexico* and headed south, publicizing their findings on stops along the way. In Sitka the *Alaskan* newspaper reported the summer exploits of both the Schwatka party and the

Glave–Dalton expedition. Schwatka had brought back with him a hunk of native copper from the White River area that was 97 percent pure, and was taking it to capitalists back in New York with the intention of developing what he believed to be the richest copper mine in the world.

The findings of Glave and Dalton, while less tangible, were important for other reasons. The newspaper quoted with approval Glave's assertion that the theory of a great ice-belt extending all the way to the Arctic Circle now could be dismissed. The two men reported having covered a considerable area of previously unexplored terrain and demonstrated the practicality of using pack horses to travel into the interior. "The inaccessibility of the interior of Alaska has barred out the miner and the prospector, but now the road is open," crowed Glave, who called upon the US and Canadian governments to follow their footsteps with surveyors and fill in the big blank chart with the lakes and streams found there. Glave mentioned his dreams of going back to Africa or developing a Yakutat coal mine, and said that he wanted to obtain the right-of-way for a road, noting they had gone to great expense to explore a suitable route.[48] This was the first time that a road over the Chilkat Trail was proposed as a viable project.

Glave repeated this account of the expedition to the Victoria *Daily Colonist*, emphasizing that if a good trail were to be built into the interior, the use of pack horses would allow thousands of miners to come into the country to prospect the rich potential of the Yukon gold fields. He stated that he would petition the government for an appropriation of at least twenty-five thousand dollars to build this road.[49] On his arrival in San Francisco in early November, he echoed his earlier reports and added that during his trip he took photographs and found a rich copper mine. The news spread around the world, but little happened to further the exploration of the Yukon region for another six years, when a gold discovery of remarkable proportions was made on a small tributary of the Yukon River called the Klondike, far into the interior north of Fort Selkirk.[50]

Upon his return to civilization, Glave embarked on an unsuccessful lecture tour in Canada, then moved to New York to work as a journalist.[51] He wrote two articles about his pack horse adventures that were published in *Century Magazine* the following year. If he intended to demonstrate that he could undertake exploration in a small party he had succeeded, but he left the Yukon and Alaska with a bittersweet mixture of feelings. He never returned to the north.

Dalton meanwhile, thanks in part to Glave and his publicity, had established his reputation as one of the premier outdoorsmen and pathfinders in Alaska. He was good with horses, he was good in canoes, he was inventive in tight situations, physically tough and not one to wilt at the first sign of adversity. Had he been more of a self-promoter he easily could have become the poster boy for pioneering the northern frontier. More importantly, however, he had a gift for seizing an opportunity when it presented itself, and he was on the verge of replacing the Chilkat control of the pass to the interior with a monopoly of his own.

History Then and Now

It was the summer of 1979. My best friend, Les, flew in from Edmonton, and I drove from Dawson to meet him in Whitehorse. We planned a hiking expedition to Hutchi, one of the stopping places on the old Dalton Trail. For me, this trip would be more than history-hunting; it was history-making. As we hit the shops around Whitehorse making preparations for our hike, Les watched me buy an engagement ring for my future wife. I carried that ring with me during the trip that followed.

On the third day of our hike, I found the old cabin. The weather was warm and dry. We had been making good time and we were hot and thirsty, so we decided to take a break and remove the weight of our packs from our shoulders. Hiking with a heavy backpack is arduous, and I was glad of some relief from the monotony of placing one foot in front of another all day long. I decided to wander around in the surrounding area to see if there was anything interesting.

Not far from the trail I noticed a scattering of decaying old tree stumps—a sure sign that someone had been cutting timber in this area at some time in the past. Sure enough, not far away I saw through the trees the remnants of an old log cabin. Les joined me and together we examined the derelict structure. I quickly realized that this was a true historical treasure because I recognized its origin. Constructed during the gold rush in 1898, it once was called Camp Storey.

Camp Storey was part of a network of temporary cabins and caches along the Dalton Trail built by a mining party known as the Mysterious Thirty-Six. All its members had been sworn to secrecy as they spread into the Kluane region in a cooperative venture that had been organized with military precision. They were just one of many syndicates formed during the gold rush so prospectors and investors could pool their resources, both human and financial, and reduce their risks in the expensive and dangerous hunt for gold.

Most of these syndicates focussed on the Klondike area, but there were a couple that came to the southwest Yukon. One ill-fated party known as the Dietz expedition attempted to reach the Klondike by travelling through the difficult terrain from Yakutat. Their travails were heartbreaking and soul-destroying, and it was incredible that any of them survived at all. None, to the best of my knowledge, ever struck it rich.

The Mysterious Thirty-Six fared better than the Dietz party since no one perished and some of them found gold. Working mainly in the area to the west of Klukshu and Dezadeash lakes along what is now the Haines road, they also built cabins at Pennock's Post, Champlain's Landing (now known as Champagne) and Cannon Creek. At the point of their deepest penetration

The cabin at Camp Storey was built as a temporary depot for supplies while members of the Mysterious Thirty-Six prospected for gold in the region in 1898. MACBRIDE MUSEUM OF YUKON HISTORY COLLECTION 1989-30-113

into the Yukon interior, they built their most remote shelter, Camp Storey. It was this last building upon which Les and I stumbled.

One of the members of the Mysterious Thirty-Six took a photograph of Camp Storey just after they built it in 1898. I had seen that photograph. It showed a small structure, perhaps ten feet square, with a sod roof sloping from front to back. The rear looked barely tall enough for a man to stand up in, while the front was perhaps half again as high. From where the photographer took the picture, there are no windows or doors visible in the simply constructed shell.

In the picture a dozen men posed beside the building while another man was bent over a fire in front of them. Someone had stuck an axe in a freshly cut stump in the centre foreground. All around the cabin a barren landscape of fire-killed spruce stretched to the edges of the photograph. On our visit to the site eighty years later, the remains of the fire-killed trees were still there, but Mother Nature was recapturing the land and making it green again.

I examined the building up close, snapping photographs of interesting details. The construction of the cabin was unusual. There weren't many cabins built with a single-pitch roof like the one at Camp Storey; most were

Although the roof had fallen in, the cabin at Camp Storey was still standing in 1979. MICHAEL GATES COLLECTION

peaked in the middle. As I peered at the logs I could see that their thickness and orientation matched what was visible in the original photograph. What was not evident in the picture was a surprising detail: there were no nails holding the building together. Instead, tiny wedges of wood had been used to fix things in place. The logs were notched and locked together, but the builders had used an auger to drill holes and fitted them with handmade wooden pegs to keep the logs in position. Finally, I noted evidence of saw cuts. I concluded that the men had erected the entire building with the use of only three tools: axe, auger and saw.

Over my years of studying old buildings in northern Canada I have come to admire the variety and ingenuity of techniques that settlers used to build in the north with the limited materials that were available. Collectively, the old structures reveal a number of common features that represent the classic northern log cabin: the small size; notching of the corners; sod heaped around the foundations; mud and moss used to chink the spaces between the logs; more sod covering the roof. Usually the sod roofs would grow grass, but sometimes early pioneers were known to plant vegetables on them. I once saw an abandoned log cabin with a large tree growing out of the roof. Eventually the sod that made the northern cabins so easy to build and that provided such effective insulation from the elements would also contribute to their decay and collapse.

That the Camp Storey cabin survived for eighty years was something of a miracle. Decay had not felled the structure, although the sod roof had caved in. It had been spared the ravages of fire, but it was apparent that the forest was encroaching. Les and I saw it standing there thirty years ago. I wonder what remains of the shelter now.

CHAPTER 3

1892–1896: Dalton's Trail

After their departure from Alaska late in 1891, Edward Glave and Jack Dalton spent much of the winter promoting the potential of Yukon development to investors in the lower states. On the east coast, Glave used his reputation as an intrepid explorer to add credibility to the route he and Dalton had pioneered into the northern interior.

The entrepreneurial opportunity presented by a trail over the Chilkat Pass impressed New York businessman Richard H. Hoag, who decided to use it to establish a trading post in the interior. Hoag headed for Alaska in April with a large stock of goods. At Juneau, en route to the Chilkat Inlet, he announced he had contracted Jack Dalton to handle the pack trains that would deliver the goods to the new trading post which would be managed by F.M. Stevens, formerly employed by Kohler and James, Juneau merchants. In an interview published in the *Juneau City Mining Record*, Hoag argued that few furs from the interior were reaching the commercial market because the Chilkat Tlingit were using their control of the trails to restrict trade with the outside. Hoag declared that his proposed trading post would create an outlet for furs and also provide a resupply point for prospectors interested in the rich mineral potential of the region.[52]

Upon arrival at Chilkat, Hoag began operating under the business partnership name of Major and Hoag. He built a store adjacent to the village at Chilkat and purchased pack animals to transport supplies to the planned

Pyramid Harbor provided safe moorage for ships coming to the cannery (foreground), or to the start of Dalton's trail (centre left). LIBRARY AND ARCHIVES CANADA / 3941372

trading post inland. Jack Dalton, pleased by his possession of a contract for one hundred dollars per month, commenced construction of a warehouse in which the partnership would store its inbound and outbound trade goods.[53]

Theirs was not the only development underway in Chilkat Inlet in the spring of 1892. There were three fish canneries operating, two on the eastern side of the inlet at Chilkat and one on the western shore at Pyramid Harbor. A three-mile road from Chilkat crossed the narrow neck of land sheltering the inlet from the Lynn Canal and led to a third busy settlement, Haines Mission. Chilkat itself was booming with four saloons, a dance hall, two trading posts and a post office. It was a tough place that was said to contain more "petty, trifling criminals and shady men" per capita than anywhere in the United States.[54] Across the inlet at Pyramid Harbor, there was a wharf and seasonally operated cannery. Within a short time after its construction, Chilkat Native workers had settled nearby in a small cluster of houses built of hewn log and bark. Everywhere in the inlet booze was plentiful in all its forms and variants, and its associated problems were rife in these tiny coastal enclaves.

Despite its initial promise, Hoag's enterprise fizzled. Hoag disappeared without paying Dalton, so in the fall of 1892 Dalton sued Hoag for breach of contract and was awarded $929, which he realized through the sale of Hoag's Chilkat property. Dalton spent the winter acting as a watchman at one of the Chilkat canneries with his friend John Lindsay, a job they did not do very well: the cannery burned to the ground December 14, 1892.[55]

The Birth of a Dream

Dalton did not give up on the dream of founding a new trade route into the interior. Within a few months, Lindsay was in San Francisco announcing that he and an unnamed partner, probably Dalton, planned to return to Pyramid Harbor with supplies, horses and an outfit to transport goods north across the Chilkat Pass to the Yukon River at a point below the Five Finger Rapid. They proposed to provide more convenient transportation of goods into the interior than what was offered by the route in use for more than ten years over the Chilkoot Pass. The Chilkoot Pass, where travel was restricted by Tlingit packers, involved a steep climb to a summit frequently coated with ice and a descent to the headwaters of the Yukon through a series of lakes and treacherous rapids.[56]

By the spring of 1893 Dalton had plans to advance his packing scheme and establish himself in the interior, but he was acutely aware of the resistance to this notion by the Chilkats of Klukwan, traditional guardians of the gateway to the Chilkat Pass. He knew his endeavour would be hazardous. The Chilkats had controlled the pass and trade into the interior for generations, and recognized the implications of Dalton's potential intrusion into their trade empire. In 1852 they had dealt with a formidable economic competitor and won—by destroying the Hudson's Bay Company post at Fort Selkirk. During the intervening forty years, however, the political landscape had changed, and so had the economic realities of the region. The control of the Chilkat Tlingit over their territory was already on the wane.

The Struggle for the Passes

America had purchased Alaska from the Russians in 1867 but for many years the government exerted minimal authority over Native people in the sprawling territory. Tlingit traders continued to rule the mountain passes.

The situation changed in 1880 when the American government was able to open the Chilkoot Pass to white travellers by diplomatically stepping into the middle of a dispute between rival factions of the Chilkat Tlingit. In 1879 the renowned warrior chief Kohklux, while trying to settle disharmony and prevent serious intertribal warfare among his people, was seriously injured during an altercation. Lieutenant Lester Beardslee, commander of the navy vessel *Jamestown*, offered assistance to Kohklux in settling the dispute in exchange for the chief's permission to allow miners access to the headwaters of the Yukon River. Kohklux decided he would permit the miners to cross over the Chilkoot Pass, provided they did not compete with the Chilkats in the fur trade.[57]

At first the agreement between the American authorities and the Tlingit worked in favour of the Tlingit as they assumed a monopoly over guiding and packing along the Chilkoot Trail for the inflowing miners. By 1886 there were two hundred packers making a lucrative living working on the Chilkoot Trail under the oversight of the local Tlingit chief Klanot. This workforce consisted of men from both the Chilkoot and Chilkat Tlingit, as well as interior Natives from Tagish (most notably Skookum Jim or Keish) and some women and children.

Eventually the number of miners wanting to go into the Yukon exceeded the capacity of the Tlingit to handle all their requirements, and the packing arrangement deteriorated. In 1888 a shortage of Native packers led to delays that outraged the impatient miners, who knew they would have to contend with a short mining season and harsh conditions in the interior. Tensions built until a party of five miners, including brothers Hugh and Albert Day, announced their plan at Haines Mission to pack their own supplies in without paying tribute to the Chilkats. They would have been massacred had it not been for the intervention of the missionary and his wife.[58]

The demands and needs of the miners increasingly conflicted with the interests of the Chilkoot Tlingit who claimed proprietary rights over the use of the Chilkoot Pass. John J. Healy, who had set up a trading post at the foot of the Chilkoot trail at Dyea, observed presciently: "At present the only practicable relief is for some enterprising party to construct a pack-trail through the Chilcat [Chilkoot] Pass, place pack animals upon it, and set the Indians at defiance."[59]

His intentions enraged Chief Klanot. Klanot was already angry with Healy for his interference in the Chilkoots' fur trade with the Stick Indians of the interior, and now Klanot saw Healy developing the Chilkoot trail for pack horses, further eroding the economic base of the Tlingit people. Healy soon undercut the Tlingit packing rates as far as Sheep Camp, and left the Tlingit only the more difficult packing from Sheep Camp to the summit. Eventually he tried to supplant even this concession by hiring Tlingits from Sitka to handle the shipment of goods over the entire pass.

When a number of Sitka Tlingit arrived under the command of their chief, Jack, to commence packing over the trail, Chief Klanot intervened with a demand for a percentage of any money the Sitka Tlingit would make. The chiefs fell into furious combat and killed each other in front of Healy's trading post. The following day, chastened by the deaths of their leaders, the two groups of Tlingit worked out a suitable compromise to resolve the conflict.

Perhaps because they could see their grip over the Chilkoot Trail loosening, the Tlingit fiercely guarded what they considered as their much more important trail over the Chilkat Pass to the west. Despite their determination, the pressure of American colonization and exploration was relentless, and the signs of intrusion and change were appearing all around them. The Chilkat Tlingit in particular were experiencing a sometimes unsubtle and inexorable imposition upon their way of life. Europeans and Americans were moving into the Chilkat region in growing numbers, introducing schools, a new religion, a cash-based economy and a demand for the resources that were the very livelihood of the Tlingit people.

One of the economic pressure points was the salmon run. In the 1880s salmon canneries had been set up in the Chilkat Inlet area to process and export an expanding volume of fish from the region. The canneries' demand for fish began to hurt the Natives' local subsistence fishery, and while the economic damage was masked for a time by good-paying jobs for Native people in the canneries, these jobs started to disappear when Chinese labourers, who would work for lower wages, were imported to do the work.[60]

By 1892 the Chilkat were nursing numerous grievances regarding the salmon fishery. They were being displaced from lands and waters that they traditionally used, even being forced to vacate their own homes. Although the Tlingit possessed documents signed earlier by Alaska governor Brady supposedly securing their fishing rights, the canneries were injuring the very basis of their subsistence. They did not want the canneries taking their fish and they threatened the white cannery staff constantly and cut the cannery fish nets.

The availability of alcohol in the community inflamed the situation and on July 4, 1892, a group of Chilkats clashed with whites in a local saloon. In the melee, a Native died. The next day, apparently in retaliation, an innocent white man was killed. Head Marshal Orville T. Porter appointed Jack Dalton to act as a special deputy marshal to investigate the case. While Porter sent for reinforcements, Dalton identified the killer, a Chilkat named Tom, and went after him. Accompanied by his partner, John Lindsay, and another man named J. Wade, Dalton sneaked into the woods behind the Chilkat village three miles up the inlet and lay in wait.[61] By the time a contingent from the naval gunboat *Pinta* arrived, Dalton was already returning to Haines Mission with Tom and two other Chilkats in custody.[62]

A few days later, the *Pinta* brought Governor Lyman E. Knapp and a party of officials from Juneau to Chilkat, where for several days they listened to the grievances expressed by two hundred Chilkats. Their major complaint was that the price paid for their salmon had dropped by half from the previous year. Eventually tensions eased, and there was a grudging shaking of hands.[63] Whether or not the shooting incident inflamed Chilkat animosity toward Dalton, he certainly became the lightning rod for their antipathy, and from that time it took little to ignite their hostility toward him. His plans to take pack trains into the Yukon and establish a trading post were bound to aggravate their resentment. Any gossip in the community of Chilkat about his plans, whether accurate or not, fuelled the fire.

The combination of Chilkat anger and Dalton's own mercurial nature was a recipe for disaster. Dalton had a reputation as a sober and hard-working man, but he also had a temper that could go off like a stick of dynamite, and he wouldn't back down from a fight. His personal history was filled with episodes of violence. Before coming to Alaska in 1885 he had run a lumber camp in Burns, Oregon, where he lived under the pseudonym of Jack Miller. When he fired a man named Matt Egan, Egan challenged him to a fight. In the ensuing struggle, Dalton killed Egan. The authorities deemed the incident a case of self-defence, so he was not charged with murder. Not long after that killing Dalton got into another vicious fight and had to flee on a borrowed horse to escape a pursuing posse. After heading north and landing in Alaska he got into trouble again, spending some time incarcerated in Sitka together with some crewmates from a sealing schooner after they were apprehended while hunting illegally in the Aleutian Islands.

The Shooting of Dan McGinnis

Dalton's temper and the simmering threat of trouble from the Chilkats came together with tragic consequences in the spring of 1893. On March 6 at about ten o'clock in the morning, Daniel McGinnis, a twenty-seven-year-old clerk in the store belonging to Murray's cannery at Chilkat, was sitting and talking to a customer named Patrick Woods. Dalton walked into the store, accompanied by a local trader named Dickinson and a group of Chilkats. According to the testimony of witnesses given later, he strode across the room, passed the counter and came to a stop in front of McGinnis. He didn't waste words:

"What's this I hear McGinnis about you talking to those Indians about my going inside?"

"I don't know what you mean," replied McGinnis.

Dalton turned to Dickinson and asked him to translate. Dickinson exchanged words with one of the Natives in the Tlingit language. Dickinson repeated the comments in English: "Dan says that Jack Dalton is going in there [the Yukon] and make a trading post and we get poor."

Dalton turned back to McGinnis and repeated, "I don't want you to be talking about me going in there."

McGinnis again denied the charge made by Dalton. As he reached over to put down his pipe on the writing desk beside him, Dalton grabbed his left shoulder and shoved him back down into the chair. Reaching into his pocket, Dalton pulled out a pistol and started hitting McGinnis over the head with it. With each blow, he repeated: "You are a liar!"

After the third blow the small clerk started to struggle, grabbing Dalton by the shoulders. Dalton, in response, struck him a fourth time with the gun. There was a deafening explosion: McGinnis was shot in the shoulder and gasped, "My God I am hit." Dalton struck another blow to his stomach and the gun went off again, wounding the stunned clerk in the abdomen. He staggered back against the chair.

Woods, the visitor, left the store and made for the stairs at the rear of the building that led to McGinnis' apartment on the second floor. When he found the door locked he returned to the front of the building where McGinnis emerged, bleeding profusely from his various wounds. Woods helped the wounded man to his second floor room, then quickly arranged for a fishing boat to transfer him to Juneau where he could receive medical attention. As friends carried McGinnis down to the wharf, they saw a blood-spattered Dalton watching them with a rifle on his shoulder. McGinnis survived the passage to Juneau but died on the beach while Woods went hunting for a doctor.[64]

A warrant was issued for Dalton's arrest and a marshal was sent to take him into custody at Chilkat, where Dalton surrendered without resistance. He was returned to Juneau to await trail. The news of the killing by a deputy marshal stunned the community. Dalton told his version of the story to the press, saying that he had worked hard over the winter preparing a trail for transporting supplies into the Yukon, but a faction of business people, including McGinnis, felt that Dalton's plans would hurt their own fur trading and did everything they could to stop him.[65] Dalton claimed that when he entered the store that morning he was exasperated by the opposition to his plans. He said that during an argument McGinnis attacked him with an axe.

Edward Glave, the explorer who had been Dalton's companion on their adventurous trek through the Yukon interior, was quick to write a letter in Dalton's support to the *Alaska Journal* in Juneau. "Jack Dalton is by no means a quarrelsome man," he said, ". . . though he has a determined disposition and is thoroughly capable of defending himself."[66] Glave went on to praise Dalton for his tactful relations with the Natives and stated that Dalton's work was essential to the development of Alaska.

The trial commenced on June 17 in the Juneau courthouse, with Dalton pleading not guilty. John F. Malony, a Juneau lawyer, was the defence counsel. His primary strategy seemed to be to badger the main witness and to imply that McGinnis had attacked Dalton with an axe. Testimony took three days, after which the jury members retired to deliberate. They returned a verdict of not guilty. Alaskans were abuzz with the news; some defended the decision, while others, outraged by the verdict, alleged that the jury had been bought off. A few days after the trial a mob reportedly considered lynching the acquitted killer, but decided instead to give him three days to leave town.[67] Dalton shipped out for San Francisco on the *Topeka*.

The jury may have found him not guilty, but the government prosecutors remained convinced of his guilt. They weren't the only government officials disgusted by the trial outcome. Subsequently, Israel Russell of the US Geological Survey, who had named a glacier in Disenchantment Bay on the Alaskan coast after Dalton, asked that it be renamed Turner Glacier.[68]

The trial hurt Dalton's reputation, but it did not break his determination. In spite of the ill will against him prevailing in much of Alaska, Dalton returned north in 1894, again in partnership with John Lindsay.[69] "I am now on my way to Chilkat where I have a pack train," he said in Victoria to a reporter from the *Daily Colonist*. "I intend to go into the trading business there again, taking provisions into the Yukon country and bringing furs out."[70]

Dalton's Trail

Dalton's plan was to take a pack train over the Chilkat Pass to the Yukon River, and from there float the goods down the Yukon River to Forty Mile, which, since the discovery of gold on the Fortymile Creek in 1886, had become the major mining community along the river. Farther down the Yukon, west of the Alaska boundary, gold had been found in the Birch Creek mining district in 1892, and a new community named Circle City was growing rapidly nearby. There would be lots of customers for Dalton's goods.

The route was a good choice for pack trains; it had a gentler climb and lower elevation than either the Chilkoot or White passes and it circumvented the wind-swept lakes at the headwaters and the succession of turbulent canyons and rapids of the Upper Yukon River.

By the end of May 1894 the traditional Chilkat expedition had passed through Klukwan on the annual trading trip to the interior. It is probable the Chilkats were aware of Dalton's activities as he came along behind them; he departed from the coast with a pack train in early June, accompanied by Joe Kinnon. The two men reached Yukon Crossing, on the Yukon River below the Rink Rapid, where they built rafts, loaded their supplies onto them and headed for Forty Mile. The plan changed when they reached the mouth of the Pelly River. There a man named Dawson bought the entire outfit and

Jack Dalton is standing beside his trading post at Dalton House, 100 miles into the interior from Pyramid Harbor, 1898. MACBRIDE MUSEUM OF YUKON HISTORY COLLECTION, 1989-30-132

floated it down to Circle City to take into Birch Creek. Another miner named Ray Stewart bought Dalton's horses and took them down to Circle City, where he planned to use them for hauling supplies into Birch Creek.[71]

Kinnon turned back at Pelly and returned over the trail in twenty days time. In his account in a Juneau newspaper, this route is referred to as the Dalton Trail for the first time. Dalton continued down the Yukon River all the way to St. Michael.[72] In that remote corner of Alaska, he learned that a grim report of the McGinnis killing had preceded him. Persuaded by the sententious missionary Sheldon Jackson, the commander of the US Revenue cutter *Bear*, Captain Michael Healy, refused to give passage out to Dalton. There were other vessels in the area, however, and Dalton eventually was able to make his way back to Juneau in the fall.[73]

By then he knew he would face some competition on "his" trail. Ike Martin, a merchant from Chilkat, also went across the Chilkat Pass in the summer of 1894, intent on building a trading post in the interior.[74] Dalton had a strategic response to Martin's challenge: as soon as he had the chance, he hired Martin.

At the beginning of 1895 Dalton was already making preparations for the forthcoming summer. By late January he had shipped thirty-five tons of freight from Seattle along with fourteen horses and a wagon for use in packing over the trail.[75] Dalton's dream was coming closer to realization. On his return voyage to Chilkat in early March, he stopped in Juneau long enough to sign the legal papers making John F. Malony, the lawyer who got him off for killing Dan McGinnis, a partner in his new business, to be known as J. Dalton and Company.[76]Among the products that Dalton was rumoured to be hauling into the interior were those of the wet variety. According to various accounts, this was the second season in which Dalton engaged in the profitable importation of liquor into the Yukon.[77]

Dalton vs. the Chilkats: the Trade War

Dalton spent the summer of 1895 establishing a trading post 117 miles from Pyramid Harbor in the interior not far from Neskatahéen and searching for the copper deposits rumoured to be located on the White River.[78] In the fall he returned to the coast in the company of William Stanton and James Cannon, leaving behind Ike Martin, who was now in his employ, in charge of the new post. Martin probably had realized that it was wiser to work with Dalton than against him.

Relations with the Chilkat were going badly and Dalton was at the centre of the trouble. That Dalton now posed a serious threat to Chilkat trade interests was clear from his construction of a trading post near Neskatahéen; they could ignore him no longer. It was obvious that Dalton's new post threatened the established Native fur trade in the interior. Dalton's enterprise was not the only challenge facing the Chilkat people. On the neighbouring Chilkoot Trail, John J. Healy was circumventing the local packers to move goods to the interior and a new tramway constructed at the Chilkoot Pass by Peter Peterson was threatening their packing business over the most difficult section of the trail. The Chilkat resolved to resist all encroachments on their traditional rights. The *Alaska Searchlight* predicted that trouble was imminent.[79] In July Judge H.W. Mellen and translator Edward Armstrong prepared to go to Chilkat to look into the matter.

For months the Chilkat did their best to intimidate Dalton. Chief Caotawat (Kudawat) offered five hundred blankets to anyone who could stop him, and the personal threat to Dalton became more serious. In February, 1896, he made a winter trip over the Chilkat Pass to see how Ike Martin was doing at the new trading post. The weather was brutally cold, reaching sixty below zero Fahrenheit on February 12. On his way in he cached supplies at intervals along the route over the Chilkat Pass for his return trip. Chilkats following him emptied these caches, knowing that the loss of his supplies would mean he would perish on the return journey.

When he headed back to the coast, Dalton found the first cache missing. Thinking that some animal had broken into the cache, he carried on. He did not realize the truth of the situation until he discovered the second cache was also missing.

Now in serious trouble, he struggled through the cold and snow to his third cache, which, to his good fortune, had been overlooked by the saboteurs. By then he was so exhausted he barely had the energy to prepare camp and make a meal. If he had been caught in a storm at this point he surely would have perished, but luck was with him. Rationing the supplies from the undisturbed cache, he was able to survive even though he found that the next two caches had been looted.

The Chilkat did their best to intimidate Dalton. Chief Caotawat (Kudawat) offered 500 blankets to anyone who could stop him from going into the interior to trade.
COURTESY OF THE SHELDON MUSEUM & CULTURAL CENTER, HAINES, ALASKA

When he arrived at Klukwan after several days of exhausting travel, the surprised Chilkats greeted him with some consternation. Subsequently it was rumoured that a number of those involved in the sabotage mysteriously disappeared.[80]

As Dalton invested more effort, time and money on the Chilkat route from 1896 onward, he became increasingly proprietary about his trail and protective of his control over it. Not only did he face high risks because of animosity from the Tlingit Chilkat and the basic challenges of wilderness weather and terrain; many other potential hazards threatened his business, including competition from other entrepreneurs. Interest in the mining potential of the Yukon valley was growing as new finds of placer gold were being made on the Stewart River, in the Fortymile and Sixtymile districts and at Birch Creek, near Circle, Alaska. Dalton was opening his route to the goldfields at an opportune time, and people along the Yukon River at Forty Mile and Circle City became increasingly aware of the usefulness of his trail.

Hundreds of miners were now streaming into the Yukon valley each summer. By July 1, 1894, 435 prospectors had entered the Yukon district over the Chilkoot Trail, according to a report from Inspector Charles Constantine of the North-West Mounted Police.[81] The logistics of policing the vast area were difficult in the extreme. The North-West Mounted Police established a post at Forty Mile during the summer of 1895, and they needed a reliable supply of goods and mail service. Dalton saw there was the potential for lucrative government contracts. The stakes of the game were increasing rapidly and Dalton, with his fierce determination, wanted in.

Dalton was well positioned to address economic opportunities that changing times presented. According to Dalton authority and biographer Mark Kirchhoff, "Dalton considered the trail his and his alone—he had pioneered it, he had improved it by cutting trail and building bridges, and he owned a trading post on it. The deal now was, if you wanted to use it, you better get permission."[82]

This would be made clear to one businessman during the summer of 1896.

The First Cattle Drive to the Klondike

Willis Thorp was from a cattle-raising family and had been involved in cattle raising and driving as a youth. He had moved to Juneau in 1886 and opened a butcher shop. He built a slaughterhouse on the southern outskirts of the town and began bringing in live animals by ship, so it is unsurprising that he decided in 1896 to drive a herd of cattle into the Yukon to supply the demand of the miners in the small communities along the river. Juneau was the starting point for prospectors going to the interior and the first civilized port on

Willis Thorp was the Juneau butcher who brought the first herd of cattle into the Yukon in 1896. *SEATTLE POST-INTELLIGENCER,* NOVEMBER 29, 1897

the way out. In Juneau it would have been hard for Thorp to ignore word of the booming business at Circle and the continuing mining activity around Forty Mile. Real estate in the interior was getting expensive; lots in Forty Mile were reported to be selling for eight thousand dollars each.[83] It seemed that a prime market opportunity was opening up and it was Thorp's intent to supply the hungry miners with beef.

Thorp assembled a party consisting of ten men and a herd of forty to sixty head of cattle at Haines Mission in June. They did not leave for Fortymile until July 6, a date many knowledgeable locals considered too late for him to get his animals to market before the bad weather set in.[84] Twenty of the steers were each loaded with two hundred pounds of supplies to be used by the men on the way in. With animals picked for their endurance and covered in canvas capes that hung down to their knees, he planned to move the cattle in over the Chilkat Pass using the trail that Dalton claimed as his own. Dalton, who had expended his own resources to clear brush and build the trail to allow easier access to his trading post in the interior, was angry when he heard about the drive.

Initially the going was tougher than Thorp and his team had expected. Thorp walked and swam the herd for ten miles up the strong current of the Chilkat River, which he likened to "the mill race of hell." [85] Despite the best efforts of the experienced herders, by the time the herd reached Klukwan, only twenty miles up the Chilkat Valley, some of the animals were already footsore and lame, and the journey had only begun.

According to an account in the *Douglas Miner*:

The first night after reaching Klukwan, while the party of cattle drivers was encamped upon the trail, Willis Thorp called his men together and delivered to them a short address in which he told them that they must expect to encounter trouble from the owner of the trail upon which they were camped but that they must stand up for their rights and be ready to give the enemy a warm reception should the latter be so indiscreet as to come within shooting distance. After advising his men to look well to their arms, to have them cleaned and loaded and ready for instant action, Thorp brought his address to a close. No pitched battle occurred during the night . . . but early upon the following morning a single horseman could be seen coming rapidly up the trail. The newcomer rode into camp and up alongside Willis Thorp who meanwhile stood motionlessly gazing at the visitor.

There was no mistaking the identity of the horseman. It was Jack Dalton and his only weapon was a revolver which he carried in a belt strapped around his waist.

"Thorp, I want you and your crowd to get off this trail and I want you to keep off it, and I want you to be damn quick about moving." These said to be the words which Dalton addressed to Thorp, and the latter is said to have meekly replied "All right Mr. Dalton, we will get off your trail at once."[86]

To enforce his demand and to ensure that Thorp's cattle stayed off his trail, Dalton followed the herd as it made its way into the interior. The Thorp party kept off Dalton's trail, cutting their own route over the mountains and down to Kusawa Lake, then overland along a track, part of which subsequently became the wagon road from Whitehorse to Dawson. It became known as the G. Bounds trail, named after George Bounds, a relative of Thorp and a member of the cattle drive.[87]

Eventually the Thorp party reached the Yukon River and followed its western shore downstream to a point below Five Finger Rapid, where they built a raft to transport the herd to Circle. Most of the cattle arrived at the river in good condition, although four of the heaviest animals had become footsore and had to be shot on the way in. The cattle drivers never made it to Circle. When they reached the junction with the Klondike River in early October, they found hundreds of prospectors there, stampeding to get in on a new gold strike. The miners were all hungry for beef.

It was good timing for the Thorp party as they were able to stake claims for themselves. They sold most of their beef for sixteen thousand dollars in Dawson and hauled what remained to Forty Mile. When members of the party left in the spring, the newspapers announced that they were the first party to leave Dawson, poling up the Yukon River and then travelling overland following the Dalton Trail. They brought with them eighteen thousand dollars in gold dust that they had raised from the sale of the cattle and from their claims on Eldorado Creek.[88]

Not all of the meat stayed in Dawson and Forty Mile. Thomas O'Brien, who had been operating from Forty Mile before the Klondike strike, packed and shipped a ten-pound piece of beef 250 miles to Circle City, Alaska. According to the newspaper account, when the O'Brien meat hit town, it caused a sensation when it was displayed in the window of a Circle trading post:

> Everybody wanted a piece of the fresh meat, and the prices offered would have resulted in a mining camp quarrel or bloodshed if it had not been decided to raffle the steak off for the benefit of a hospital which Bishop Rowe is trying to establish for the miners at Circle City.
>
> At first, only five dollars per pound was offered for a slice of the steak, but the bidding became brisker as the meat was sliced, and as high as $35 per pound was offered. Finally, in order to avoid complications, it was decided to sell tickets at 50 cents to $2.50 for the privilege of drawing for a slice. After $480 worth of tickets had been sold the draw began and to the relief of the managers of the sale no trouble resulted in the disposition of Circle City's first beefsteak.[89]

Meanwhile, Dalton had taken his annual pack train to Forty Mile. He wanted to assess the potential opportunities for doing business with the Canadian government. Floating down the Yukon River, he stopped at Joe Ladue's trading post at Ogilvie, located on an island opposite the mouth of the Sixtymile

River. Dalton had sold horses to Ladue previously, and they were well acquainted. Ladue was running out of timber for his sawmill, and Dalton suggested he should look at a location some distance downstream at the mouth of the Klondike River.

In mid-August when they arrived at the site, they learned that gold had just been discovered on a tributary of the Klondike. American George Carmack, his Tlingit brother-in-law Skookum Jim (Keish) and Jim's nephew Charley had been looking for prospects on Gold Bottom Creek when, while returning over the hills, they discovered gold on a small stream named Rabbit Creek. Their announcement in Forty Mile of this discovery sparked an immediate stampede and a week later, on a hill overlooking the creek, a miners' committee renamed the creek Bonanza.[90]

Ladue decided immediately to stake a lot nearby on the river for his sawmill. Within days he had laid claim to 160 acres on the flats on the north side of the confluence of the Yukon and Klondike rivers. He named this site Dawson City, in honour of George Mercer Dawson, head of the Geological Survey of Canada. Dawson, who in 1887 was one of the first government officials to enter the area, had predicted that a find like this was bound to happen somewhere in the Yukon some day. By September 1 Ladue had completed the construction of the first building on the site, a small log cabin twelve feet by fourteen feet square. He then returned to his sawmill upriver, which he disassembled and floated down to the new site.[91]

Unlike Ladue, Dalton didn't seem to take news of the strike seriously at first, and didn't join other men in the area in their stampede to stake on Bonanza Creek. Focussed on his own business plan, he continued on to Forty Mile where he met with Canadian government surveyor William Ogilvie and Inspector Charles Constantine of the North-West Mounted Police. To them, Dalton sang the praises of his trail. He was prepared to quote a price for supplying goods for government use.[92] Ogilvie was interested in Dalton's claim that he could bring two to three tons of goods from tidewater to the Yukon River in ten to twelve days. Dalton tended to be close-mouthed about the particulars of his trail, but Ogilvie was able to make detailed notes about the route described by Dalton that included the general path it followed and conditions along the way.

Plans were made for either Ogilvie or one of Constantine's men to accompany Dalton out over the trail when he headed back upriver on September 10, but those plans changed once the implications of the gold find near Dawson became apparent. Nevertheless, Constantine took careful note of Dalton's account and saw the potential in opening up a wagon road or a railroad over Dalton's route.[93]

Having seen many gold strikes come and go, Dalton was quite prepared to resist any temptation to stake a claim. He chose to cast his lot with the development of his trail, hoping to expand his trade, bring in cattle and facilitate transportation for his customers. Despite his planning he was not ready for what was to come. Dalton missed his chance to get in on the ground floor in the Klondike, but he didn't realize that in the fall of 1896. It wasn't until the following year that he found an opportunity to profit from what became the great Klondike gold rush.

A Burning Question

During my years of hiking on the Dalton Trail I have passed through many areas remarkable for their old burnt tree stumps and, in some places, impenetrable deadfall. These decaying remains suggest fires were very common at an earlier time, an idea that is reinforced by historical photographs of the trail. Several gold-rush travellers who went in over the Dalton Trail have left accounts that make reference to fire devastation. The Mounted Police mentioned fires, too.

"Miles and miles of blackened stumps marked the ravages of forest fires," noted Edward Glave in 1891:

> The Indian, when resting on his journey and suffering from mosquitos, sets fire to the twigs and leaves around him, creating a smoke which keeps the pest at a distance, and, when refreshed, he straps on his pack and moves along the trail, of course without extinguishing his fire; when announcing his approach to friends at a distance, he sets fire to a half-dead spruce- or tamarack-tree, and the column of thick, black smoke is the signal, to be acknowledged in the same manner by those who see it, so as to direct the traveller to their camping-grounds. In the summer everything is crisp and dry, and the timber is saturated with turpentine. The trees left to smolder are fanned into flame by the slightest breeze; the flames

creep among the resinous trees, and spread till whole forests are destroyed.[94]

Old photographs of the period show a more open landscape that contains plenty of evidence of burnt-out forests. The fact is that fire is essential to a healthy northern ecosystem. It boosts both variability in food sources and the total productivity of the land.

In 1972 when I travelled into the Tatshenshini valley by pack horse, the undergrowth was dense and unrestrained. The willow was so thick that it was possible to move forward by stepping from one branch to the next without ever setting foot on the ground. Art Brewster, our guide, stated that the Jacquot brothers, noted big game outfitters from Kluane Lake, used to set fires in places like this to provide more browse for moose. They clearly understood the value of fire in improving the moose population. But that hadn't been done for decades when we passed through. In fact, the dense growth of vegetation was undoubtedly one of the results of the depopulation of this area in the late nineteenth century.

Gold seeker hiking through a burn near Champagne. Fires, or evidence of past fires, were evident everywhere along the trail. ALASKA STATE LIBRARY, FRED HOVEY PHOTOGRAPH COLLECTION, P352-71

The Mounted Police didn't like fires and in 1898 they posted notices that they would arrest anyone who abandoned a campfire without first extinguishing it. Their concern was the harbinger of a new perspective, one in which fire was not to be welcomed, but fought at any cost. Today, to protect property and the forests, forest fire fighting has become a major industry, and victory over a fire has become one of the premier symbols of our mastery of the environment. The Smokey Bear culture prevails.

I see two cultures with conflicting views of fire. One, embraced by indigenous peoples, recognized the value of fire as a tool in managing their landscape to improve the production of foods upon which they relied. They did not view timber as an economic resource, and they had not made major investments in property that had to be protected from the ravages of fire.

The other culture, imported to the Yukon during the massive influx of people and government during the gold rush, saw timber as a commodity that was destroyed, or devalued, by fire. Major investments in buildings, bridges and other constructions had to be protected.

If we champion the prevention of fire, we are also promoting the uniformity of the landscape, and ultimately the creation of "a world of great trees, dark and silent."[95] Gone would be the succession species that make up the complex web of nature's interrelationships and produce a rich and varied landscape. First Nations people knew this better than the newcomers and they accepted fire as a normal part of things. Fires promoted variability in natural plant regimes, creating a mosaic of ecosystems that boosted the variety of food sources and increased the productivity of their natural food basket.

The land is a dynamic and vibrant entity and I recognize the beauty of its complexity even as I know I cannot comprehend it completely. Whenever I seek historical adventure on the land, it presents me with questions about its web of changing relationships. Rather than viewing a forested landscape as a pristine wilderness stretching from lakeshore to treeline, devoid of the human touch, I see evidence of people everywhere that I go. Archeologists interpret this evidence, and they can chart a human imprint in the Yukon extending back at least twelve thousand years, maybe more.

It is a common misconception that Europeans landed on American shores and found an untouched wilderness extending across the continent.

The ancestors of the modern First Nations are often presented in earlier European literature as innocent savages, but the reality is that they lived in complex societies all across the northern and southern continents. Far from living savagely, the people of the pre-contact Americas often dwelled harmoniously in densely populated regions. Many were occupants of cities that rivalled or surpassed the contemporary European centres in their size and population. The original inhabitants of North and South America effectively exploited the terrain and became integral components of the ecological balance of nature. In fact, so important were people to the ecosystems of the American continents that they should be viewed as a "keystone species"; in other words, a species that affects the survival and abundance of many other species.

Remove a keystone species from the ecosystem and everything goes out of kilter in unpredictable and sometimes devastating ways. When Europeans arrived in the "New World," part of their contribution to the Columbian exchange was a cascade of diseases against which the indigenous people had no natural defences. In some areas, the populations may have declined as much as 90 percent. This decimation made it impossible for the existing cultures of the Americas to maintain the lifestyle and practices of the past. Many societies collapsed. Vast areas once part of complex agricultural systems fell into disuse. Many wildlife species moved into the vacuum that this human depopulation created, a development that may explain the presence in the nineteenth century of tens of millions of bison across the prairies, and the huge flocks of passenger pigeons that blackened the skies for days as they flew past.

The population of the southwest Yukon was once much larger than it was when Europeans arrived. Edward Glave, the English explorer, observed the remains of abandoned buildings in various villages during his 1890 journey, a fact that suggests many more people once lived here. Disease had ravaged the people prior to Glave's coming and the population declined dramatically from the levels probably known in earlier days.

Anyone who compares photos taken in the Yukon in 1898 with views of the same places today must observe that forests now occupy a greater portion of the landscape than they once did. Untended, the regrowth makes travel difficult. Early accounts of travel through Dalton Trail country describe an open landscape suitable for grazing large herds of cattle that, in fact, gained weight while travelling over the trail. Those open vistas were probably the result of the use of fire for land management by people dwelling on the land for many generations.

Indigenous people everywhere else across North America were aware of the value of fire as a tool for improving the productivity of the country; I can't imagine that it would be any different in the Yukon.

CHAPTER 4

1897: The Stampede Begins

At the beginning of August in 1896, the country at the confluence of the Klondike and the Yukon rivers was mostly moose pasture. On the upstream side of the junction was the First Nation settlement known today as Tr'ochëk; a half mile below the mouth of the Klondike, George Carmack and his family were camped, catching salmon. The quiet of the valley changed forever at mid-month when Carmack, Skookum Jim and Dawson Charley made an excursion into the hills and found gold in Rabbit (later called Bonanza) Creek. Word spread up and down the Yukon valley "like a giant stage whisper."[96] By the middle of September, there were five hundred men— and three women—in the Klondike.[97] By Christmas 1896 hundreds more miners from up and down the Yukon valley had descended upon the new gold strike. Joe Ladue, who had moved his sawmill downriver from his trading post at Ogilvie in late August and filed a claim on 160 acres just north of the river confluence, had the federal government surveyor, William Ogilvie, lay out a townsite. Ogilvie established a reserve of forty acres for government use, and around it Dawson City began to grow. By early spring of 1897, in addition to Ladue's sawmill, a scattering of thirty log cabins, a second sawmill and a saloon were spread out along the waterfront facing the Yukon River.

The population of Dawson soon ballooned to fifteen hundred while Forty Mile and Circle were virtually abandoned. The North American Transportation and Trading Company (NAT&T Co.) and the Alaska

Commercial Company were building stores and warehouses at the Dawson townsite by the summer of 1897.[98] The best town lots were selling for two thousand dollars, and as the season progressed, the price just kept escalating.[99] As spring turned to summer, more and more people arrived at the new town, optimistically expecting to make their fortunes in the boom.

Word of a big gold strike spread outside of the Yukon valley to Juneau and beyond, where thousands prepared to get in on the action. Regular reports from William Ogilvie and Inspector Constantine alerted the Canadian government in Ottawa to the developments in the region as the government began considering what administrative actions the Klondike would require. Meanwhile, entrepreneurs far to the south got ready to take advantage of opportunity.

Early Cattle Drives

One of the interest-generating newspaper accounts to reach the Outside was the report of the sale of Willis Thorp's beef at Circle City.[100] A price of $480 for a ten-pound beefsteak got the attention of ranchers on the Canadian prairies where beef was selling for only a few cents per pound. One cattleman attracted by the stunning potential for profit was Ed Fearon of Maple Creek, Saskatchewan.[101]

Fearon smelled a cattle market in the north, even before the news of the Klondike gold discovery inflamed public passion. In the spring of 1897 he assembled one hundred head of longhorn cattle bearing the "V" brand of Conrad and Price, ranchers north of Maple Creek.[102] On the understanding that he would pay forty-five dollars a head for the cattle that he took north, he shipped the livestock, horses and supplies to Vancouver by Canadian Pacific Railway, then up the coast aboard SS *Capilano* of the Union Steamship Company, which had been fitted out to accommodate the cattle herd plus twenty horses, men, hay and a ton of supplies. Fearon also took Bessie, his family milk cow, because of the calming influence she would have on the other livestock. [103] Fearon did not attempt to use Dalton's trail over the Chilkat Pass; instead, he landed his animals at the head of the Lynn Canal and took them over the shorter but steeper White Pass route to the Yukon River. On arrival in Dawson City he sold ten thousand pounds of meat to the NWMP at $1 a pound, and then sold the remainder to the general public at

$1.50. It wasn't a bad markup for meat that would have sold for nine cents a pound back in Saskatchewan.

The success of Thorp's 1896 cattle drive had impressed Jack Dalton. Dalton started making plans early in 1897 to take a herd of his own across the mountains to Dawson City. He shared the enterprise with his lawyer, John F. Malony, and another backer by the name of Nowell, presumably a member of the prominent mining family of that name from the Juneau area.[104] The partnership contracted with the NAT&T Co. to bring forty head to Dawson at the price of seventy-five cents a pound. In addition, they bought more animals that they planned to sell to the miners for the best possible price they could get.[105] By the time Dalton's arrangements were in place for the trip, his party included some unlikely travelling companions: his lawyer partner, Malony, and a mining developer named Henry Bratnober who was representing the investment interests of the powerful Rothschild family of London.[106] A government surveyor, J.J. McArthur, would join the group at Neskatahéen. McArthur was commissioned to survey the route Dalton had described so eloquently the year before to NWMP inspector Constantine and government surveyor William Ogilvie.

The ship hauling Dalton's livestock and horses to Pyramid Harbor arrived on June 21, and the herd, consisting of forty oxen, two milk cows and sixty Hereford steers, departed for the interior around July 8, arriving at his trading post a short distance from Neskatahéen a few days later.[107] The arrival of the cattle caused a commotion in the community as these were the first such animals that the Southern Tutchone residents had ever seen. After watching them cross the river a mile upstream, the villagers retreated in trepidation to safe vantage points to observe the strange creatures. [108]

Dalton was greeted enthusiastically by all the villagers. The crowd implored him to trade with them for their furs, so he set aside his plan to depart immediately with the cattle herd and negotiated for the furs, demonstrating yet again his wiliness as a businessman. In exchange for their furs, Dalton gave the village people coloured tickets of different values, and they quickly redeemed these for goods in his store. According to Jimmy Kane, a Native man who was young at the time: "we use tickets. . . . We never see cash. I think one dollar is yellow, fifty cents, red, 'two bits', blue, 'six bits' was kind of green, no ten cents. Two bits were the lowest money."[109]

The *Farallon* transported people, animals and freight up the coast of Alaska during the gold rush. YUKON ARCHIVES, H.C. BARLEY FONDS, #5159

Dalton and his party departed with the cattle on July 15. Soon the herd was trailing Dalton, and falling farther behind as the days progressed. His herders had to contend with the unpredictable behaviour of their cattle in the variable and often challenging trail conditions. They encountered quicksand and extremes in weather, and they had to watch over the horses, which took advantage of the long hours of northern sunlight to wander off great distances during the twilight hours. To discourage the wandering of the horses, Dalton would take his blanket up the trail a short distance and sleep on the path to prevent the animals from going past him.

The work of the herders was tough and physically demanding, especially when they had to cut their way through spruce and willow thickets. Because of the mosquitoes, they dared not strip down to cool off. They often had trouble with the oxen who were supposed to carry the supplies. The crafty animals soon learned how to scrape the panniers off their backs by manoeuvring under low-hanging tree branches. Some of the herders were inexperienced and had difficulty keeping the animals moving during the early stages of the trip. Fortunately, they had an intelligent little shepherd dog that would round up the oxen and ensure that all of them made it to camp each night.

Every time it rained, the livestock got spooked and scattered far and wide, but the faithful shepherd dog would round them up again. Water posed other problems; there were many streams to be crossed and rivers to be forded. The cattle could swim across the deep water, but the men usually crossed on horseback. Sometimes two or three men would climb up on the back of one of the large oxen, and the animal became accustomed to waiting for them to mount whenever they reached a stream.

Swamps were hazardous for the animals and the trail gang struggled to avoid them. Whenever they came to a beaver dam, they had to detour around the obstacle. In one case, this was not possible. The dam was a half a mile long and stood fourteen feet out of the water. It took the crew three days to clear the brush growing out of the crest so that the cattle could cross on top of the dam, one at a time.[110]

The worst thing the horsemen had to endure was not the hard work or the trail conditions; it was the insects. When the wind died down, hordes of voracious mosquitoes descended upon them. Each night as they tried to sleep, the insects plagued them without mercy. It was impossible to keep the bugs out of the food. According to McArthur, the surveyor:

One of Dalton's herds at Montagu, not far from the Yukon River. MACBRIDE MUSEUM OF YUKON HISTORY COLLECTION, 1989-26-69

We had mosquitoes boiled with rice, fried with bacon, warmed with beans, and in fact everything had more than a flavouring of mosquitoes. At first we attempted to pick them out of the food, but for every one we picked out, two would drop in. We soon got used to swallowing them, and I think some of us were almost glad of the chance to get even.[111]

The Dalton party moved ahead of the herd, finding the best route for the cattle to follow, and arrived at the Southern Tutchone village of Hutchi on July 19. They left the following morning, but instead of following the trail down the Nordenskjold River, they turned west, crossed the valley and headed for Aishihik Lake. Dalton wanted to test another approach to the Yukon River at Fort Selkirk.

On the trek between Hutchi and Fort Selkirk, one of the oxen staggered into the underbrush, lay down and died. There was some anxiety that a disease had taken the beast and that other animals would succumb, but after a few days without any more deaths, the tension eased as they moved north.[112]

The herd made it to the Nisling River by August 5, arriving at Fort Selkirk a few days later in surprisingly good condition.[113] Because there had been so much grass for them to eat on the way, the animals gained a total of two thousand pounds on the trail to Fort Selkirk, and every pound was money. Hot on their trail were two other herds, one of sixty animals belonging to Cameron, Franklin and Heaney, and another, smaller herd of twenty-eight, belonging to a man from Seattle named Baker.[114]

Surveying for a Road

Government surveyor J.J. McArthur was glad to go on the trail ride with Dalton, but not because he appreciated Hereford steers. The government had assigned him to travel over Dalton's trail and evaluate its suitability for the construction of a wagon road or railway. Constantine and Ogilvie had wanted to conduct the survey the year before but had been prevented by the first onslaught of the gold rush. The authorities suspected Dalton's route would be the best candidate for such construction, but they simply did not have enough information upon which to base a decision. McArthur's job was to fill in the gap, and the report he made influenced government thinking and government map-making for years afterward.

McArthur was an independent and resourceful man. Arriving at Pyramid Harbor early in the morning of June 5, 1897, he found himself well ahead of the boat that was carrying the cattle herd and the animals for his pack train. Instead of hanging around on the coast, McArthur took the opportunity to explore the southern end of the route. McArthur led his party in to the Klehini River in a trip lasting four days and waited there to meet up with their pack train. Because the ship carrying the horses and cattle did not arrive until June 21, the pack train did not reach the Klehini River until July 4, and it was two days more before it arrived at Dalton Cache. McArthur's plan had been to travel with Dalton and the herd, but the surveyor and his assistants decided to precede the main body with four pack horses, setting out on July 7. This small party climbed up and over the Chilkat Pass, then followed the general trend of the land to the north, where they encountered and followed the Tatshenshini River to a point opposite Dalton's trading post.

According to McArthur's account, they were greeted enthusiastically with a volley of gunshots by thirty local residents, some of whom had not seen horses before, and the barking and howling of a hundred dogs. The riders mounted the packs atop the horses in order to make the crossing and provided much entertainment for the crowd who watched the animals floundering amid the boulders in the rapidly flowing river. By the time they arrived at Dalton's post, a large crowd had assembled. Everyone seemed disappointed that Dalton was not a member of this leading group. The Natives watched as the horses were unloaded. One of the ponies was a newly broken bronco, who, startled by the curious crowd and irritated by a loose strap, broke free of his handler and started a display of bucking that scared the crowd away. Two men stayed behind to spy the action from a hilltop two hundred yards away, but the rest of the spectators did not come back until the pack train departed.

Dalton showed up two days later with four others, including his partner, John Malony. After that, McArthur travelled with Dalton and his party ahead of the herd, marking the way and travelling fifteen miles per day. The rate of progress was slow enough to allow the surveyor to explore the countryside, carrying out his work. Having left the trading post July 15, they followed

Dalton's pony express, June 30, 1898. YUKON ARCHIVES, J.B. TYRRELL FONDS, 82/15, 28

the Unahini (Klukshu) River to Klukshu, and then headed northeast, skirt-ing Dezadeash Lake and following the eastern shore of the Dezadeash River. Generally, McArthur would leave camp, either on horse or on foot, and zig-zag along the way to make his observations. His total distance travelled was always far greater than that of the main party, and he usually would arrive in the evening camp a couple of hours after the others had stopped for the day.

They continued north until July 19 when they reached the village of Hutchi, which consisted of two cabins and the frame of another located be-side the most northerly of a string of three small lakes. At this point Dalton made a decision that later caused some confusion in official records. Instead of continuing down the Nordenskjold River to the Yukon along his usual route, he took the exploratory party west toward Aishihik Lake. McArthur opted to accompany Dalton, but sent his survey team to investigate the Nordenskjold River trail.

Dalton, McArthur and their companions travelled over high ground to the north end of Aishihik Lake and reached the village of the same name. The trail to this point turned out to be very trying, requiring them to climb above five thousand feet. From Aishihik, they continued north along a well-defined trail, crossing the Tahte (Nisling) River on July 23 and arriving at Fort Selkirk on July 30 as the last of their supplies ran out. To their dismay, the trading post was bereft of flour and bacon; the only things edible in evidence were "slabs of dried beef nailed to the side of the house up under the eaves." There they learned that up to the end of July, 1,149 people had floated by Fort Selkirk headed for the Klondike.[115] Fortunately, a passing trader came in with two scows full of supplies. Their food needs were met quickly and Dalton secured a ride with the trader as far as Dawson City for most of his party.

Now a team of two, McArthur and Dalton started to backtrack from Fort Selkirk July 31, reuniting with the cattle herders at the Nisling River August 5. Bidding farewell to Dalton at this point, McArthur continued on to Hutchi with a Native guide and one pack horse, arriving there the evening of August 8. The remainder of his survey team, which he had sent along the other trail following the Nordenskjold, had already returned from that reconnaissance low on supplies.

McArthur continued his return to the coast, making a side-trip to Kusawa Lake. From there he and his assistant headed for Dalton's trading post, travelling eighteen hours every day on half rations, and reaching Neskatahéen on August 18 feeling light-headed. For three days prior they had eaten nothing but boiled rice and some mouldy caribou meat. Leaving Dalton's post August 21 after recuperating for two days, they arrived back at Chilkat August 28.

McArthur had covered hundreds of miles of previously uncharted terrain. Because of McArthur's reported observations, the route Dalton had chosen on that journey via Aishihik Lake to Fort Selkirk subsequently appeared on numerous maps as the Dalton Trail, and the misattribution persisted for years. Inspector Jarvis of the Mounted Police tried to clear the matter up in a report he made in 1898:

> Mr. Dalton once did go through to Selkirk but says he will never attempt it again: he had to cross over a range of mountains 5500 feet high, and the trail, or what was called a trail was something awful. He and other parties now going in go down the Hootchai, or Nordenskjold River to Five Finger Rapid.[116]

Although it would be marked on many maps, the Aishihik route was never the main track or even a secondary branch of the Dalton Trail.

McArthur summarized the potential for developing a wagon road at the end of his trip report. The route was possible, he said, with the easiest portion being that from Hutchi to the Yukon River. He estimated that for a cost of sixty thousand dollars, a permanent wagon road could be built from Pyramid Harbor to below the Five Finger Rapid. In Juneau in a newspaper interview, he extolled the potential of this route for rail and wagon roads, suggesting that all future mail would be carried over this route, and stating that San Francisco capitalists proposed to lay a cable telephone line to Dawson City.[117]

Fear of Famine

The rumour of a gold strike draws miners to an area like bees to sugar. In the stampede to Dawson City, seasoned veterans and rank amateurs alike were joined by their hope of getting in on the ground floor of the Klondike bonanza. The population in the Klondike had exploded. Many stampeders incautiously ignored their own experience and travelled light in order to get there at the head of the rush. As a consequence, supplies had been short during the winter of 1896–97; food was scarce and the miners were even killing off their sled dogs for food.

Dawson City, summer 1897. Only months before this photo was taken, the site of Dawson City was nothing but moose pasture at the mouth of the Klondike River. PRINTS AND PHOTOGRAPHS DIVISION, LIBRARY OF CONGRESS, 1897

"If you could see the food we had to eat," said early pioneer Frank Buteau, ". . . you might laugh, but if you found yourself a thousand miles from civilization, without roads, as it were, it might bring tears to your eyes."[118]

There was never enough food; the miners were usually short of something, and often went without important staples for months. The quality of food available to the early prospectors left much to be desired.[119] When the steamer *Bella* arrived in the spring of 1897, it brought with it a shipment divided between food and liquor. Rejoicing, the miners, who had just gone through a winter on slim rations of flour, beans and bacon, indulged themselves:

> In less than an hour the old *Bella* was tied up to the bank, loaded equally with liquor and food, which were rushed ashore immediately. What few saloons there were opened up with free drinks; the ban was off, and *everybody* got drunk. This included the temperance men.[120]

Dawson had been nothing but swamp the year before. Over the winter it had consisted of a small cluster of crude log buildings and tents. When spring arrived, the small community could boast a population of approximately fifteen hundred souls. New buildings were popping up faster than spring crocuses. With ten saloons operating round the clock, but only three restaurants, liquor was more abundant than food. The food shortage would soon become a big issue in Dawson City.

As soon as the ice broke more newcomers began arriving each day. They were the forerunners of the big stampede, those who had made their way over the passes and into the Yukon basin during the winter, or had arrived from more distant points in the Yukon valley. By mid-summer the population had reached thirty-five hundred, and thousands more were struggling over the Chilkoot Trail and down the Yukon River, trying to reach the city of gold before freeze-up. Many of these were travelling without adequate provisions for the long, isolated winter. No one knew how many more would be coming to Dawson, and the residents of the new city did not yet appreciate the impact on the world that news of the Klondike would have when two ships outbound from Alaska, the *Excelsior* and the *Portland*, arrived at San Francisco and Seattle in the middle of July.

America had for years been gripped in the clutches of a devastating economic depression that reduced thousands to poverty. In the northwest, many families lived from hand to mouth; some resorted to living off clams dug from the coastal beaches. As the breadwinners lost their jobs, more and more women and children were forced into the workplace. Thousands of men lay idle for want of a decent job. This era even spawned a popular song titled "Everybody Works but Father."[121] It is not surprising that thousands of men, who for years had languished in the humiliation of unemployment, would go to the Klondike on a quest for fortune and, no less, for adventure. Many of these were inexperienced clerks and labourers who would set out poorly equipped and unprepared for the ordeal ahead of them.

Many of those arriving came without enough food to carry them through the long winter that would follow. As summer progressed an ominous unease grew in Dawson City about the food supply needed to feed the growing population in this isolated boomtown. The managers of the trading companies were losing sleep over the pending shortage. The NAT&T Co. publicly cautioned people Outside not to go into the Klondike without adequate provisions, a warning that the Canadian government soon echoed.[122] The North-West Mounted Police, under the direction of Superintendent Sam Steele, responded to the situation by instituting the one-ton rule that required each stampeder to bring enough supplies to feed himself for a year. This rule undoubtedly saved the hides of many inexperienced gold-seekers the following year, while it increased the demand for food and other goods at various ports along the Pacific coast. Of these, Seattle enjoyed the most economic benefit as the stampeders stocked up there before boarding their ships. Yet despite the warnings, many inexperienced and ill-equipped people with dreams of making their fortune were flocking to the Yukon without adequate provisions.

By the middle of September, with the level of the Yukon River falling and making passage difficult from Alaska up to the Klondike, the expected supply boats from down river had not reached Dawson City. Only the *Weare* arrived with 125 tons of supplies, followed by the *Bella*, but the *Bella* had a light load because many of the goods consigned to her for Dawson had been taken off by force at Circle City. It was said that the *Bella* arrived carrying a cargo of whiskey and billiard balls.[123]

Captain J.E. Hansen of the Alaska Commercial Company went downstream on the *Margaret* to see what additional shipments of supplies could be counted on that fall. He discovered that the company ships *Alice*, *Healy* and *Hamilton* were all stranded in the shallow flats at Fort Yukon, unable to move their shipments to Dawson. Captain Hansen returned from Fort Yukon by poling upstream in order to get word to the worried community that more supplies were not to be expected. Hansen moved around town speaking to groups of men wherever he found them, and his message was not good: "Go! Go! Flee for your lives . . . Do you expect to catch grayling all winter?"[124]

There was reason to be concerned. Inspector Constantine, the officer in charge of the North-West Mounted Police station in Dawson, posted an announcement that read:

> For those who have not laid in a winter's supply to remain here longer is to court death from starvation, or at least a certainty of sickness from scurvy and other troubles. Starvation now stares everyone in the face who is hoping and waiting for outside relief. Little effort and trivial cost will place them in comfort and safety within a few days at Fort Yukon, or at other points below where there are now large stocks of food.[125]

Hurried meetings were held, and fifty men left town in small boats and scows. More took passage on the *Weare*. Inspector Constantine made arrangements for the *Bella* to take more men down the river before it was too late. Then a mass meeting was held and speeches were given encouraging more to leave town. The *Bella* left with 160 passengers on board, each supplied with five days' worth of food.

The old-timers knew what lay before them with a shortage of food. As Pierre Berton wrote: "A man could have half a million dollars in gold—as many did—and still be able to purchase only a few pounds of beans, but it was some time before the newcomers could understand this. They found it hard to comprehend a situation in which gold by itself was worthless."[126]

Another eighteen hundred people, unaware of the impending famine, were reported to be headed for the Klondike, coming up the Yukon River on various boats. Only forty-three actually made it; of those, thirty-five were without supplies, and they quickly turned around and fled back down the river. Although the Mounted Police had implemented the rule that incoming travellers should bring with them a year's supply of provisions or be turned back at the passes, it was too late to catch those already in Dawson or in transit on the Yukon River.

Some tried to corner the market in key supplies. The price of flour went out of sight. According to one man who was trying to find a winter supply of food in Dawson:

> Money was plentiful and everyone wanted to buy, but no one wanted to sell. A man who had five or six sacks of flour was looked on as an aristocrat and was respected and bowed to by everybody he met who knew he had the flour. It soon leaked out that I was short on flour, and I was watched by the police and shunned by everybody. I had enough of other provisions to last me for several months, but had only a part of one fifty-pound sack of flour. If I had two sacks of flour beside this, I could have stayed in Dawson ... I found a man who had two sacks of flour to sell but wanted $120 for them. I told him that he was asking too much, but I would give him a dollar a pound for the flour, and that was enough. He insisted on the price he had asked so I left him. In about half an hour I returned and told him that I would give him his price for the flour, but he refused and raised the price to $160.[127]

The food situation was bad and getting worse. John Brauer, who was the US mail carrier up river from Alaska, noted:

> The only things you could possible [*sic*] buy were sugar, baking powder, spices, and some dried fruit. No bacon or anything of that kind could be purchased from any of the stores, simply because they did not have them ... The stores are practically cleaned out. All they would sell was five pounds of sugar to the man. Flour could not be bought at all. One or two sacks were quickly picked up at $250 per sack.[128]

When I left Dawson, the men who were there had on an average of four month's food supply. Some did not have a month's supply. . . . The restaurant closed the night I left. It had been selling nothing but beefsteak, for which the hungry paid $2.50 a steak.[129]

The price of food of all sorts was rising rapidly, and restaurants were closing because of the lack of fresh meat. Two men caught stealing food were killed immediately.[130]

While many fleeing miners went down the Yukon River into Alaska, some chose to leave by going up the river, intent on trekking across the mountains and reaching the coast before winter set in. Most of them veered off the river at George Carmack's abandoned trading post near the mouth of the Nordenskjold River, and tackled the overland route via Dalton's trail. That winter, before the Chilkoot and White Pass trails became the predominant routes for stampeders making their way to and from the Klondike, the Dalton Trail was the preferred escape route.

Escape from the North

There were two good reasons to leave Dawson City late in the autumn of 1897: the first was to avoid starvation; the second, for the newly rich, was to reach the coast with their gold before the Coast Mountains became impassable. Although things were about to change, the Yukon was still a geographical isolate during the long winter months. Extreme cold, great distances and mountain passes filled with storms and deep snow all conspired to make the Klondike one of the most difficult places on the continent to get to—or leave—in the winter.

The seasoned veterans of the Yukon campaign knew the challenges and hazards of trying to leave the Yukon after the snow started to fly. They viewed the Dalton Trail, with three hundred miles of reasonably level ground, no major streams and its low summit in the Chilkat Pass, as at least as easy a means of exiting the Yukon as poling upstream against the strong Yukon current, through rapids, across lakes and over the snow-shrouded Chilkoot Pass. Because of the existence of a trading post at Dalton House and two established supply caches, one at Hutchi and another thirty miles south of Dalton House, the departing stampeders knew there was a chance that they could pick up supplies along the way. Without horses, however, they would have to travel light in order to carry their gold and make reasonable time. All who travelled out over Dalton's trail that fall encountered hardships of one sort or another, and as the season progressed, conditions worsened. Some men became lost, and most ran short of rations. They encountered harsh weather, heavy snow and frostbite, but not one miner was reported to have perished on the trail that autumn.

Earlier in the summer before the food crisis became apparent, a party of four men had poled up the Yukon River, then hiked out over the Dalton Trail with light packs and heavy pokes. Notable among them was Ed Thorp, who had helped his father bring the first herd of cattle into Dawson the previous fall. For Thorp and his companions, the trek was not an escape from famine but merely a return to their base in Juneau, and Thorp was planning to bring in another herd of cattle.[131] They relied heavily on procuring game along the way but their hunting met with only sporadic success and left them very hungry at times during their trip. They arrived in Juneau in mid-August carrying with them eighteen thousand dollars in gold produced from their gold claims and from the sale of cattle the previous fall.

Many other miners travelled out over the Dalton Trail during late summer and into the fall. They came in pairs and they came in larger groups, travelling by water for the first leg of the journey. The tiny steamer *Kiokuk*, an "old, rickety, and utterly broken down" steamboat, left Dawson headed up the river September 27 with fifteen passengers, each of whom had paid a fare of $250 to be taken as far as Fort Selkirk.[132] At a time when food was scarcer than gold, this price was a bargain. After disembarking, they trickled out of the Yukon over Dalton's trail. As many as three hundred stampeders made the trip that fall.[133]

While some were leaving just to escape hunger, others were taking a fortune in gold with them. Many hoped to return as soon as possible. One party of five men lugged out one hundred pounds of gold along with blankets and provisions. Despite having a Native guide and one member who had previous experience of the Dalton Trail, they got lost and wandered for days over hills and up valleys before they reached Hutchi, gaunt and hungry. There, they bought what supplies they could and continued on their way. A couple of days later they met men guiding a flock of sheep headed for Dawson, from whom, presumably, they were able to pick up additional supplies. They arrived, exhausted, at Dalton House, where they joined a pack train headed for the coast.[134]

Pat Galvin, weighed down with gold dust, came out over Dalton's route with his wife, Mary Ellen. An Irishman from County Kerry, Galvin had been in the Yukon before the gold rush, operating a hardware business and fabricating sturdy Yukon stoves for his eager customers. He was already doing well when the Klondike gold was discovered. Galvin seemed to have the Midas touch and was able to sell some property for a million and a half dollars. When he travelled out in the autumn of 1897, he was on his way to Britain to form The North British American Company. Later his steamer, the *Mary Ellen Galvin*, would be one of the first of the new paddlewheel vessels on the Yukon River. Galvin's party started out with eleven pack horses. By the end of their journey, only four survived.[135]

John Brauer wasn't carrying gold, but mail from Circle City, Alaska. He set out from Circle City September 14, poling three hundred miles up the Yukon River in eleven days. From there, he continued on his laborious journey with three other men, pushing a scow up the ice-clogged Yukon River. At Sixty Mile he was compelled to layover for five days; every couple of days after that, they had to take their tiny boat out of the water to remove the ice caked on the hull, until they reached Carmack's Post and turned landward over the Dalton Trail. He and his travelling party plodded on through three feet of snow for twenty-five days with a dozen horses. All the horses died before he was half the way to his destination. And for this service, his patrons paid a mere two cents per letter.[136]

Some individuals with substantial reputations on the Outside went out over the trail that autumn. A former military man named Lieutenant S. Adair went out on the trail in September but declared he had big plans for returning to the area the following summer. Henry Bratnober also took the Dalton Trail out. Bratnober was a celebrated and colourful Prussian-born mining speculator with a bigger-than-life personality. Guided over the trail by Jack Dalton earlier in the summer, he had investigated prospects in the Klondike gold fields for the Rothschilds of London, but his real interest was in copper.[137]

Severe hardship waited for those who left their exit until late in the season. One unfortunate party departed from Dawson September 24. It included Joseph Whiteside Boyle and "Swiftwater" Bill Gates. Tall and imposing, Boyle was a fight promoter and entrepreneur with a scheme to dredge the Klondike for gold, and he was on his way to eastern Canada to look for backers. Gates was, by comparison, a short man, standing five feet five inches tall with a dark beard and eyes that never stopped scanning their surroundings. Gates was the lucky owner of claim number thirteen on Eldorado Creek and was worth a fortune. He was on his way out for business—and pleasure. He liked to draw attention to himself and was notorious for living extravagantly and pursuing the infamous Lamore sisters, one after another.

The Boyle party battled intense cold as they worked their way up the Yukon River. Their boat was coated inside and out with ice and so badly battered from ice floes that it was barely seaworthy when they arrived at Carmack's Post. During their trek over the trail, the temperature varied from fifteen degrees below zero during the days to forty degrees below zero at night. They had to burrow into the snow at night with nothing but their dogs and a blanket to keep them warm.[138]

They started out with eight horses, but eventually had to kill them all to feed their dogs. At one point, Boyle forded a river waist deep in water, then carried across the others in the party and their packs, one at a time. If it hadn't been for Boyle's leadership, the members of the party would not have reached the Alaskan coast alive.[139] When they finally arrived in Seattle, they had a dinner at which all of those present contributed to the purchase of a gold watch and chain that they presented to Boyle in appreciation of his leadership.[140]

It was very late in the season when Thomas Magee and his son, accompanied by H.A. Ferguson and an Indian guide, departed from Dawson on October 14, in a canoe containing six hundred pounds of personal gear. Magee had first attempted to book passage down river on the steamer *Kiokuk*. Captain Hansen dissuaded the party from going downriver, so Magee resolved instead to take the tiny vessel two hundred miles upstream to Fort Selkirk.

According to Magee:

Seven days were spent upon this steamer and instead of taking us to Selkirk, she took us a distance of thirty-five miles only. Her machinery broke down from one to eight times a day and she was constantly running aground.

On one occasion, through mismanagement, she was driven ahead at full speed onto a rocky shore, where her bow was torn away and her whole frame shaken. But for double protection in her bow she would have sunk. At the end of the seventh day, surrounded by heavy pack ice in the river, the trip was given up, and we all returned to Dawson. This move cost us $200 apiece.[141]

They tried again, battling their way upstream in a small boat against heavy ice floes for nine days, at which point, Magee stated, "The ice in the main river grew daily worse until . . . when in a slough, with raging current, high banks, and overhanging trees, we were caught in nearly ice-closed water. Further travel seemed impossible."[142]

The obstacles they encountered drove the Native member in the party to despair. Having exhausted his vocabulary of profanity in both English and his native language, he broke down and cried, refusing to go any further.

Then they had a stroke of good fortune. Jack Dalton and a Native companion arrived and joined forces with them. Dalton, with his business partner John Malony, had purchased an interest in Klondike mining claims and was eager to return to the Outside before winter shut off the Klondike entirely.[143] Dalton's small river craft, with its passengers and two hundred pounds of cargo, was nearly wrecked in jamming ice, but the travellers continued for another four days of "difficulty, doubt and danger" until they arrived at Fort Selkirk, where they rested for two days before moving on.

They left Fort Selkirk on October 28, using five pack horses, but the going was so bad that Dalton and two others returned to Selkirk for a boat that would lighten the horses' loads. They were now struggling through more than a foot of snow, cutting brush to clear a path as they worked their way up the eastern side of the Yukon, crossing back to the west side two miles below Five Finger Rapid and travelling on to Carmack's Post. It snowed for the next three days, by which time they were breaking trail through two feet of snow on level ground.

Dalton, one of the most seasoned veterans of the northern trails, urged the party to turn back, but, determined to return to civilization, they refused. They were low on supplies and the river was practically frozen shut; they knew, if they turned back, they would find no food to buy at Selkirk. Instead, they continued with Dalton.

At Carmack's Post they turned on to the trail, and after five days of toil, but without new snow, they arrived at Hutchi. Beyond Hutchi, the weather changed. Heavy snows and gale force winds impeded their progress. The surrounding mountains were shrouded by dense clouds, "as black as the densest smoke."[144] At some point they drank tainted water and were stricken with severe cramps and hemorrhages.

When they were able to eat, they got only two meals daily. Breakfast, prepared between four and five o'clock in the morning, was eaten in the dark, as was their dinner, which was prepared between four and five o'clock in the afternoon. The daylight at this season was too short for them to stop to prepare a lunch. Finally, after six days on the trail from Hutchi, they reached Dalton Post and ravenously consumed a meal of corned beef, fresh-baked bread and cold tomatoes.

Two of Dalton's horses had died en route to Dalton Post. The men left their remaining horses there and continued on foot, trudging on through the deepening snows for two days toward a cache that Dalton had set up along the trail near the summit. From dawn until well past dusk they travelled, and in pushing on so hard, they became lost. After a night out huddled behind a large boulder, exposed to strong winds at temperatures of twenty degrees below zero, four members of the party had frozen feet.

Still they continued their journey over the summit, their pace a running walk. Once past the Chilkat Pass, they were over the worst of their travels. Relieved to have survived the forty-two-day ordeal, Thomas Magee stated: "Part of the time I did not in the least care whether I lived or died. Had I been assured any morning of the trip that I would be dead before night, I would with none the less appetite have eaten my full share of bacon and beans and drunk my coffee in contentment."[145]

All of these weathered sourdoughs brought with them news of the pending famine in Dawson City. Thomas Magee described to newspapers, who eagerly reported his statements, how flour was selling for two dollars a pound, and at that price, only by the fifty-pound bag.

Ironically, while making their way out of the Yukon, these travellers couldn't have missed the hundreds of head of sheep and cattle being herded over the Dalton Trail to the Yukon River, where they were being butchered and shipped down river to Dawson City, yet seldom did those going out with their gold or those coming in with their livestock ever make mention of each other.[146]

Meanwhile, nobody starved in Dawson City from famine that winter, though the rumours trickling to the Outside would have some practical and some bizarre repercussions. Unbeknown to the officials concerned for the welfare of the community, plenty of livestock was being brought in.

Bringing the Meat to Market

Dalton had delivered his herd to Fort Selkirk in late August. Not knowing whether there would be any feed for it when it reached Dawson, Dalton slaughtered sixty of his animals and had the meat transported to Dawson aboard a little steamer belonging to Red McConnell. The remaining beasts were herded onto rafts constructed from local wood. Dalton placed Jack Brooks, one of his trail crew, in charge of the flotilla and pushed them off into the Yukon River. The plan was for Brooks to pull ashore each evening so that the animals could graze, but this was a challenge beyond the skills of the inexperienced pilot. Before they reached Dawson City, the steers had lost a lot of weight and their hunger made them restless and hard to handle.

When the Dalton consignment reached Dawson, forty head were transferred to the NAT&T Co. at the previously arranged price of 75¢ a pound, and the remaining beasts were slaughtered and sold to the ravenous Klondike miners at $1.50 to $2.50 per pound. An elderly Jack Brooks later remembered: "Many [miners] would have bought whole animals, but it was sold in smaller lots to give everyone a share."[147]

Brooks reminisced further: "They had no butcher paper, so they sharpened sticks, and when someone selected a piece of meat, it was impaled on a stick and handed across the counter. Even the offal sold for twenty-five cents a pound, for dog feed. And that alone yielded enough to pay off the expenses of the entire drive."[148]

Dalton was not the only one to recognize that every morsel of the animals had value. The bones could be used by restaurateurs for making soup and hides were sold at fifty cents a pound, cut up, hair and all, mixed with rice and oatmeal, boiled, frozen and used for dog food. One enterprising party of travellers never made it to the Klondike that winter. Passing the slaughter yards left upstream by cattlemen, they recognized the potential of the huge gut piles, and spent the winter parcelling the offal and selling it to dog mushers at a dollar a pound for dog food.[149]

Other investors besides Dalton were driving animals to Dawson City in 1897. Some were operating on a small scale: Joe Winterholm and two partners headed in over the trail in late September, using four big steers and six heavily loaded pack horses to haul quantities of beef extract, desiccated beef and other grocery products for sale in Dawson City.[150]

Some were major importers of meat on the hoof, and among them the spirit of competition was intense. The cattlemen knew that whoever got to Dawson first would get the best price for their product. Charlie Thebo was trailing a herd over the Dalton Trail, while a number of rival wranglers were coming in over the White Pass from Skagway and down the Yukon River, including Archie Burns with a small herd of ten animals.[151] Burns was hoping to reach Dawson a few days before Dalton.[152] Three other herders were on their way via this route, including G.F. Miller with one thousand sheep. Both groups planned to drive their livestock as far as possible overland before placing them on scows for transport downriver

Late in the season, Pat Burns of Calgary dispatched a herd of eighty-five five-year-old steers and old work oxen, under the command of seasoned herder Billy Perdue.[153] His animals arrived in Skagway on August 28. The gentle oxen had the heavy task of hauling in the supplies for the party. Although the team lost a reported twenty animals in quicksand on the way, most of the herd and the Burns trail riders reached Five Finger Rapid safely. There the gang butchered the herd before floating the meat down to Dawson. In spite of the hazards associated with their late travel, they managed to make Dawson City by November 4. They were able to sell their beef carcasses, weighing about eight hundred pounds each, for one dollar per pound. This was probably the last meat shipment of the season to arrive before winter set in for good.[154]

Timing was everything, and some herdsmen arrived too late in the fall of 1897 to make it over the Dalton Trail. One of the stragglers was Willis

Thorp, who left Haines Mission September 10 with forty head of his own cattle,[155] another forty that were the property of Thomas Morgan and some animals belonging to other smaller investors. The winter snows came early to the Chilkat Pass, so when outgoing miners James Clark and C.E. Brown encountered Thorp and his herd at the summit, they saw that most of the party was discouraged and wanting to turn back. The cattle were sound, but the horses were dying daily.[156] What lay ahead for the cattlemen were a hundred miles of snow with no feed for the beasts. They pressed on, but day after day the horses succumbed to the cold and overwork, and their bodies were left on the trail with their valuable packs of provisions. This continued until thirty horses had died.[157] It was so cold, Thorp reported, that if he turned his face away from the campfire, ice would immediately form on his beard.

A vicious killer storm took twenty of their horses in one night. Thorp finally turned the herd around, and in the teeth of the biting Arctic winter, found his way back over the snow-covered trail by following the line of dead horses, discarded harness saddles and provisions that had been abandoned. On regaining the coast, he rerouted his herd over the trail from Skagway to Bennett, where the surviving animals were slaughtered and frozen. The meat was sold at Bennett to passing stampeders, or was served in the hotel that Thorp constructed there.[158]

Thorp's son Ed, however, had been determined to forge ahead over the Chilkat Pass trail, despite the harsh conditions. Ed and a dozen others loaded twenty-eight of the surviving horses with supplies for his uncle, who was mining in Dawson, and continued to the interior. On reaching the Yukon River, they encountered an outward-bound party including Joe Boyle, Swiftwater Bill Gates and others. The Boyle party bought the twelve animals that were the only survivors of the inbound journey, and these long-suffering creatures were soon heading back up the trail into the cold and snow.[159]

Another large herd of four hundred cattle and eighty men financed by Boston banker Pierre Humbert came late to Chilkat Inlet and was stranded on the coast, unable to fight through the snow pack to the summit of the Chilkat Pass. Thorp commented on the likelihood of the failure of this party. Humbert's plan called for each of the pack animals to pull a sled. "What do they expect to do with sleds across a country blanketed one to ten feet with snow?" asked Thorp when he was interviewed later in Seattle about the prospects of the Humbert herd getting through. "What are they going to feed their animals on—wind? Did you ever figure how many pack animals it would take to carry food for 100 head of cattle on a sixty-day journey? It would take 1,800 head of pack animals."[160] Without Jack Dalton, who knew better, to guide them through the snows to Dawson, they were stuck at the start of the trail, and the whole affair was abandoned by the spring.[161]

A third party attempted and failed to take cattle over the Dalton Trail that fall. Henry Waechter and Sons landed one hundred live turkeys and 134 head of cattle at Haines, and their group started over the trail on September 12 with Herman Waechter and Herman Steuber in charge.[162] Having caught up with the Thorp party in the Chilkat Pass after struggling through the ice-fields and deep snowdrifts, they joined the Thorp herders in their retreat to the coast.[163] Waechter and Steuber then opted to go over the White Pass and got their herd as far as Bennett before the ice prevented their advance. They slaughtered and froze their animals, rather than feed them all winter, and then moved the shipment forward in the spring. Faced at that time with warm weather and thawing beef, they cut and salted their shipment then floated their product into Dawson just after breakup of the Yukon River in 1898. Bringing in Dawson's first shipment of meat after a long winter, they sold the entire load to eager hungry buyers for two dollars a pound.[164]

Despite the short season, desperate hardships and poor preparation by some of the cattlemen during the summer and fall of 1897, there was still a large quantity of meat that reached the Klondike. J.J. McArthur, the Canadian government surveyor, estimated that two thousand head of sheep and four hundred of cattle were on the Dalton Trail that summer, all expected to reach the gold fields in late September and October.[165] Although food staples eventually ran short in Dawson City, the much-feared winter famine never materialized.

Hutchi

May 1974. I was walking alone on the old Dalton Trail.

The path was taking me north from the Alaska Highway toward the Hutchi Lakes, and this section was still well defined and easy to hike—a superhighway in the bush. In recent years this section had been maintained by outfitters for pack horses.

The trail led through country that had been filled with gold rush stampeders and livestock seventy-five years earlier. Fifty years before that, Kohklux and a party of Chilkat raiders returned to Klukwan over this route after destroying the Hudson's Bay Company trading post at Fort Selkirk. In 1898 a member of a prospecting party travelling this way took a photograph of grave houses at the village of Hutchi. This abandoned cemetery was my destination. Once a busy settlement, Hutchi declined in population in the early twentieth century as residents slowly gravitated to Champagne, a trading site on the Kluane wagon road that later became the Alaska Highway.

The spring sun beat down on me. The snow that had fallen the night before was gone and there was little likelihood of more precipitation. I had a good trail to follow and my destination clearly in mind. I should have been in good shape. But I was in pain.

The night before, when I retired, I placed my boots outside my tent. I woke in the morning with a blanket of white covering everything, including the boots. I laced up my wet footwear and set out on the trail, certain that I could deal with the problem later. In a little while, I found a dry place where I had camped the year before with my friends, archeologist Steve Cassidy and anthropologist Alice Legat. We had set out on the same quest, but had lost the trail and failed to reach Hutchi. This year the place was hauntingly quiet. I set a fire on a bed of fine gravel, and once the fire had settled to a warm bed of coals, I dug down into the gravel, scooped some of it and placed it in my boots. Dry them from the inside out like a good boy scout, I told myself, and I did.

The boots shrank, and became hard and inflexible. By the end of the day my feet were covered with blisters from toe to heel. My sturdy stride had been reduced to a painful shuffle. I decided to set up camp for the evening.

As soon as I removed the boots and saw my feet, I knew I was in trouble. I was on my own, twenty-five miles away from the nearest road, with ten more to cover before I would reach Hutchi. Fortunately, I had brought a new pair of cotton sneakers. Useful when crossing streams and easily dried, they were comfortable to wear at the end of a long day of slogging along the trail when my hiking boots felt like lead weights. For the next few days I wore them, loosely laced, and limped along. I fashioned two walking sticks out of branches and used them like cross-country ski poles. They helped a lot. Nothing was going to stop me from getting to Hutchi this time.

Along the way, there were many features that revealed the history of the region. Not far after leaving the Alaska Highway at the beginning of the trip, I found the collapsing remains of a hastily constructed temporary sawmill used in the war years during the construction of the Alaska Highway. The most notable feature of the abandoned building was the large pile of cast-off beer cans that had accumulated there. I wonder how many fingers were cut off by drunken soldiers while operating the saw. At the end of the first day's hike, I had camped beside a noisy stream, and then noted some poles and other signs of a campsite, apparently decades old, that revealed this as a stopping place for another party before me. I never found out who they were.

At my campsite the second night, I found a recently abandoned brush shelter under the canopy of two large spruce trees. As an experiment, I decided to sleep out in this traditional structure to see what it felt like. I fell asleep in front of a small campfire and woke in the morning after a sound twilight sleep. Night has little meaning at this latitude because by May it never gets dark.

Near this camping spot I climbed a rock terrace. From the wind-swept treeless prominence I could see for miles in every direction. At my feet in the loose gravel I discovered small chunks of granular rock and a scattering of tiny stone flakes. I realized these flakes were the by-product of tools manufactured at this small quarry by long-ago hunters. Probably they, too, had scanned the surrounding landscape for signs of other people, or for game.

I plodded painfully toward my destination, and finally entered a grassy opening along the shore of the last Hutchi Lake. After a few minutes of searching, I located the old graveyard. Once, tiny grave houses stood neatly on posts above ground, each enclosed in a wooden fence, but most of these structures had collapsed. I could still see some of the details of construction and they matched those in my photograph. The landscape behind the dilapidated structures corresponded perfectly with the old photograph.

I aligned myself where I guessed the earlier cameraman had stood, and took my matching photograph. This was the first of many then-and-now photographs I have taken over the years. I then walked about the site snapping more photographs of what I saw, agonizing over which images to capture with my limited supply of film.

I spent the next day surveying the site, locating numerous structures, caches and more clusters of graves, and that evening I slept on the floor of an old abandoned cabin. The following morning I made my way back down the trail I had followed to reach Hutchi. I noted with interest and apprehension that my footprints from the day before were partly obscured by bear tracks. I followed these tracks on the trail for the next two days, as I limped back toward Champagne. I was hypervigilant as I hiked, careful to keep a clean camp and cautious to hang belongings and food well away from where I slept and prepared my meals.

When I reached Taye Lake, I found the excavations of famed archeologist Richard MacNeish who, a decade before, had uncovered an ancient campsite overlooking the lake. The departing scientists had not backfilled the tiny square holes and, despite a softening of the smooth even walls of the holes from natural forces, the dig had remained undisturbed over the intervening years. The ancient campsite was another reminder of the human imprint left on the landscape thousands of years before. Ironically, the excavation of MacNeish had obliterated some of it.

At the lower end of the lake, where Mendenhall Creek ran off to the south, I found a derelict log cabin, once the home of local resident Bobby Kane but now long abandoned. Beside it I was pleased to find the camp of Sue Van Bibber and her sister, Grace Chambers, who were on their last beaver hunt of the season. They had a large tent frame covered with canvas and a team of dogs tethered nearby. They were expecting the arrival of a third sister, Belle Desrosiers. The three sisters were the daughters of Tom Dickson, a former Mountie who had established a homestead at the mouth of the Kluane River at the turn of the twentieth century and raised a family while running an outfitting business from there.

I introduced myself and explained the purpose of my quest, and in the course of our conversation I brought up the topic of the bear whose tracks I had been following for two days. Oh yes, they were well aware of the bear. It had walked into their camp and agitated the dogs before coming up to the entrance to their tent.

"What did you do then?" I asked Sue Van Bibber.

"I got out my .308 and shot him," was the concise reply.

She delivered this remark in a casual manner, as if the event was nothing more unusual than a walk to the creek for a bucket of water or to the woodpile for a few sticks of firewood.

When Belle arrived, she brought guests: a long-time friend from the United States and his daughter who was on her first visit to the Yukon.

The three sisters invited me to watch them prepare a special treat of moose nose for the guests. This northern delicacy proved to be too strange for the young girl, and she turned up her nose. I, as an onlooker, was not offered a taste, and secretly I was relieved to be spared the test of my palate.

Later in the day, Sue instructed me in the art of skinning a beaver. According to Sue, separating the pelt from the carcass is easy as you work the knife up to the backbone. At the backbone, she said, the task becomes much more challenging and special care must be taken when cutting along the spine, or you risk nicking the pelt. She pulled out a large knife and deftly honed it on a sharpening stone before handing it to me and walking away. I looked down at the beaver. I felt honoured that she would trust me to rise to

the challenge and skin it. For a trapper, I realized, the pelt represented a substantial investment, so I resolved to take special care to remove the skin without damaging the fur. Following her instructions, I carefully separated the
hide, which came away easily as Sue had predicted. Then I reached the critical
point on the backbone. There, I slowed down and paid close attention to the
immediate task. I slid the knife in carefully along the spine, using minute
strokes of the blade. It seemed to be working when, faster than I could react, I
made a fatal incision. I'd nicked the hide! The pelt was ruined! I had betrayed
the trust that had been placed in me. I felt shame; I had let down the person
who had showed so much trust in a young stranger. Like a coward, I returned
the knife. I didn't have the nerve to show Sue my butchery. I had learned that
some tasks are not as easy as they seem.

Later, in a final act of generosity, Sue Van Bibber drove me the rest of
the way to the highway in her pickup truck, thus sparing me the considerable
effort of hiking out with my backpack and my blisters. Soon I managed to
hitchhike back into Whitehorse. Despite the pain in my feet, I felt enriched
by my trip. I had reached my objective—the cemetery at Hutchi—and I had
met some unexpected challenges and new experiences along the way.

From this terrace overlooking one of the Hutchi Lakes, I could see for miles
and centuries. MICHAEL GATES COLLECTION

CHAPTER 5

1897–1898: Bold Dreams and Crazy Schemes

By the fall of 1897 Klondike mania was at a fever pitch. Reports of a remarkably rich gold strike in northern Canada (or Alaska, as many mistakenly believed) had electrified the globe. The news of the bonanza was enough to jolt the depressed North American economy from the financial coma it had been in for most of the 1890s. A flood of spending gave industry a massive and sudden kick-start. After years of unemployment and despair, idle family men had something to hope for again. Thousands of men and a few women from all over Canada, the United States and around the world dug out the savings hoarded under the floorboards to buy an outfit and hurry north.

The Klondike continued to be front page news throughout the winter as squadrons of would-be miners prepared to leave for the Klondike or were already on their way. Most of the stampeders were ill-prepared for the arduous journey that lay ahead on the rough transportation links to the Yukon interior, including the Dalton Trail, that had been established during the previous fifteen years.[166] Few had any idea of where they were going or what conditions to expect, and the news trickling out of the isolated north was confusing.

Some news accounts described discoveries of great riches, while others spoke of despair and disappointment: optimists repeated the promise of fortunes to be made; pessimists stated that all the rich ground had been staked.

There were journalists reporting starvation among the miners, and journalists assuring their readers that nobody would be hungry. Whatever the news, accurate or inaccurate, there was plenty of it to go around.

One widely published account, based on stories from some miners who had just come from the Klondike, stated that there were lines of men a quarter of a mile long in Dawson City, waiting their turn to get supplies from the stores. Food was being doled out so that everyone would have a share. Another newspaper, under ominous headlines proclaiming "RICH MEN STARVE," warned: "There would be great suffering from hunger, if not actual starvation, in Dawson City this winter."[167]

Crazy Schemes

Such ill-omened warnings did not stop the frenzied odyssey to the Klondike. Instead, the dire news reports seemed to inspire wild ingenuity in some of the stampeders. One party went north in the fall of 1897 with one hundred turkeys with the intention of carrying them over the Dalton Trail to Dawson and selling them for Christmas dinners at fifty dollars each. "In view of [the unsuccessful experience of Willis Thorp]," reported one newspaper, "... the probability is that there will be no Thanksgiving or Christmas turkeys in Dawson this year."[168] Another party sailed from Tacoma in December, loaded down with five tons of sausage and other cured meats, blithely expecting to take them immediately to Dawson by way of the Chilkat Pass.[169]

There was a report that a telephone line was under construction over the Dalton Trail (there wasn't); another announced that a twenty-six-year-old blind street musician named James D. Gibson was preparing to make the trip. "He plans to go over the Dalton Trail with a spotted cayuse he has commenced training," said one newspaper, and "... when the trail becomes rocky, he will slide down from the cayuse's back and grab its tail with both hands and follow it along."[170]

Then there was Mrs. S.A. Hicks of Newark, New Jersey, who left home headed for Portland, where she would outfit for the Klondike. The fifty-seven-year-old woman, who weighed two hundred pounds and was slightly lame, planned to purchase four hardy mules to transport her ton and a half of supplies and trek in over the Dalton Trail with her adopted son, riding one of the sleds and hobbling along with her walking stick for part of each day.

She said she would attach herself to Jack Dalton, or at least follow the mail carrier, arriving in Dawson the third week of January.[171]

Jack Dalton was nowhere near the trail at the time Mrs. Hicks planned to arrive in Alaska, nor would he have been interested in leading her over the Chilkat Pass in the dead of winter. He was busy back in the lower United States sizing up his opportunities for making money out of the stampede that was heading north.

The truth was that no one was going far on the Dalton Trail in the deep snow and biting cold. All the people who attempted to drive cattle in over the trail in October, including the experienced Willis Thorp, were forced to retreat. One party of wranglers with three hundred horses made it to Dalton's trading post but became stuck there, 110 miles from the coast.[172]

The difficulty of using the Dalton Trail in the winter left an indelible impression on Israel A. Lee, one of the hopeful travellers who attempted it late in 1897. Lee had talked to Ed Thorp, who had come out from Dawson with his pockets full of Klondike gold, and Lee had been heartened by Thorp's words: "It is hard work and a hard country, but there is plenty of gold."[173] Thorp returned to the Klondike in the fall with a herd of cattle, and Lee planned to tag along.

"We shall take three or four horses to carry our packs and travel as light as possible," he wrote his mother. "I think . . . we may be six weeks on the trail and if you do not hear from me in that time or longer, do not worry. There may be no mail get through all winter. I shall be safely housed in Dawson City or Indian River."[174] He didn't consider the possibility that if the mail couldn't get through, then perhaps he might not make it either.

Lured by the potential for making nine thousand dollars in profit in Dawson, Lee made a deal to take in ten horses and ten head of cattle. Things started out reasonably well for him. In mid-September the horses were healthy, despite the constant rain. After ten days of travel, though, things had changed. Only fifty miles along the trail, with another two hundred to go, the first horse dropped dead from exhaustion. All Lee's gear and clothing was getting wet and mouldy. Had he been aware of the conditions ahead of him, he would have waited till spring; instead, now committed, he was determined to carry on.

Six weeks later Lee arrived at Dalton Post. He had learned a harsh lesson.

All of his horses had died from overwork and he had hauled sixteen hundred pounds of supplies on his own back, seventy-five pounds each trip, over the final stage of the journey to Dalton's trading post. Although he was warm and well fed at the stopping place, he felt alone and isolated and he gave up any thought of travelling farther. He sold his outfit to Jack Dalton and returned to the coast through sub-zero temperatures and harsh trail conditions. Leaving Pyramid Harbor, he turned to the White Pass where thousands struggling over that snow-covered trail were keeping it open all winter. When he joined the throng, he met men from two other outfits who also had been defeated on the Dalton Trail.

Railroad Dreams

Despite the harsh conditions presented by the Chilkat Pass and Dalton's trail, there was plenty of potential to lure investors to this route. The early reports of government surveyor J.J. McArthur about the favourable topography of the Dalton Trail drew capitalists to the trail as if pulled by a magnet. In September 1897 the *Seattle Post-Intelligencer* announced that Andrew F. Burleigh, a Seattle lawyer, proposed to build a railroad over the Chilkat Pass and the Dalton Trail. Burleigh said passengers would be able to take the train to Kusawa Lake then go on by boat down the Takhini River and the Yukon to Dawson. For a construction cost of $2,500,000, Burleigh expected soon to transport people and goods from Seattle to Dawson in five days at a good price.[175] George Dickinson, Burleigh's general manager, stated that the Chilkat Pass was the only feasible route because of its "long easy ascent."[176] By January, however, Burleigh's group had raised their cost estimate to $8,000,000.

The Rothschild family of London, England, with Henry Bratnober as their agent, also announced they wanted to proceed with the construction of a railroad over the Chilkat Pass. It was a different enterprise, however, that began actual groundwork for a rail project.

A millionaire Boston banker, Pierre Humbert Jr., sent a large expedition to Pyramid Harbor in mid-October. It was transporting six hundred tons of equipment and feed, 278 horses and 400 head of cattle, and among its eighty men were members of a railroad survey team. Within a month the surveyors were thirty miles up the Dalton Trail and by the beginning of 1898 they had penetrated one hundred miles into the interior. The chief engineer, W.C. Alberger, dispatched a smaller advance party of ten men and five dog teams to the northern terminus of the Dalton Trail at Fort Selkirk, and these men were within one hundred miles of their destination by December 10.[177] Alberger planned to commence construction of the railroad by January 1, but severe winter conditions and substantial depths of snow compelled him to change the plan. By late January he had pushed back his start date to May 1.[178]

There were many warning signs that Mother Nature brutally opposed the railway project. At the end of January Alberger more or less abandoned the undertaking and sent all the equipment and the livestock to Skagway for sale.[179] A year later, however, Humbert was still making optimistic pronouncements in Boston about completing the work. The money was waiting, he said; all that was required was a charter from the Canadian government and his company would be on its way.[180]

Of all the proponents of a Dalton Trail railroad, the most realistic was the Rothschild agent, Henry Bratnober. Bratnober, who had already been in and out over the trail, had seen it at its best and its worst. He harboured no misconceptions about the physical challenge that lay ahead. By December 1897, he was announcing his intention to build a railroad over the Dalton Trail. [181] He filed for thirteen acres of land for a terminal at Pyramid Harbor and he estimated the cost of the line's construction would be between seven and eight million dollars.[182]

By the end of February the Rothschild interests had made an offer to the Canadian government to construct a railroad from Pyramid Harbor to the foot of Rink Rapid if the government granted certain concessions: no charter for another railroad in the Lynn Canal for five years; approval of freight rates advantageous to the Rothschild railroad; and title to portions of land along the right of way of the rail line. One of the principals involved in this proposal was Andrew Onderdonk, who had been a supervising engineer in the construction of the Canadian Pacific Railroad. Canada had until March 10 to agree to the terms.[183]

Assuming the plan would get government support, Bratnober went ahead with preliminary work. On March 5 the steamer *Walcott* arrived at Port Townsend, Washington, en route for Pyramid Harbor with forty men and equipment for building a harbour. Some employees from the Treadwell mine at Juneau were instructed to rent a tug and go to Pyramid Harbor to squat on the land proposed for a new townsite. A survey for the new town was submitted to the Surveyor-General of Alaska. Andrew Onderdonk's son was appointed as engineer in charge of the construction.[184]

By April blasting had commenced near Pyramid Harbor, and in May, Bratnober and the younger Onderdonk were in the interior traveling over the proposed route for the railroad. While the purpose of building the railroad was ostensibly to extend track from Pyramid Harbor to the Yukon River, Bratnober had another idea in mind. If sufficient mineral deposits could be found in the southwest Yukon, a railroad would provide a convenient means to haul the ore to smelters in more accessible locations. Bratnober was especially interested in the rumours of copper to be found in the White River region.

Meanwhile, however, a rival railroad was being constructed quickly from Skagway over the White Pass. The Canadian government, conscious of a challenge to its sovereignty in the north, delayed approval of Bratnober's railroad and promoted an all-Canadian route via the Stikine River. [185] Facing such deterrents, those who had trumpeted a grand railroad along the Dalton Trail eventually abandoned the idea.

Response to Famine

Stories of a looming famine in the Klondike emanated from the north throughout the winter of 1897–98. In Washington D.C., President McKinley and his cabinet were aware of, and alarmed by, reports that American citizens were suffering. By some estimates about 80 percent of all Klondike stampeders were American. Humanitarian feeling inspired wide public concern, but the alleged hunger in the Klondike was also an issue of interest for a political reason: the precise location of the international boundary had yet to be established and it was in the American interest to assert some authority in the situation.

In mid-September Joe Ladue, the newly wealthy and influential founder of Dawson City, visited with Russell A. Alger, the American secretary of war. Secretary Alger was already aware of public concern for the hungry miners, having received several telegrams urging immediate relief for the north.

There was some self-interest in the calls for action from the west coast cities of Tacoma, Seattle and Portland. Several communities in Oregon and Washington saw opportunity arising from the perceived horror of the situation. The Portland Chamber of Commerce wired Secretary Alger extolling their city as the transportation hub to Alaska and requesting that any relief expedition heading north depart from their city. A citizens' committee in Tacoma sent their own telegram, as did the Seattle Chamber of Commerce.

Alger introduced Joe Ladue to President McKinley, and Ladue delivered shocking news: there were six thousand people in Dawson City and there was food for only three thousand. He suggested that stations be set up on the route to the Klondike and that supplies be sent in using relays of dog teams. The secretary of the interior, Cornelius Bliss, proposed an alternative to dog teams: reindeer. Bliss argued that reindeer would be good for transport because they could move swiftly, haul three hundred pounds of supplies each and forage off the land along the way.[186]

President McKinley and his cabinet did not take action immediately, in part because they wanted to hear a report from Captain Patrick Henry Ray of the 8th Infantry, whom they had sent to Alaska to investigate the alleged Klondike famine. With assistance from Lieutenant W.P. Richardson, Ray was to determine the conditions among the miners flocking north and the adequacy of the food supply. While waiting for the dispatches from Captain Ray, Secretary Bliss issued a warning to American citizens of the possible consequences of being trapped for months in the northern wilderness, far from the reach of any aid. Yet thousands continued to travel north in a motley fleet of steamships and rustbuckets to get in on the action.

While the cabinet considered a number of options for moving relief supplies to the Klondike, Secretary Alger instructed the military to be prepared to oversee a major relief operation. By the middle of October it seemed that he was favouring reindeer for carrying this relief inland, but that was not the only transport that he had in mind.

Secretary Alger had first-hand knowledge of another option: steam-powered snow locomotives. He had used these two-ton devices for hauling logs through the snow on his own property in Michigan. George T. Glover, the inventor of the device, extolled it as the best solution to the problem of hauling relief supplies to the goldfields. In Michigan, the snow steam locomotive could haul payloads of up to forty thousand feet of logs at a speed of twelve miles per hour. Built on a heavy steel frame, it had a wood-fired boiler that delivered power to the wheels by means of a giant cog-toothed drive shaft.

Glover was confident that getting these massive machines over the pass was not an insurmountable challenge. He thought that the operators simply would use the steam-powered windlasses on the machines to pull themselves over the steepest part of the summit. He estimated the first train would take no more than forty-eight hours to cross the pass. Glover consulted the crude maps that were available for the interior and misinterpreted the geography of the region, asserting that the grade on the Dalton Trail would make for easy steaming to Fort Selkirk. From there, he said, the locomotives would travel on the ice of the Yukon River and make a fast trip to Dawson City. One veteran of the Yukon, upon hearing of this proposition, described it as a Jules Verne fantasy.[187] Joe Ladue also dismissed as totally impractical the suggestion that supplies could be brought in by these "ice engines."

Not heeding the warnings of men with experience in the Yukon, Glover was as supremely confident of the abilities of his equipment as he was ignorant of the local conditions and the terrain. Glover proposed to deliver several of his machines to the trail head by the beginning of February. They would be ready to start for the Klondike two weeks later, and he was sure they would chew up the miles on the Dalton Trail. [188]

In early January Charles Strauss, a lawyer representing the newly formed Snow and Ice Transportation Company, announced that he had a contract in place with the army for a northern relief expedition. His company would provide the snow steam locomotives and thirty-five cars carrying supplies, and the supply train would be escorted by a company of US Army soldiers under the command of Captain Brainard as it took the food through Canadian territory to Dawson City. Strauss said the company's general manager was E.J. Rosenfeld and he claimed that Joe Ladue had organized the whole endeavour.

Strauss said the cost of building each train and transporting it to Dyea would be less than thirty-five thousand dollars. The Snow and Ice Transportation Company, which owned the rights to the locomotive, would charge the government twenty-five cents a pound for transporting three hundred tons of relief supplies. Once in Dawson City, he said, four of the machines would be used to transport supplies to the gold fields, while the remainder would return to the coast to make a second trip to Dawson before the end of winter. The company started taking reservations for passengers.

In the end, the whole thing appeared to be a fraud. Joe Ladue, who was advertised as the president of the company in the newspapers, was quick to tell the Seattle Chief of Police that he had nothing to do with the business. Anybody who had laid down four hundred dollars to book passage feared never getting to the Klondike or seeing their money again. In February 1898, Mrs. Minnie Cronin of Seattle had the local agent for the company, J.A. Smiley, and his assistant, Phillip Hanna, arrested for obtaining money under false pretences.[189] Meanwhile, agent Smiley continued to claim he had a government contract to haul the relief supplies.

Hot air drove this enterprise, but it wasn't able to drive the actual snow locomotives very far. When the first of the much-heralded engines arrived in the north, a demonstration of its prowess failed miserably, much to the amusement of local citizens. Instead of making the advertised progress to the Klondike, it could barely move forward on a level path. It was obviously incapable of hauling people and supplies over the steep passes and through the rugged Yukon terrain, and the project was abandoned.[190]

Reindeer Relief

When the secretary of the interior suggested using reindeer in a Klondike relief effort, he was picking up on an idea that had been around Washington for some time. It had been proposed earlier, apparently as a divine inspiration, by the famous Alaskan missionary, Sheldon Jackson.

Jackson had been elected as moderator of the General Assembly of the American Presbyterian Church in May of 1897, the first missionary to hold the highest position in the church. After his election as moderator, Jackson continued his missionary trips to Alaska while at the same time cultivating well-placed contacts in Washington. He became an advocate for Alaskan causes, constantly moving between Washington D.C., where he spent his winters, and Alaska, where he spent his summers.

Since his first encounter with reindeer on a trip to Siberia, Jackson had been a passionate publicist for introducing the animals to the American side of the Bering Strait. He believed that the lot of Alaskan Eskimos would be improved if they could be trained in reindeer husbandry.

"It will do more than preserve life," he said of his idea, "it will preserve the self-respect of the people and advance them in the scales of civilization. It will change them from hunters to herders."[191] Despite the failure of an initial effort to introduce reindeer, Jackson continued to champion their importation to Alaska at every opportunity.

He found money to purchase herds of the animals and recruited herders who could teach the Eskimos how to tend to these herds properly. From the outset Jackson preferred the Lapps to the Siberian herders because, among other reasons, the Lapps were literate. He established a reindeer station on the Seward Peninsula north of Nome, then another at the Cape Prince of Wales mission, garnering support from Congress.

In 1897 Jackson took a trip up the Yukon River as far as Dawson City, arriving there on the steamer *Portus B. Weare* July 25, and departing for St. Michael the following day. He advocated the use of reindeer for hauling freight in the Yukon, telling the newspapers, "I believe the mines of the Yukon can never be fully developed without the use of reindeer. The animals are absolutely essential to the successful prosecution of the mining industry under the conditions that exist in that country."[192]

By the time he returned to Washington November 2, the issue of starvation in Dawson City was on everyone's mind. Having both the connections in the halls of power in Washington and the experience of having been to Dawson recently, he was well situated to influence any decision Congress might make with regard to famine relief for the miners.

Though Jackson's presence in Washington was advantageous to swaying opinion in favour of a proposal to use reindeer, the seed was already planted in the minds of the decision-makers. Secretary Alger clearly was considering reindeer as early as October 23 as the best means of hauling supplies to the Klondike, but the decision to take action had not yet been made, nor was the opinion unanimous that starvation was imminent in Dawson City.[193]

On November 29 the Seattle Chamber of Commerce got in on the action, sending a telegram to President McKinley expressing concern for the welfare of the starving Klondike miners. The following day McKinley talked with his cabinet about the situation, discussing various options for transporting relief supplies, including reindeer, dog teams and even Glover's steam tractors. He instructed Secretary Alger to gather as much information on the situation as possible. Congress was to be asked to approve an appropriation for relief measures to be overseen by the War Department.[194]

Communication with Jackson must have been good, or perhaps the secretary of the interior had issued instructions. In either case, there was some confidence that the eventual outcome of the deliberations of Congress would be favourable, because on December 1, William Kjellmann, who was the superintendent of the Teller Reindeer Station north of Nome on the coast of the Bering Sea, was dispatched to Lapland to begin the process of assembling a herd and procuring the necessary herders and equipment for the relief expedition.[195]

A few days later the competition for the lucrative relief contract increased when the Portland Chamber of Commerce upped the ante by offering to provide one hundred tons of food to the relief expedition. It is not known if the government took Portland up on its offer, but within a few weeks a tender call was being prepared for the provision of relief supplies.[196]

Debates regarding a relief expedition began in Congress December 9, 1897, when Oregon senator McBride, presumably because of the interest of the Portland Chamber of Commerce in the matter, introduced a joint resolution. This resolution called for the distribution of the relief supplies provided by the Chamber, and also called for an appropriation of $250,000.

A few days later, on December 14, Secretary Alger submitted his report on the matter to the Senate. The report affirmed the belief that that there wouldn't be sufficient food for American citizens in the Klondike. It further stated that five hundred reindeer should be purchased in Lapland, and permission given to allow a number of Lapp herders into the country because of their knowledge of herding these animals. The report did not state that the supplies necessarily should be distributed for free since, though food was in low supply in the Klondike, gold was not.[197]

Debate of the bill followed, and minor revisions were made to it. With the permission of the Canadian government, this relief would be extended through Canadian territory.

If the decision to use reindeer was made in the minds of Congress, it is also clear that the ever-optimistic George Glover did not give up hope of selling his snow locomotives to the government as part of the package. While the bill was being debated in Congress, the *New York Times* reported that Glover had approached Secretary Alger with a proposal to use his steam engines to haul supplies to Dawson in quick time to save the miners from starvation.[198]

On December 18 the die was cast: President McKinley approved an act of Congress to supply, with the approval of the Canadian government, relief to the starving miners in the Yukon either free, or at cost. The secretary of war was authorized to bring in the supplies using reindeer and Lapp herders. Once the supplies were delivered, the reindeer could be sold off to recover some of the costs of the expedition.[199]

Jackson, with pockets full of government money, immediately set off for Norway, where he secured Lapp herdsmen, 538 reindeer plus 250 tons of reindeer moss to sustain the animals on the long journey ahead. The herders and their animals set off across the Atlantic, departing on the *Manitoban* from Bossekop, Norway, on February 4, 1898, and arriving in New York more than three weeks later, February 27.

In the north, the immediate reaction to the reindeer plan was not altogether positive. Jack Dalton, undoubtedly the most capable and experienced packer in the Yukon, immediately criticized the use of reindeer in a newspaper interview in Seattle. He said that while there was no doubt there was need for a relief expedition, the notion of using reindeer to provide relief supplies to Dawson City was preposterous. In his view the best approach would be to use horses, provided they were adequately fed, to haul the supplies from Dyea over the Chilkoot Pass and down the Yukon River.[200]

Dalton, always looking for a good business opportunity, offered to lead a relief expedition himself, but his proposal was turned down by Captain Robinson, the army contract quartermaster at Seattle, who stated firmly, "A good army officer could make his way in with an expedition. Montana horses should be used."[201]

By late December, four officers and fifty men from the US 4th Cavalry, Company H, 15th infantry, were headed to Dyea to establish a camp to handle the relief supplies for the miners. The Army was hedging its bets; while rapidly advancing the acquisition of a herd of reindeer, they were also evaluating other options. Quartermaster Captain Robinson, basing his judgment upon Dalton's own evaluation of conditions on his trail, said that the Dalton Trail was not the way in for a relief expedition. He further pointed out there was a large supply of seventy thousand pounds of beef, together with horses and feed (probably belonging to Waechter and Sons, or Willis Thorp), that was already located at Bennett.[202] This would make the problem of supplying the starving miners much less challenging as food was already only a few hundred miles from its destination. Meanwhile, another procurement officer was in Chicago, preparing tender calls for the provision of the relief supplies.[203]

While all of these preparations were under way, word was trickling out of the north that the food situation in Dawson was not as bad as originally thought. By mid-January all plans to procure emergency supplies were put on hold. The need for a relief expedition was disappearing at the same time that Sheldon Jackson and William Kjellmann were hurriedly assembling a herd of reindeer, herders, reindeer fodder and supplies half a world away.

By the beginning of March the decision to cancel a relief expedition was official, but by this time the large herd of reindeer had already landed at New York City, accompanied by the colourful entourage of Lapp herders. From there, the herd was transported to Seattle by rail, where they were transferred to a three-masted bark, the *Seminole*, which was towed by the tug *Sea Lion* to Alaska.

By the time the reindeer expedition arrived on the west coast, the government had concluded that the miners of Dawson City would not need help after all. The necessity for a relief effort was gone, yet, spurred on by the vague commitment of the Klondike, Yukon and Copper River Company to purchase the animals when they reached Circle City, the organizers of the reindeer expedition carried on to Alaska. The most foolish episode in the Klondike saga was underway.[204]

Ironically, the reindeer expedition was soon suffering from the same problem it had been intended to solve: starvation. Reindeer require a specialized diet of moss and cannot live on the grasses commonly fed to cattle and other livestock. Four died in Seattle while waiting for transport to Alaska, and another eight expired on the voyage north. The situation did not get any better when the herd arrived at Haines Mission (now Haines) Alaska on March 27, 1898. They were dropping like flies. Observed one of

People watched with amusement and fascination as the reindeer relief expedition slowly made its way through the wilderness to the Klondike, arriving more than a year too late to provide any relief. YUKON ARCHIVES, J.B. TYRRELL FONDS, 82/15, #96 AND #368

the herdsmen: "They are so hungry that they ate the bark of spruce trees and licked each other a little, and even bit into our clothing, which was pitiful to see."[205]

Under the supervision of Hedley Redmeyer, the herd was moved toward the mountains where there was some food available, but the deep snow in the mountain passes blocked their way to an abundant supply. By April 15 they were able to move over the mountains on the Dalton Trail but in the middle of May only 164 would still be alive. [206]

The reindeer trail drive started out with the reindeer pulling their provisions in pulkas, the traditional boat-like sleds of Lapland, but with the disappearance of the snow the trail gang had to stop to fashion packs. In the warm weather the herd shed their winter coats, and then made for the ice and snow of the uplands to escape the flies. In order to avoid the heat the herders kept the reindeer at higher elevations rather than following the trail.

All that summer the reindeer expedition wandered about the southwest Yukon. Their human food supply was limited so eight of the fifteen men were sent back to Haines and then on to Seattle. This staff reduction ensured the food supply for the remaining seven would last until the end of September.

By June 23 another eighteen animals had perished. The animals frequently wandered off into the nearby mountains and had to be brought back to the trail. After crossing the summit the herd turned west and followed the Tatshenshini River for several days before doubling back. They took to the peaks on the east side of the Dalton Trail and by the time they got to the Mendenhall River the herders had to send a party forty miles back to Dalton Post to get more supplies. Meanwhile, the main party moved on, across swamps, over mountain peaks and through dense brush, crossing raging streams and suffering from the constant hordes of mosquitoes. By the end of September they had made it as far as Hutchi. From Dalton's trading post located there, they were able to obtain additional supplies to last them until the middle of December.

They turned west at Hutchi, crossed the Aishihik River and moved northwest past Aishihik and the Nisling River all the way to the White River. By the middle of October they were fighting the early winter snows. The men were not prepared for the cold and they were running out of supplies again. Some of the herdsmen began suffering from frostbite. The reindeer were getting thin and weak and they were attacked by wolves. One herder drove a reindeer wearing a bell ahead of the main body of animals, which had four more herders pushing them on. Finally, two more herders, each handling six animals hauling their provisions, brought up the rear.

They finally reached the White River and followed it down to the Yukon where they were able to obtain provisions near the mouth of the Stewart River. Christmas came and went. Eventually, on January 27, 1899, they passed through Dawson, where, with the help of the Mounted Police, they were able to pick up a month's supply of food. A month later they arrived in Circle, Alaska, their final destination. Only 114 reindeer completed the trip.

Eighteen months after the original food panic the reindeer relief expedition had arrived at and passed Dawson City, their original destination, more in need of aid than those they originally had been intended to assist. In the end, this was one of the biggest boondoggles of the entire Klondike gold rush.

At the completion of the ordeal, one of the Lapps approached their leader and said: "Do you think there is any hell worse than this one?"

"No," he responded, "I think this is all the hell we want."[207]

INTERLUDE

Charting the Trail

Not all my history hunting has been conducted on the far-reaching trails and rivers of the Yukon; some of it I undertook in the confines of libraries and archives at several different locations across the continent. I think the best history hunting combines both elements—the physical and the cerebral.

Maps ancient and modern have revealed the story of the Dalton Trail to me in a way that goes beyond geography. They detail how individuals and cultures have perceived the realities of the landscape. The European maps are criss-crossed with imaginary lines that represent the concepts of latitude and longitude and the artificial boundaries between nations, provinces, states, municipalities and other jurisdictions. If you go out and stand on the land itself, the lines are not visible, but they are real and they are powerful. They divide the land and define people's understanding of how land can be used.

In the centuries of European and American imperialism, maps were important tools for the colonizing nations to define their territory, carve up the landscape and call it their own. Maps played an important part in the boundary dispute along the Alaskan panhandle involving the United States, Britain and Canada between 1899 and 1903. Contemporary maps, although they were abstract fabrications, had significant implications in the shaping of relations between nations.

Often maps of the north have been produced for a specific economic purpose. During the Klondike gold rush, all eyes were looking toward the Yukon. The big transportation companies saw an opportunity in this stampede of travellers to the distant gold fields and produced promotional brochures with maps showing the convenient routes to the Klondike using their shipping lines and railroads. Railroads that didn't come within a thousand miles of the Yukon or Alaska were quick to show their location in relation to the Klondike. On these promotional maps, the details in areas beyond the reaches of the sponsoring transportation networks are seldom entirely accurate and sometimes highly imaginative. What happened to their passengers after they disembarked at their transit points—whether it was Vancouver, Seattle, Skagway, Dyea or Pyramid Harbor—was of little consequence to the map-making companies. The message hidden in their maps is this: if you make it all the way to the Klondike, good luck to you.

On the other hand, there are maps that were produced by indigenous people who saw their world in a different way. Until white men challenged them to mark the landscape on paper, the long-time inhabitants carried their knowledge of the region in their heads. When they came to make maps, they based them upon the first-hand knowledge obtained by those who travelled through the land. Latitude and longitude have no place on these maps. Rather, they trace pathways by marking their connections to important features on the landscape, and they measure distance in days of travel by foot, rather than miles or kilometres. Each map is a distinctive work of its creator because each individual carried with him or her a unique set of personal reference points.

Sometimes different Native groups would create maps of a shared area and bestow different place names in different languages on the same features. Thus, some places on early Native maps will have several different names to describe them, a source of confusion for early white map makers— and often for me today.

The place names on Native maps are more than geographical markers. They are also cultural mnemonics, prompts to stories that hold special meaning for Native people. The stories associated with a place name can carry useful information for a traveller hoping to pass that way.

Like the Europeans, the Native people of Alaska and the Yukon had their own sense of territory and boundary, a sense that defined ownership and access. Just as the European colonial nations were protective of the territory they claimed, the Chilkat were proprietorial about access to and use of the mountain passes they controlled, for these access points enabled them to command the trade between the coast of Alaska and the interior.

A significant distinction between the two traditions of defining and marking the landscape appears in their respective methods of transmission. The European tradition relied heavily upon the use of paper maps, while the traditional indigenous means of sharing personal knowledge was by verbal communication. When I examined the early Native maps like the ones drawn by Kohklux, those gathered by Glave at Neskatahéen and the one produced farther to the north by Paul Kandik, I was amazed.[208] These maps represent a newly emerging interface between two cultures' definitions of the landscape.

When I first started to explore the land of the Dalton Trail, I relied upon the national topographic maps produced by the government. Those that I purchased during the 1970s still showed where the traditional trails traversed the region. These dotted lines became important for me because they defined the routes I followed during my personal journeys of discovery. Upon them I scribbled notes of my own about where I went, where I camped and what I observed along the way. I suppose my maps are now a blend of the European and the Native styles.

Inspired by photographs, maps and written accounts both published and unpublished, I sought to find and reconstruct the extent of the Dalton Trail and the places along it. My reconstruction, of course, became a personal memory of the landscape with my own individual points of reference. Here was the place where I found an old abandoned camp. There was where I stopped to dry my soaking boots. Climbing that hill I encountered a spectacular view that inspired contemplation about the meaning of the land around me. In my maps I created my own vision of the landscape with my own places of personal or shared meaning. Yes, my old maps preserve the route of my travels, but they also do more. They pinpoint the places where special experiences defined my growth into a history hunter. These maps chart the shape of my past and my future.

To develop a good map of the Dalton Trail I collated my personal experiences and observations with those of previous travellers such as Kohklux and Glave, McArthur and Thompson, and I talked with people who knew

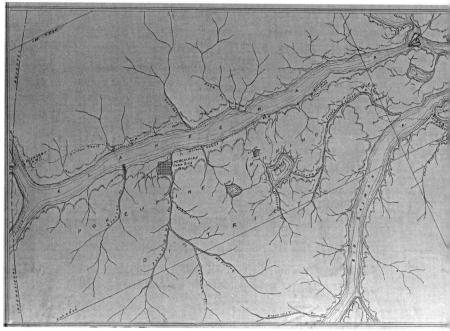

An unexpected find, this is the map that Dalton commissioned to show the precise route of his trail and the location of surrounding communities and features. ALASKA STATE LIBRARY AJ MAP 39-A-97 (AJ-074)

the country well.[209] Each narrative that I collected added some detail to the larger picture. Each person I spoke to put more flesh onto the cartographic skeleton. I compiled these references into a lengthy reference table that I arranged in a linear fashion that detailed all the important points along the way.

During my research I often encountered intriguing details about some interesting places. These provided me with the incentive to revisit the route of the trail, to see what I hadn't seen before, to discover what I had walked past on a previous expedition and to add meaning to the already rich landscape that I was constructing from my own experiences. It took me three hikes along the trail over a span of five years to locate the remains of Camp Storey and another to find Pennock's Post. The cabins were erected in 1898 by the Mysterious Thirty-Six.

In some instances an old photograph intrigued me and prompted me to determine the exact place where the photographer stood when the shutter

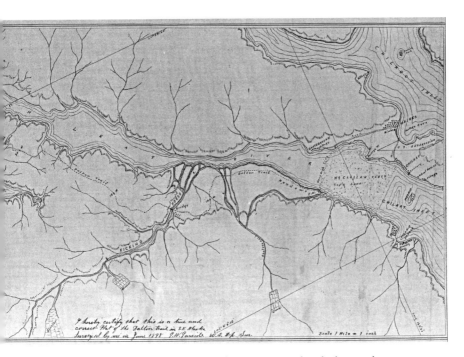

was pressed. I enjoyed the sense of excitement, the slight tingle in my spine when I stood where someone had stood a hundred years before while setting up the camera for the exposure. Snapping my own photograph from the same vantage point gave me satisfaction and provided a then-and-now comparison.

I had the pleasure of sharing some of these experiences with others. While I was able to determine the general location of some of these old places through my research, my friends sometimes saw what I couldn't when we got out on the land. It was Ron Chambers, who travelled with me on the Dezadeash River in 2008, who actually found the rotting and almost invisible remains of Pennock's Post. Ron and I were focussed on the River corridor on that voyage of discovery. In the following year when I revisited the area with my neighbour, Mark Iceton, he helped me spot the vestiges of the old trail that I had overlooked on my previous quest. On other expeditions to old waypoints on the trail my wife, Kathy, was a helpful archeological sleuth.

I had my helpers on the land and I had others in the library. On one occasion I was searching for photographs at the Alaska State Historical Library in Juneau. The staff there had been especially helpful to me, so when I completed my planned assignment ahead of schedule, I had some time at my disposal. What more can you show me, I asked? They led me to a computer that contained several databases they thought might interest me. I opened the file of maps and drawings and typed in "Dalton Trail" in hope of finding something useful. One of the items captured in my search was a map of the Dalton Trail. This was something new. It's worth looking at, I thought, so I requested the document. The archivist couldn't find it for me, so she suggested that I come back the following day. Meantime, several of the staff combed the storage in search of the missing item.

When I returned the next day they had found the misplaced document. They brought it out and carefully unrolled it for me to examine. It was one of those moments of discovery when time suddenly stands still. On the table in front of me lay exposed the official survey map of the trail from Pyramid Harbor to Pleasant Camp, commissioned by Dalton more than 110 years before. Each turn and twist in the trail was plotted, each bridge noted, each point of interest identified. The precise location of Dalton's toll booth was indicated as were obscure places such as Walkerville, Camp Sunshine and other stopping places along the route. Here was the precise charting of the road built by Dalton.

Immediately I knew this map was yet another challenge for me to go out onto the land and retrace the historic route followed during the gold rush. Here, on a table in a library far from the Yukon, was the starting point of another quest.

Each of these journeys into the landscape of the Dalton Trail provided me with more than a correlation of historical fact with physical location. They also gave me intense personal experiences: the "aha! moment" in the archives; the splendour of a magnificent view from a sun-drenched hilltop; the eerie mystery of the loon's call and the sight of a rich array of birds in a remote wetland; the thrill of catching grayling for dinner at the end of a long day of travel; and the terror of a chance encounter with a grizzly.

Maps always give me one more journey to look forward to. I need them.

CHAPTER 6

1898: The Great Stampede

Gold seekers surging into the Klondike during the winter of 1897 and the spring of 1898 had to choose a route carefully, and every route carried hazards.[210]

Those who had enough money could travel by boat up the Pacific coast and across the Bering Sea to the mouth of the mighty Yukon River, where a fleet of river steamers took them fourteen hundred miles up the Yukon into the heart of the continent. Many who tried to reach the Yukon interior this way found themselves frozen in, marooned along the banks of the Yukon River until the spring thaw. Stampeders with smaller bankrolls headed for the more southerly gateway to the White Pass, the thriving port of Skagway on the Lynn Canal. Others set their course for the neighbouring settlement of Dyea that was the starting point for the most fabled route of all—the Chilkoot. Over these two steep trails, tens of thousands of determined stampeders trudged with one thing in mind—to reach the Klondike as soon as possible.

Some prospectors coming in from the Outside took a longer and more arduous overland route to Dawson City. Starting at Edmonton, they travelled north to the Athabasca River and followed it to Lake Athabasca, continuing down the Slave River to Great Slave Lake. From the lake they could enter the great river road of the north, the Mackenzie. They followed the Mackenzie and its tributaries until they could portage across the Richardson Mountains and come down into the Yukon. On this route, many died from starvation, drowning and scurvy, and when survivors straggled into the Klondike, usually a year and a half to two years after setting out, the excitement of the gold rush had subsided, the good claims were already staked and opportunity had passed them by.

The Canadian government promoted another all-Canadian route into the Klondike, urging prospectors to come in from the Canadian west coast up the Stikine River then over the Telegraph Trail to Teslin Lake. From the lake they could take the Teslin River to its confluence with the Yukon and let the river carry them on to Dawson. This was the route used by two hundred members of the Yukon Field Force, an expeditionary unit of Canadian soldiers dispatched to Fort Selkirk to maintain Canadian law, order and sovereignty.

Some of the most ill-fated parties to depart for the north were those who elected to cross the massive Valdez glacier from the Alaskan Pacific coast. Nearly 3,500 souls attempted the glacier traverse and suffered horrifying consequences. Of these, only 1.5 percent ever reached the Klondike.[211]

People with experience in the north knew that travel over the coast range in the winter time was virtually impossible. Those who tried to cross the mountains and icefields in the winter faced bitter storms that raged for days on end and snow in quantities great enough to bury them alive. One tragic story that should have been cautionary for the stampeders was that of Tom Williams, a prospector from the interior who had perished in the winter of 1886 when he tried to come out from Fort Nelson at the mouth of the Stewart River, carrying mail announcing the discovery of gold on the Fortymile River.[212]

In the gold rush winter of 1897–98, even the formidable geographical barriers of the northern interior could not hold back the human tide. By sheer force of numbers, would-be prospectors packed down the trails. At the steepest part of the Chilkoot Trail they carved steps out of the ice and snow that clung to the rocky mountain sides. The iconic image of the human chain of men climbing to the Chilkoot summit was etched indelibly in the memories of all those who attempted the ascent that winter.

The Chilkoot Trail was known as the "poor man's route," and even this route cost considerable money, time and effort. First the prospector had to travel to a port on the Pacific coast, and then purchase a ton of supplies, enough to last a year. Next he had to find passage to Dyea on a northbound steamer. Everything along the way cost dearly in money and spirit. Once the gold seekers landed at the trail head, they had to carry their supplies thirty-three miles over the Chilkoot Pass to Bennett Lake, where they built a raft or scow for transporting their outfit from the headwaters of the Yukon all the way to Dawson City.

After the famine scare of 1897, the Mounted Police enforced a strict policy that required each person entering the Klondike to bring a year's supply of food and equipment so that the panic of the previous year would not be repeated. Anyone transporting an outfit over the trail had to relay this heavy load forward, backtracking two dozen times or more to bring everything to the next stop along the way. Thus, a prospector moving a thousand pounds or more of supplies from Dyea to Bennett at the headwaters of Yukon River navigation would have to cover a cumulative distance of more than fifteen hundred miles before he was finished.

The White Pass was another route to Bennett Lake, and although the distance was greater, the grade was easier than on the Chilkoot, and horses could be used to transport supplies. The White Pass crossing was a cruel path that earned a name of infamy among the stampeders: the Dead Horse Trail. Thousands of horses perished on the White Pass from the horrific conditions they endured and the brutal treatment they suffered at the hands of their owners. Obsessed by the lust for gold, the miners let their humanity slip a couple of cogs as they dropped the veneer of civility. The relentless human tide would not halt to move a dead animal off the trail. Instead, thousands of pairs of feet simply ground the carcasses into the mud or snow. And woe to the sick and injured men or beasts, for no one seemed willing to spare the time to offer assistance.

While miners poured over the Chilkoot Trail and White Pass throughout the winter of 1897–98, there was little traffic over the Dalton Trail after Thorp, Waechter and others failed to get their cattle and horses across the Chilkat Pass in the autumn. The trail was not as well publicized as the steeper but shorter routes that started at the head of the Lynn Canal. It also presented greater logistical difficulties because few stampeders could carry their own goods over its length of three hundred miles between Pyramid Harbor and the Yukon River at Five Finger Rapid. To take the Dalton Trail, a miner had to bring his own transport and pay Dalton a toll, or hire Dalton to pack his gear for him. One way or another, those who chose this access to the interior would be compelled to pay Jack Dalton for the privilege of using it.

That winter Dalton was far away from the Yukon. After making his brutal trip out from Dawson City in the fall, he arrived in Seattle with dozens of other bedraggled and weather-worn escapees from the Klondike, many of them laden with gold. Dalton tried to avoid publicity on this visit, but occasionally he responded to reporters asking about conditions in the north. Although he spoke with authority and accuracy, he was unable to scotch the rumours of impending famine. When he said there would be no starvation in the Klondike that winter and denounced as impractical the various schemes for relief being proposed by the US government, his words fell on deaf ears. Nonetheless, because he was a figure of note in the north, Dalton's views were sought out by serious businessmen as well as the thousands of schemers and dreamers eager for information about the Klondike. To satisfy the questioners, he eventually provided the newspapers with some rules of the trail to guide their readers.[213]

Dalton's Dreams

Dalton was more interested in chasing business opportunities than in talking to the press. He and his lawyer partner, John Malony, went east for a few weeks, looking for capitalists willing to invest in the construction of a Dalton Trail railroad. When Dalton returned to the west coast, he was invited to Vancouver, Washington, to speak to General Henry R. Merriam, the government's point man on the initiative to get relief supplies to the starving miners of Dawson. Dalton submitted a hastily assembled proposal, but it simply added to the growing list of schemes being considered by the government. His idea died with all the others when the relief project was called off, except for the reindeer expedition that blundered across the southwest Yukon for the next twelve months.

Meanwhile, Dalton went forward with plans of his own. Soon he had organized the Dalton Trail Company in partnership with Malony, Henry Bratnober (representing the Rothschild family), Fred Nowell from Juneau and Ed Hanley from Oregon. Hanley had known Dalton for many years and was his trusted friend. (A decade earlier, after Jack Dalton had shot and killed an adversary in Oregon, then got into further trouble with the law, it was Hanley who provided Dalton with a horse upon which he escaped from his pursuers.) The partners knew Dalton well, they knew the north and they knew about money. Together, these five men raised $100,000 to develop Dalton's trail.[214]

The Dalton Trail Company proposed to carry passengers, light express freight and mail between the Chilkat Inlet and Dawson. It planned to charge $250 to transport each passenger with up to forty pounds of personal luggage by horseback between Haines Mission or Pyramid Harbor on the coast and Five Finger Rapid on the Yukon River. At the river the passenger would transfer to a riverboat for the last leg of the journey to Dawson. Dalton's group purchased five hundred horses, intending to assemble them into pack trains of fifty to sixty animals and station them at various points along the trail.[215] The pack trains would run on a regular schedule. Every party of travellers would have its own cook on a trip estimated to take eleven days.[216] The company placed advertisements in a Seattle newspaper announcing the new service.

Dalton and Hanley quickly assembled the horses and equipment they would need for their operation in the north. In the spring of 1898 Dalton returned to a property he owned in Haines and Hanley accompanied him to help set up the project. Dalton realized he needed some land in Pyramid Harbor to build a store and corrals, and he knew that Bratnober and Andrew Onderdonk, operating as agents for Rothchild's London Exploration and Development Company, had secured a charter from the US Government for land at Pyramid Harbor to establish the terminus of a railroad.[217] With no difficulty he convinced his friend Bratnober to lease some of the railway allotment to him.

Dalton quickly set about making improvements to the trail. Hiring more than eighty men, Dalton formed them into five work gangs to cut lines along the trail, build corduroy over boggy ground and construct bridges to span the rivers and streams. He also hired a surveyor to plot the route from Pyramid Harbor to Dalton Cache, a point forty-four miles up the trail near the Canadian boundary. (The North-West Mounted Police later established a detachment nearby to assert Canadian sovereignty on the north side of the border crossing.)

On his trip south Dalton had met Secretary of War Alger, and with a shake of the hand they had agreed that if Dalton expended money to develop a trail to the interior, Alger would compensate him for the investment. Alger subsequently broke his promise, but Dalton went ahead with the project at his company's expense.[218] The Dalton Trail Company invested more than fifty thousand dollars on trail improvements, of which between seven and eight thousand was expended on the Canadian portion.[219]

By June Ed Hanley had arrived in Chilkat Inlet with the horses, and the first pony express trip of the Dalton Trail Company left Haines Mission on June 10.[220] The express was set up as planned in five outfits of fifty horses each to carry freight from Pyramid Harbor to Five Finger Rapid and back.

Meanwhile, the company made arrangements to accommodate customers wanting to make a trip out to the coast from the Klondike. Steamers picked up passengers in Dawson City and transported them upriver to connect with the north end of the Dalton Trail. It was rumoured that Dalton and Malony had paid $27,500 to buy the steamer *Willie Irving* so that she

Dalton improved the trail through the coastal rainforest by widening, levelling, laying corduroy and building bridges across numerous streams. MACBRIDE MUSEUM OF YUKON HISTORY COLLECTION, 1989-30-060

could take customers from Dawson to Rink Rapid where they would transfer to the trail division of the enterprise.[221] On the first voyage of the *Willie Irving*, the little steamer carried twenty-two passengers, ten of whom transferred to Dalton's horses at Rink Rapid, headed for Pyramid Harbor, while the remaining twelve set out on foot. The members of this out-going group were said to be carrying $50,000 in gold.[222]

In April 1898 Yukon Commissioner J.M. Walsh instructed the NWMP to see that letter mail was carried monthly from Dawson to Skagway by the Dalton Trail. The Alaska Commercial Company steamer *Victoria* left Dawson June 14 carrying passengers and the first mail of the season to connect with the Dalton Trail.[223] The *Victoria* ascended the Yukon River to the Pelly, where the mail was transferred to a police boat that took it to Five Finger Rapid. There it was transferred again to a horse packtrain and taken by NWMP constables to Pyramid Harbor. This service was to have been performed monthly until mid-October 1898, but the government dropped this route after one trip because it was discovered they could send the mail more cheaply and quickly on the new river steamers that were running successfully on the Upper Yukon lakes.[224]

A week later the *Victoria* left Dawson again, but it was the last trip on which it would connect with Dalton's pony express; by the time the little vessel returned to the Klondike, it had been demonstrated that small steamers could negotiate the Five Finger Rapid and carry passengers upriver at a lower price than Dalton was charging for the longer journey on horseback.[225] After months of preparation and great expenditures of capital, Dalton saw competition from the riverboats kill his pony express enterprise almost before it could get underway. Given the choice between a week in the saddle on a long trail and a few days in comfort on a river steamer at a lower price, travellers made the obvious decision. Despite lowering his price, Dalton found that the pony express could not match the appeal of the steamer service.

Just as it was becoming apparent that the horse transportation service was going to fail, Dalton ran into even more serious trouble from his old adversaries, the Chilkats. In his haste to capitalize on Klondike fever, Dalton had rushed the construction of corrals, a warehouse and a store on the property he had leased from the London Exploration and Development Company. To put up the new structures he destroyed some gardens the Chilkats had been cultivating on the land which was theirs traditionally. The resentment of the Chilkats toward Dalton became deep and bitter, and in mid-June it burst into violence. Dalton was leading a party of six men along the banks of the Chilkat River a few miles from the town of Chilkat when two gunshots rang out. The first bullet whistled past Dalton's ear, but the second one hit him squarely in the chest and would have inflicted a fatal wound if it had not struck a pocket book and a few coins that he kept in a vest pocket.[226]

The would-be assassin broke cover and ran, with Dalton and his party in pursuit, but the seven men pulled up short when they realized that a large group of Chilkats were lined up on the trail ahead, challenging them. Dalton and the prospectors saw they were outnumbered and quickly withdrew back to the settlement. Dalton took the first steamer to Juneau, where he filed a complaint about the Chilkat man known as "Jim" whom he identified as his attacker.[227] The police issued a warrant for attempted murder, but emotions were too inflamed in the Chilkat Inlet for them to make the arrest. Pyramid Harbor residents, who feared for their lives because of the turmoil, petitioned the government to send military protection. In response Captain R.T. Yeatman of the 14th Infantry, together with 112 enlisted men, immediately went to Chilkat to find out what was going on and to prevent more violence from erupting.[228]

Yeatman found that it was the Chilkats who needed protection, rather than the whites. He acknowledged that Dalton and his fellow entrepreneurs had summarily removed the Chilkats from their land and destroyed their gardens without compensation. Further, he noted that several Chilkats claimed that Dalton never paid them for work they had performed.

"These Indians are quiet and law-abiding people," he said. "They originally showed this trail to Mr. Dalton, who promised them work. This he not only refuses them they say but warns them from travel on the trail. What right he has to do this is not apparent."[229]

Finally, Yeatman recommended that no more land patents be issued until the whole matter was investigated. A special agent of the General Land Office was sent to Pyramid Harbor. Dalton tried to protest to him that he was only leasing land from a friend, but eventually he agreed to compensate the complainants.[230]

The Toll Trail

Ever resilient, Dalton accepted the failure of his pony express enterprise and figured out another way to make money from the trail he had appropriated as his own. Having invested so much labour and capital into the Dalton Trail, he was determined that others weren't going to use it without paying him for the convenience. He posted a sign on the trail that read, "People unwilling to pay toll please keep off the road."[231] Thirteen miles up from Chilkat, where the trail met the Takhin River, Dalton set up a toll station.

Although Dalton had applied for, and later would receive, a license from the American government to charge a fee for use of the road, he had no charter or official permission to operate a toll road in 1898. In the meantime, he charged all users anyway, maintaining control through his reputation for "gentle persuasion." Dalton did not dare to charge any fees on the Canadian side of the boundary, so he planted his toll booth firmly on American soil. He charged for everything that passed: two dollars and fifty cents for every cow, horse or burro; fifty cents for each goat, sheep or hog; five dollars for two horses with a sled or wagon, and ten dollars for four. His toll on shipped merchandise was one cent a pound, and every foot passenger with a pack of more than twenty-five pounds had to pay Dalton a dollar. Brazenly he compelled the Natives, who had used this route for centuries, to pay like everyone else.

The toll station consisted of:

> A pole barrier across the road, and a shack in which a man was stationed at all times. There was a big sign hanging there, stating the prices charged for each horse and head of cattle that went over the trail. A sort of private toll gate proposition. As a period on the sign was stuck a large rifle cartridge. It had its implications.[232]

Billy Henry, a cattleman from Alberta with a herd of 180 heavy cattle, passed through this point and reported later that Dalton had "some well armed men with the faces of desperados" waiting to collect their dues. Needless to say, Henry, and all the other cattlemen who used the trail, paid up.

The work Dalton had conducted meant the trail was now in good condition as far as the summit, and it offered access to the Chilkat Pass from either side of the Chilkat Inlet, Haines Mission being the starting point on one side and Pyramid Harbor being the start on the other. Dalton used different crossing points and routes of access at different times of year, depending on conditions such as water levels.

At Pyramid Harbor, where there was already a fish cannery and the remnants of a Chilkat village, Dalton had his cattle pens, a warehouse and a store nestled in the narrow confine between the shore and the tall mountains. This was the main branch that became known as the Dalton Trail.

The trail began at the north end of Pyramid Harbor and followed the shore line for the first four miles. Access to this portion was easiest when the tide was low.[233] As it left the shore the trail ran parallel to the Chilkat River on the western side until, at thirteen miles up, it reached the Takhin River and the toll station.

From the toll station the trail climbed a ridge overlooking the river for ten miles, then descended into the valley for the next eight miles until it reached the Klehini River, which it paralleled until it crossed the river two miles below Boulder Creek. Boulder Creek was an excellent camping place with fresh water and good feed for livestock. Dalton had graded the next section of trail from Boulder Creek to Pleasant Camp, forty-four miles from

Dalton's toll station was located at the bridge over the Kicking Horse River. Users paid $1.00 per person to use the trail. Dalton charged $2.50 a head for horses, cattle, mules and burros. Even the Chilkat people had to pay to use their own trail. MACBRIDE MUSEUM OF YUKON HISTORY COLLECTION

the start of the trail. Near Pleasant Camp he set up a post that subsequently became known as Dalton Cache.[234] The building that stands there today was constructed in 1898; prior to that, it is likely that the cache was either a tent frame or an actual cache designed to keep predators out. The Mounted Police soon established a post within spitting distance, just across the border.

Dalton's other way of approaching the American–Canadian boundary was rather more problematic. It was the branch of the trail that went from Haines Mission up the eastern side of the Chilkat Inlet. In the summer, travel conditions on this east-side trail left much to be desired, so it was used more often in the late fall, winter and spring, when the Chilkat River was frozen.[235] The east trail was so bad that carts broke down on it frequently, and the last two miles were nothing but massive boulders.[236] This track passed the Chilkat village of "Yinda Stucky" (Yandestake).

Fifteen miles beyond Yandestake was Klukwan, the largest and most powerful Chilkat Tlingit settlement in the region of the Lynn Canal, with twenty or thirty longhouses constructed in a row facing the Chilkat River. Just beyond Klukwan at a junction that became known as Camp Sunshine, the eastern and western approach trails linked up, and users from either

The Dalton Trail south of Dalton House, 1898. THE THOMAS FISHER RARE BOOK LIBRARY, UNIVERSITY OF TORONTO

route would carry on thirteen miles to Dalton Cache and Pleasant Camp at the international boundary.

The trail beyond Pleasant Camp rose to an elevation of seventeen hundred feet, but after several miles on the heights it dipped down into Rainy Hollow. Rainy Hollow got its name from S. Hopkins, a man who packed along the trail for Jack Dalton in 1894 and experienced continuous rainfall at this location for eighteen consecutive days.[237] Near here, parts of the trail were so steep that horses had fallen over backwards while ascending it.[238] After Rainy Hollow the trail made its ascent to the barren and rocky summit of the Chilkat Pass at nearly thirty-five hundred feet above sea level. Past the summit the trail carried on north across a treeless plateau on which, in the spring of 1898, were strewn the rotting remains of horses that had died on the failed cattle drives of the previous autumn.

Not far from the summit was Glacier Camp, and beyond that the trail was good except for occasional swampy areas and boggy lowlands. Sixty-nine miles from the start of the trail, at an elevation of 3,275 feet, it crossed the north-south divide. On one side, water flowed to the south and ultimately drained into the Chilkat River; on the other, it flowed north in the Tatshenshini watershed.

Crossing a stream in the Chilkat Pass . Numerous river crossings had to be made before arriving at the Yukon River. YUKON ARCHIVES, J.B. TYRRELL FONDS, 82/15, 15

The next stopping place was twenty-five miles along at Bear Camp, and from there the trail crossed the valley to the west side of the Tatshenshini and stayed on the high terraces, except where it had to descend into two steep-walled canyons. A mile beyond the second canyon the country started to fall off toward the north. The trail continued north to a point where the Tatshenshini River curves around from the southeast to the west through a canyon more than three hundred feet deep. The descent into this valley followed a steep path next to the river and led to Dalton's main trading post. It was possible to cross the river here, but not easy. The water ran fast, the bottom was full of boulders and the river was 150 feet wide.

Dalton's trading post consisted of small log buildings and canvas-covered frames. The interior of the trading post, according to one report,

> was not unlike that of a country store . . . the shelves being piled high with calicoes, ginghams, shoes, hats, tin pans, plates, and cups, while from the roof beams depended kettles, pails, steel traps, guns, and snow-shoes. Ike [Martin, the storekeeper] informed them [members of a prospecting party] that he kept a small stock of flour, bacon, rice, sugar and other provisions in a storehouse near at hand . . . and that the establishment traded principally with the Stik Indians, whose village lay nearly a mile down-stream to the west.[239]

The trail then led to Neskatahéen, a substantial village a mile and a half downstream sandwiched between the Tatshenshini River and a small salmon stream. It was the home of one hundred Southern Tutchone and contained a dozen impressive structures built in the style of coastal Chilkat longhouses.[240] Neskatahéen was the most important place for the exchange of trade goods between the coastal Chilkats and the Southern Tutchone people of the interior. This was also the most substantial settlement along the Dalton Trail between Klukwan and Fort Selkirk.

The trail climbed the high terrace behind the village. For the first six miles along the steep walls of the river, the trail kept high up on the wooded hills to the west to avoid several deep ravines. The valley then became broad and the river flowed for some miles through a marshy flat. About ten miles

Neskatahéen was the largest settlement along the trail. It consisted of a dozen substantial long house structures, inhabited by a hundred Southern Tutchone residents. YUKON ARCHIVES, J.B. TYRRELL FONDS, 82/15, 18

from the post the trail crossed to the east and continued for another six miles to Klukshu Lake.

At the southern end of Klukshu Lake, beside the mouth of Klukshu Creek, there was a small encampment consisting of a few rudimentary shacks and drying racks where Southern Tutchone fishers would catch and smoke the abundant salmon that migrated here to spawn during the summer. Nearby were the remains of several decaying, overgrown cabins, indicators of what had once been a more populous settlement.[241]

The trail followed the eastern shore of the lake for a mile and a half and then trended to the northeast through high undulating land covered with spruce and poplar. The trail crossed the Kluhini River, which empties into Dezadeash Lake a short distance to the west, and then it climbed through the gap between two conical peaks. Beyond this pass it followed the eastern shore of the Dezadeash River until it cut through thickly forested country between prominent mountains to the east and west.

Where the Dezadeash makes a sharp westward turn, the trail left the water and continued through a gap in the mountains to the north, beyond which it crossed the Mendenhall River over a substantial bridge that had been constructed by Dalton in 1896. An alternate branch of the trail left the Dezadeash River here and headed to the northeast until it passed Taye Lake, then followed the Mendenhall River to rejoin the main trail at Dalton's bridge crossing. After the bridge, the trail followed the valley of the Mendenhall north to the Hutchi Lakes, a string of three small bodies of water.

Beside the most northerly of the little lakes was the village of Hutchi. Hutchi consisted of only two or three cabins, but the nondescript appearance of the spot belied the importance of the settlement.[242] Hutchi was a key transit point for travel through the Nordenskjold River watershed to the northeast and the Aishihik Lake region to the northwest. Here during the gold rush Dalton established a crude, ill-supplied station consisting of a supply tent, where "everything cost a dollar a pound except coffee, for which he charged $2.50 a pound."[243]

The trail continued along the eastern side of the lakes and then followed the Nordenskjold River for some fifty miles to Carmack's Post on the Yukon River. This portion of the trail was the forerunner of the modern-day Klondike Highway between Whitehorse and Carmacks. The grade through this country was very gentle, and the trail crossed the river a number of times. Carmack's Post, now the village of Carmacks, was a simple log cabin established by George Carmack for trading purposes (a post Carmack later abandoned for greener pastures). From this point, the trail offered travellers a choice of two alternate routes. The first paralleled the western side of the Yukon River for twenty-five miles to a point beyond Five Finger and Rink Rapid. By carrying on past these notoriously treacherous reaches of the river, the trail enabled users to board vessels below the rapids and thus avoid the most hazardous aspect of the downriver journey to Dawson.

The Five Finger Rapid is the more formidable of the two river obstacles.

Here the water divides into five channels flowing around four rocky protrusions that span the Yukon at a sharp bend in the river just above Tatchun Creek. Today, Five Finger Rapid is a scenic attraction and viewpoint on the Klondike Highway; then, it was a dangerous passage of turbulent, churning waters that could take the life of the unsuspecting. The seasoned river travellers knew to take the extreme right-hand channel if they wanted to get through safely. The Mounted Police established a post below the Rapid in 1898, and beside it Charlie Thebo set up a small store and a small sawmill. The mill kept busy producing lumber during the gold rush.

The second branch of the Dalton trail crossed the Yukon River at Carmack's Post and ran north along the eastern bank. This branch terminated at a point on the Yukon River near the confluence with the Pelly River just above Fort Selkirk. Before the start of the gold rush, Fort Selkirk was a small settlement consisting of a trading post, an Anglican mission and a Native village. Once the Klondike frenzy brought heavy traffic on the river, Selkirk ballooned in size to several hundred people, and for a short time it was expected to become the capital of the Yukon Territory.

Pennock's Post was a supply cabin built on the trail between Dezadeash Lake and Champagne. ALASKA STATE LIBRARY, FRED HOVEY PHOTOGRAPH COLLECTION, P352-52

DISTANCES ON THE DALTON TRAIL

Pyramid Harbor to Murphy's Flat	6 miles
Murphy's Flat to Long Bridge	15 miles
Long Bridge to Big Salmon (Tsirku) River/Walkerville	6 miles
Walkerville to Camp Sunshine	4 miles
Camp Sunshine to Porcupine	6 miles
Porcupine to Pleasant Camp	7 miles
Pleasant Camp to Rainy Hollow	11 miles
Rainy Hollow to Glacier Camp	20 miles
Glacier Camp to Bear Camp	25 miles
Bear Camp to Dalton House	15 miles
Dalton House to Klukshu Lake	20 miles
Klukshu Lake to Pennock's Post	25 miles
Pennock's Post to Champlain's Landing (Champlain)	18 miles
Champlain's Landing to Camp Storey	20 miles
Camp Storey to Hutchi Lake	11 miles
Hutchi Lake to Five Finger Rapid	85 miles
Five Finger Rapid to Slaughterhouse Slough	48 miles
Total Distance Pyramid Harbor to Five Finger Rapid	294 miles
Total Distance Pyramid Harbor to Slaughterhouse Slough	342 miles

The Tatshenshini Expedition

The grizzly bear came up the valley along our right flank, but it wasn't until he crossed the valley and started to follow us that I became uneasy.

I was a one of a party of five riders plodding down a flat and barren valley, almost half a mile across, bounded by cliffs seventy-five feet high along each side. There was nowhere to go but forward, downstream toward the Tatshenshini River. The dull, overcast day had been long and the terrain exhausting. Our horses were strung out over several hundred yards along the flat gravel stream bed and we were all tired. The curiosity of the grizzly disturbed us enough to inject new energy into our search for a camp for the night.

I asked myself: how did I get into this situation? It was 1972, and I was a recent graduate of the University of Calgary in the field of archeology. It hadn't been an easy road for me to arrive at that point in my life. When I started university I was just seventeen and I found the adjustment difficult. With some help from my family, I had worked my way through four years of study. I wanted to go on to graduate school and become an archeologist, but I had to take a year off from school to make some money and build up my savings for further study. I often had two or three jobs at one time.

One of my jobs was working at the Calgary Brewery. The pay was good and the demand for beer was high at the time, so I was working plenty of overtime, but the job was tedious and repetitive. The amusement of watching bottles of beer go by on a conveyor belt hour after hour and day by day quickly wore thin. I made mental calculations of how many bottles would pass by me if I stayed at the brewery for my working life, and the number was astronomical. While digesting the mathematics of the situation, I observed a life-long brewery employee who, after fifty years of labour, was assigned a job working the shrink wrap machine. Was this to be my destiny?

After a few months of employment, the day came when I had to undergo a physical examination as a preliminary step to joining the union. I could see my life before me—a never-ending belt of bottles that would symbolize my existence passing by me day after day. I knew this wasn't for me.

That was when I received a phone call that changed my life. Jim Bennett, a graduate student from the archeology department at the university, was looking for an assistant to join him on a project in the Yukon. Would I like to come with him? The pay was poor, but I had stockpiled plenty of funds from my multiple jobs. Anything would be better than the mind-numbing monotony that I saw in my brewery future. "When do you want to leave?" I asked. "Tomorrow," was the reply. We compromised, and two days later we were on the road in a 1949 Mercury one-ton truck. Soon we were bouncing up the dusty unpaved Alaska Highway.

I spent the next two months hiking into remote regions of the southwest Yukon. There was, I decided, enough archeology, enough wildlife and enough scenery to fill a lifetime in this vast expanse of wilderness.

One day we were at the village of Champagne, a small village sandwiched between a big bend in the Dezadeash River and the Alaska Highway, talking to elder Johnny Fraser. He was bent with age, but his eyes were bright and alert as he talked to my boss about an old village on the Tatshenshini River.

Johnny Fraser must have been around ninety years old. He was born before the first white men came into the southwest Yukon, and he was the last of the people who had lived, fished and traded at Noogaayík, a small village on the banks of the Tatshenshini River. (This river was once called the Alsek, Alsac, or Alsegh; today it is often referred to as the "Tat," while one of its tributaries bears the former name). Before the middle of the nineteenth century, Native settlements flourished along this river, but then disease, the harbinger of the European arrival on the Alaskan coast, devastated the people along the Tat. They were defenceless against the new and deadly microbes. Around 1850, another disaster struck the inhabitants. The large glacier that spans the Alsek valley upstream gave way and released a mighty wave of water that swept away everything in its path. Many people dwelling along the Tatshenshini below its junction with the Alsek died when their homes were obliterated.

Several of today's First Nations families in the southwest Yukon trace their roots back to Noogaayík, and to a period when there was regular commerce along the Tat. Johnny Fraser knew of the ancient Tatsheshini village because he had grown up there, although he and his family lived there no longer.

Through time, the traditional trade and family connections between the Tatsheshini area and the coast became fewer. People abandoned the settlements along the Tatshenshini; some moved back to the coast, to Klukwan, home of the Chilkat Tlingit people who are said to have established Noogaayík. Others moved upstream to Neskatahéen, a village at the mouth of a small tributary of the Tatshenshini that was rich with salmon. Neskatahéen sat within a large river bend where the Tat reverses its northward direction to flow southwest to the Pacific Ocean at Dry Bay. The site is deserted now, and the region is marketed as a pristine wilderness, but not long ago it was a busy commercial centre whose inhabitants traded with many other people living to the north.

Considering what he knew from historical accounts and combining it with information from Johnny Fraser's reminiscences, Jim Bennett decided he would visit the vicinity again in 1972 to study the sites of Noogaayík and Neskatahéen.

I returned to school in the fall with my former uncertainties about the future replaced by the dream of a career centred in the Yukon. Then Jim Bennett dropped out of school and gave me his field notes and specimens. While I was contemplating what I could do with these, I was offered an opportunity to return to the Yukon. One facet of that opportunity was to venture into the Tatshenshini River valley to locate the remains of the old village of Noogaayík. Which brings me back to the grizzly bear.

It wasn't the first grizzly bear we saw on that trip, nor the last; just the most memorable. When our party of stragglers formed up in the apparent safety of numbers, the inquisitive bruin disappeared and we made camp.

We were an odd assortment of individuals. I and Frances Roback, another student from the University of Calgary, were social scientists. Art Brewster, of the famed Rocky Mountain Brewster family, was our able guide. Dale, his young son, was also a member of the party. Tom Wild, an ancient cattle wrangler from Rose Prairie, British Columbia, had decades of experience with horses and wilderness travelling. In the evenings Tom regaled us with stories of his colourful past, often suitably exaggerated to enhance their interest.

We travelled with five saddle horses and four pack horses. The weather was warm and sunny, and we made good time. Our camp the first night had been at an old abandoned cabin that was nestled in a hollow beside Silver Creek, at the bottom of a steep canyon. The next morning brought me the first sign the trip would be unexpectedly eventful. I found a case of sweating dynamite exposed to the elements behind the cabin. In this condition, dynamite is very unstable and apt to explode unexpectedly. I wondered if this was an omen that danger would always be near on our journey. When I returned to Haines Junction later, I reported the explosives to the Royal Canadian Mounted Police.

The first night we camped in an old cabin at Silver Creek. The next morning, I found a case of sweating dynamite cached outside the rear wall. MICHAEL GATES COLLECTION

Later that day we ascended a series of steep switchbacks. Larry, one of the packhorses, fell off the edge and landed on the switchback perhaps fifty feet below, shaken but unharmed. We retrieved him and, after repacking, we started off again. Later, the challenges of the trail compelled us to stop and repack a second time. Art said it was the most difficult day he had ever had with his packhorses. We camped that night at Onion Lake, and the next day we headed across country with no trail to follow. An unanticipated bonus, however, was the frequent sighting of moose, bear, sheep, goats and various species of small game. At one point we observed two magnificent bull moose locked in combat.

This area had not seen many people in recent times and had become densely overgrown with willow. The thick brush slowed our advance to a crawl. Art and Tom had to hack away the dense undergrowth with axes to enable any progress at all. At one stop I dismounted from my horse, Chief, and went forward to investigate. The branches were so thickly intertwined that I was walking four feet above solid ground, and then suddenly there was no solid ground beneath me. The web of branches stretched out over a steep embankment. Below my feet and the web of branches was open air; the ground was seventy-five feet below. I carefully retraced my steps to the edge of the valley wall.

We eventually descended a steep talus slope into the barren glacial out-wash valley. That was where the grizzly started following us. This trip was giving me adventure alright—maybe too much.

After another day of travel along the bottom of the valley of a glacier-fed stream, we reached the Tatshenshini River. It was a day during which progress was slow, and humans and animals alike were exhausted and hungry.

We piled our gear unceremoniously on a sandbar and assessed our situation. Behind us was the stream we had been following for the last day and a half; in front of us was the Tatshenshini, flowing dark and fast. The area, having been undisturbed for years, was densely overgrown. The chances of finding the exposures that revealed archeological remains seemed remote. Worse yet, there was nothing for the horses to eat. Art was concerned for their well-being and advised that we should retreat to more nutritious terrain. After all our labour in getting to the area, we departed without having confirmed the location of the abandoned village.

We had another two days of difficult travel before we regained the trail that we had followed for the first part of our journey. During our trek back, another horse collapsed and fell about seventy-five feet down a steep slope. She was a mare that had been feeding a foal during our travel as well as packing supplies. She tumbled end over end, with the panniers remaining firmly fixed in place on her back, and landed at the bottom of the hill, nearly at my feet. When I approached her, I could not tell at first which end was which because her head was twisted under her body. Art was quickly beside the still beast. He swiftly cut the ropes binding the large pack boxes in place, a move that enabled her to struggle to her feet. She stood unsteadily, and then shook. Fortunately, despite the fall, she was uninjured. We transferred her load to the panniers on the other pack horses and carried on.

On the return portion of our expedition we found some indication of past human presence, but it wasn't very ancient. We camped in a small grassy meadow one evening where there were signs of an old campsite and fragments of a child-size white rubber boot. I wondered who else had been to such a remote place, but never found an answer. We endured cool, wet, windy weather for three days during our return to Neskatahéen and we were all thankful to be back at our starting point.

In the end, the pack horse journey yielded little historical information, but it provided plenty of excitement. We had travelled nine days through some of the wildest country in the Yukon. This trip was a defining moment in my life. I savoured the experience. In the years that followed I made frequent backpack trips to the Yukon and had numerous interesting encounters with Yukon history, many of them in this same region. This journey taught me that you sometimes reach your destination in a roundabout fashion, and that the trip is as important as the arrival.

After the Tatsheshini pack horse expedition of 1972, I was on my way to becoming a history hunter.

CHAPTER 7

1898: The Golden Year

The shared need for basic survival created some unusual alliances when the human parade started pressing along Dalton's trail after 1897. One unlikely accord was the one that developed, to the benefit of both parties, between Jack Dalton—an American who was a known killer—and those pillars of Canadian peace, order and good government, the North-West Mounted Police. Dalton's trail, although it wound through some of the most sparsely populated and isolated territory on earth, was attracting notice from governments in Washington and Ottawa. The opening of the trail had global political implications, and the people who had to work out some of them on the ground were Dalton and the frontier police officers.

For much of its existence the Dalton trail was in a no man's land between two nations whose boundary in this region was yet to be defined. That the local Native people had established workable boundaries long since was of little concern to powerful players on the world stage.

The Yukon and Alaska slowly had begun to enter global consciousness in the late eighteenth century when a number of notable explorers charted the coastline of the Pacific Northwest and opened the area to foreign interests. Vitus Bering drew maps of the Alaskan coast for Russia in 1741, giving his name to the sea at the mouth of the Yukon; in 1774 Perez charted some of the north coast for Spain, and his compatriot, Bodega y Quadra, contributed more information from his voyage of 1779. Captains

James Cook and George Vancouver explored northern reaches of the west coast for Britain in 1788 and 1790. After these navigators had approached the north latitudes by sea, the redoubtable fur trader Alexander Mackenzie became the first European to reach the northwest coast by land when he crossed the continent in 1793 and emerged at the mouth of the Bella Coola River.[244]

What drew Europeans at first to the northwest was the global demand for furs and the competitive drive of the great imperial powers to lay claim to potentially productive territory. Emperor Paul of Russia issued an edict in 1799 granting a trade monopoly to the Russian–American Company north of latitude 55° on the western coast of the American continent. In 1821 he issued a second decree extending that boundary south to 51°. Although the fur trade was beginning to diminish and the economic value of this remote region was in decline, both Britain and the United States, whose traders by this time were active along the west coast, protested the extension of Russia's sovereign claim.

The Alaskan coast and adjacent territories became the subject of distant diplomatic negotiations, and in 1825 the British signed a treaty with the Russians that delineated territorial interests of the two nations in northwest North America. With typical imperial disregard for topographical realities like watersheds and mountain ranges, the European diplomats drew a straight line from the coast of the Arctic Ocean south to the St. Elias Mountains. At one point in the negotiation, they gave some consideration to the 135th meridian as a possible boundary. Had they chosen that line, the western half of what today is the Canadian Yukon would have passed out of Britain's control. The Klondike gold rush, when it occurred seventy-five years later, would have been an American phenomenon, and therefore entirely different in character.

As it was, the 1825 agreement settled upon the 141st meridian, a decision that placed the future site of Dawson City and the surrounding gold creeks well within British (and then later Canadian) territory. Neither Britain nor Russia had any notion of what was to be found in the regions through which the imaginary line was drawn, as no representative from either country had set foot there yet. A government presence in the region did not come until another half-century had elapsed.

From the St. Elias Mountains and south along the Alaskan coastline, the treaty definition of the boundary was less clear and its location would become contentious in later years. The treaty described a line of demarcation that reached up from the southernmost point of Prince of Wales Island through the Portland Canal to 56° north latitude. From there, it ran north roughly parallel to the coast along the summit of the mountains till it reached the 141st meridian. The negotiators agreed that a strip of land, or "lisière," along the coast would remain Russian territory and that this strip would extend no farther than ten marine leagues (approximately thirty miles) inland from the coast. The statement was too inexact to take account of the tortuous indentations of the shoreline. Russia published a map of Russian territory allegedly based upon this treaty, and for decades the authority of the map went unprotested. Nothing would be done to clarify the precise location of the boundary line below 60° north latitude until seventy-three years later when the Klondike gold rush made the question of the border a concern to both the US and Canada—and to Jack Dalton, whose trail passed from one country into the other.

The Disputed Line

In March of 1867, just three months before the passing of the British North America Act established Canada as a nation, the United States purchased the Russian territory of Alaska for $7,200,000, and the rights and interests concerning the boundary transferred to Canada's southern neighbour. Neither country paid much attention to the finer details of delineation at this time as the region was still essentially unexplored. When British Columbia joined the Dominion of Canada in 1871, interest in defining the boundary line increased, but not to the extent that anyone was prepared to finance the cost of proper surveying. Alaska lacked any formal government structure until increasing economic development and an influx of Americans into the region called for an official presence. In the mid-1870s the Cassiar gold rush drew many American prospectors into the Canadian territory to the east of Juneau, Alaska, and jurisdictional disputes between Canada and the United States heightened concern for a formal boundary line. In the 1880s interest in the north increased again as the giant Treadwell mine began operating at Juneau and the Chilkoot Pass north of Skagway opened to prospectors. In

1884 Congress passed the Organic Act, formally establishing a government in the Alaskan territory.

The demarcation of a thirty-mile American coastal zone became increasingly contentious. Where did the coastline commence, and from where was the thirty-mile buffer zone measured? Was it from the outer coastal islands or the continental coastline? Did it include the heads of the inlets, if they were more than thirty miles from the "coast?" Neither government expressed much official interest in the matter, yet over the years, from 1884 onward, Canadian maps showed a continual shrinking of the conceptual American footprint on the Alaskan Panhandle.

In America, confusion reigned in the newspapers and popular literature of the period as writers displayed only a vague knowledge of what was Alaska and what was Canada. Journalists constantly complicated the matter by introducing their own concepts of where the boundary line should be located and what should be viewed as American soil. American voices began to argue that Canada's claims on the Alaska Panhandle were too aggressive, given the language of the treaty.

On the international stage, a dispute between Britain and the United States over the boundary line between British Guiana and Venezuela brought the two nations to the brink of war in 1895–96 and further inflamed American opinion against recognition of Canada's sovereignty over the land Canada had inherited from Britain along the north coast. Finally, the discovery of gold in the Klondike in 1896 brought to an end any indifference of the two national governments to the location of the Alaskan–Canadian boundary.

Dismay grew in Canada as America instituted a new tariff on Canadian goods brought across American territory into the Canadian north. As one Canadian writer remarked, the "most provocative and frustrating American policy was the ability of the United States to maintain the 'open door' in the Yukon Gold Rush and its boundary contentions in the Panhandle."[245] The imperialist actions of the United States in various other regions of the world were enough to alarm Canada—and Britain—about probable American expansionism in the north, and Canada realized it could ignore no longer the question of the boundary. Tensions rose further at the news that the US Congress had authorized the expenditure of funds to send the reindeer relief expedition through Canadian territory to Dawson City.

As a response to American fees and duties being charged on Canadian goods transported across the Panhandle to British Columbia and the Yukon, the Canadian government contracted the MacKenzie–Mann railroad interests to construct an all-Canadian railroad into the north, and introduced a bill in Parliament to fund a route that would commence at the Stikine River. The bill failed to pass, however, after legislators objected to a provision that gave the railroad company a five-year monopoly.

As highly charged boundary discussions began between the two nations, America contended that its territory extended inland as far as Tagish near the Mounted Police post located between Tagish and Marsh lakes. Canada proposed that its domain extended to salt water on the Lynn Canal, including Skagway. The ambiguity of the boundary situation generated some practical difficulties for those trying to conduct their business in the neighbourhood of the disputed border; for instance, American cattleman Willis Thorp was told by Superintendent Z.T. Wood of the North-West Mounted Police that he must pay a duty of sixteen dollars per head on the cattle that he had

IF THE SMALL PERSON IS NOT RESTRAINED THE EAGLE MAY LOSE HIS TEMPER.

This cartoon from the *New York Herald* portrays Canada as the recalcitrant child pulling the Eagle's Pyramid Harbor tail feather. *NEW YORK HERALD*

brought to Bennett. Thorp refused to pay on the grounds that Bennett was in American territory.[246]

In January of 1898 Minister of the Interior Clifford Sifton instructed the Mounted Police to establish posts at the summits of the White and Chilkoot passes to control the flow of traffic into the region and to collect duty on imported goods. Since the summit of the third pass in the area, the Chilkat, was more than thirty miles from the coastline and thus, in the Canadian view, well inside Canadian territory, Sifton determined to establish a post at a suitable point on the Dalton Trail at its intersection with the border. Construction of the new detachment was to start once the snow receded in the spring of 1898. Into a region once controlled by the Chilkats and recently appropriated by Dalton, came members of the NWMP as the representatives of Canadian sovereignty.

The Mounties Arrive

Yukon Commissioner James Walsh instructed NWMP Superintendent Zachary Taylor Wood early in 1898 to establish a detachment at the supposed line of the international boundary on the Dalton Trail where the officers would collect duty and watch for illegal importation of liquor. Although winter snow still blocked the trail, fifty or sixty people were waiting at Pyramid Harbor eager to set out for the Chilkat Pass once the weather permitted, and more were arriving daily. Circumstances demanded that the police establish a post as quickly as possible.[247] Walsh ordered that a second post, subordinate to the one on the border, be set up at the terminus of the Dalton Trail near Five Finger Rapid.

The comptroller of the North-West Mounted Police advised Minister Sifton that an officer and twenty men were available in Regina, ready to depart for the north to establish the post on the trail. Sifton gave the order to proceed, instructing the commissioner of the NWMP to set the post up forty miles from tide water.[248]

Those in command at NWMP headquarters were mindful of how delicate an issue the location of the boundary was, and they gave much thought to the appropriate placing of the new post on the Dalton Trail. They selected Rainy Hollow, fifty-five miles up the trail from Pyramid Harbor, as a likely safe location for the base of operations, rather than

Dalton Cache, which, at about forty-four miles, might have been too close to the coast.

Inspector A.M. Jarvis was placed in charge of this detachment on February 23 and ordered to prepare to leave for Haines Mission from Mounted Police headquarters in Regina. Jarvis was to wear many hats on this assignment, including those of stipendiary magistrate and collector of customs. Meanwhile, Inspector A.B. Perry, stationed in Vancouver, was instructed to purchase six months of supplies for the new post and secure boat transportation to Haines for them.[249]

Jarvis and his men left Regina by train for Vancouver on the morning of April 2. At the time, NWMP Superintendent Sam Steele was stationed in the north at Lake Bennett, close enough to Chilkat and Pyramid Harbor to be well informed about the number of people waiting to enter Canada over the Dalton Trail. Aware of a pressing need to supervise the early arrivals and collect fees from them, he dispatched Sergeant Major Barker with a corporal and ten men to proceed to the border point as soon as possible. They established a temporary post and awaited the arrival of the main detachment.

According to the orders given to Inspector Jarvis, his party would be supplied with various lumber wagons, bobsleighs, Red River carts, horse sleds, man-drawn sleds and twenty-one pack horses. When they arrived at Haines Mission they were to establish a supply camp and send an advance party to select a location for their detachment, where they would construct a number of buildings to house the operation.

Jarvis's objectives were clear: he was to maintain law and order on the Dalton Trail, he was to collect customs duties and he was to familiarize himself with the country through which the trail passed. Once established, he was to go into the interior and scout out suitable places for patrol camp sites and pastures. Gold had been reported in the "Alseck" country, and Jarvis was to investigate its potential and determine whether a mining recorder should be sent in.

Jarvis was also expected to undertake the mundane tasks that accompany any assignment. A regular routine, discipline and inspections were to be maintained at all times. He was to keep a detailed accounting of his expenditures. He was to act as a magistrate and report fully and promptly on the results. In addition, he was to monitor the importation of liquor over the trail.

Since he had jurisdiction over liquor above the sixtieth parallel (the Yukon border) but not below it where the trail ran through the provincial control of British Columbia, he might find it necessary to establish a small post in the interior where illegal liquor could be seized and the importers prosecuted. In sum, he was expected to establish and assert Canadian sovereignty on the trail and enforce Canadian law.[250]

Inspector Jarvis, accompanied by Sergeant Lasswitz, eighteen constables and twenty-one horses, left Vancouver for Skagway the evening of April 8 on the *Tees*, with sufficient supplies to last the party until October, and arrived in Skagway on April 12. In Skagway they transferred to another vessel and arrived in Haines two days later. They immediately set about hauling their supplies five miles up the Chilkat Inlet to "Yinda Stucky" (Yandestake) over unexpectedly challenging terrain. The ground proved to be either wet and mushy or extremely rocky, with little moderate going in between. The wagons broke down constantly and soon they had cracked two axles. On April 20, despite "shifting quicksand," they swam twelve horses and several boatloads of supplies across Chilkat Inlet at low tide. Special Constable Connell almost died in the crossing. But this was only the beginning; at least sixteen more crossings would be required as they progressed up the valley before they reached their destination.[251]

They tried using the riverbed as their highway, but their progress was impeded by quicksand, a soft mushy river bottom and heavy snowfall. On May 1 they camped above the mouth of the Klehini River. Ahead of them lay another thirteen miles of trail, and despite the fact that the snow was melting rapidly, they were forced to cut a trail through the bush for a mile and a half where the white blanket still obstructed progress.

Along the way Jarvis encountered the American reindeer relief expedition and observed that it was losing two or three animals every day to starvation. He noted several reports of placer gold claims being staked in the interior on the "Kah-Sha River." He also observed that dog salmon were running in the river and the fishing was excellent.[252]

Jarvis and Sergeant Lasswitz arrived at Dalton Cache on May 4. Here the ground was covered by snow to a depth of five feet, so they were forced to leave their supply wagons behind and travel light with pack horses. The snow got even deeper as they proceeded beyond this point on the trail. They soon learned that their destination, Rainy Hollow, was still buried under twenty feet of snow, so they backtracked and set up camp one hundred yards north of Dalton's Cache.[253] Jarvis concluded that this location was well within Canadian territory so he proudly raised the Union Jack and commenced collecting duty the following day.

He decided not to go onward to Rainy Hollow as originally planned. Not only the snow deterred him; the building site at Rainy Hollow was a dismal place slightly off the main trail, and Jarvis judged that travellers might find it easy to sneak by the post to evade paying duty. He decided that his current location, which became known as Pleasant Camp, or Dalton Trail Post, would become the permanent encampment for the Dalton Trail detachment.[254]

The building site that they chose was located on a gentle slope overlooking the Klehini River. There was plenty of fresh water, timber for construction and firewood, and a nearby source of limestone from which they could manufacture plaster for use in construction of their buildings. There wasn't any good pasture for the horses in the immediate vicinity of the post, so they fenced off eleven acres of open land and seeded it to timothy. At the instigation of Jarvis, two milk cows and fifty hens were enlisted as part of the detachment strength.[255]

The Mounties immediately established a rather imposing presence at Pleasant Camp. They built an impressive post consisting of a half dozen buildings arranged in a quadrangle with a parade square in the middle where they erected a tall flag pole. They constructed all the buildings from logs they cut themselves in the vicinity. They built a small kiln and used it to process the local limestone to produce plaster for chinking the spaces between the logs. The plaster interstices created a pleasant visual effect and heightened the comfort of the men inside. The largest buildings were a two-storey barracks for the constables and large officers' quarters with an attached dining room. They erected a smaller building for the sergeant major, as well as an office, a storehouse and chicken coop. Eventually they added a stable to the assemblage. In August they set up their secondary post farther inland, constructing a small barracks, a storehouse and a large doghouse beside Dalton's trading post on the Tatshenshini River. This post became known as Dalton House.

The Mounted Police station at Pleasant Camp. YUKON ARCHIVES, E.J. HAMACHER FONDS
(MARGARET AND ROLF HOUGEN COLLECTION), 2002/118, #425

The Mounties began regular patrols along the trail to check out the country and to keep an eye on people passing through. They took one mail consignment from Dawson over the trail before headquarters decided to send
subsequent mail shipments from the Klondike by way of the Yukon River.
Inspector Jarvis was told to expect an inspection visit from Commissioner
Walsh, and he stationed men and horses at Five Fingers, with relays along the
trail awaiting the commander's arrival. Unfortunately Walsh had to change
his plans and the letter informing Jarvis was misdirected, so the men of the
detachment wasted much time waiting for the boss.

Users of the Dalton Trail soon learned they could rely on a police presence. The Mounties patrolled the trail regularly and noted what was going
on. As one observer stated, "The Mounties were always asking their usual
question. We might lose ourselves but the Mounties would always know
where we were."[256] They monitored fires along the trail, posting warnings
of prosecution for neglected or abandoned campfires.[257] Frequently they remarked on the slow progress of the reindeer "relief" expedition.

Between constructing their buildings and riding out on patrol, the officers and men of the Dalton Trail detachment kept themselves busy. Discipline
was generally good, and they had little crime to investigate. During 1898
they collected $11,738.50 in customs duties as well as $795 for placer mining fees and $570 for miner's licenses. A man named Shorty Bigelow had

found traces of placer gold in the mountains west of Klukshu late in the previous year, so the Mounties instituted patrols to Shorty, Alder and Kah-Sha creeks to check on activity in the newly named Last Chance mining district. Hearing that prospectors were even making their way into the region by way of the extremely difficult route from Yakutat Bay and the Tatshenshini River, the Mounties prepared to collect duty from them.

Inspector Jarvis' work was made easier because of the assistance of Edward Armstrong, an American court interpreter who worked for Dalton at Dalton Cache adjacent to the new Mounted Police post. Armstrong provided the Mounties with translation of the Tlingit language as well as a heads-up on who were the "hard cases and bad men" of the region.

The Mounties worked at making themselves reasonably comfortable in the wilderness. As many men as could be spared were taught how to bake bread, and every man from the sergeant major down was taught how to throw the diamond and Colville hitches to tie down loads on the pack saddles. Jarvis gave special acknowledgement to the skills of Sergeant Major Barker, who split most of the shingles for their buildings, and to Sergeant

Mounted Police Detachment, Dalton House, 1899. CANADA. DEPT. OF MINES AND TECHNICAL SURVEYS / LIBRARY AND ARCHIVES CANADA / PA-023126

Lasswitz, who "did the work of three men during the busy season, making out customs papers, issuing miner's licenses and recording claims."[258]

As the summer came to a close, traffic on the trail dwindled to nothing. Inspector Jarvis received orders to reduce the size of the detachment left on the Dalton Trail to nine men and five horses. The balance of the detachment left Pleasant Camp for the coast to report for duty on the Chilkoot Trail.[259] Things went from busy to slow in a hurry; in the month of October only six people passed Pleasant Camp and no duty was collected. Reports of a gold discovery on nearby Porcupine Creek were drawing people away from the trail. In the month of November the Mounties again collected no duty at all at the Pleasant Camp post.[260]

Comings and Goings

Compared with the thousands using the Chilkoot Pass a few miles farther up the Lynn Canal, there were only a few hundred stampeders filing through the Chilkat Pass. Nor had the port of Haines grown to the size of the lawless little town of Skagway. There were, however, dozens of gold seekers who by

Party of prospectors hiking along the Dalton Trail, 1898. ALASKA STATE LIBRARY, FRED HOVEY PHOTOGRAPH COLLECTION, P352-66

accident had heard the rumours of gold in the Last Chance mining district, and they assembled at Haines to tackle the Chilkat Pass.[261]

Slightly over one thousand men used the Dalton Trail in 1898—and five women. Nearly three hundred of these travellers were people coming out from Dawson City.[262] Among those outward bound was Ezra Meeker, carrying several thousand dollars he made selling merchandise. Meeker was a noted pioneer and one of the founders of Puyallup, Washington. He took a steamer to Five Finger Rapid, and from there he planned to ride out on one of Dalton's pack trains. In a letter he wrote before leaving, he enthused, "I am to have a horse to ride, have meals furnished, shelter to stay in and blankets packed for $200 from here to Pyramid Harbor with a probable time of 15 days."[263]

Compared to the travellers going out, those coming in usually had minimal experience in the north. One of the more bizarre greehorns heading for the Klondike was a French aristocrat who expected the best of everything for his journey to Dawson City, so of course he chose Jack Dalton to arrange his travel. He arrived with the most useless of supplies for a journey into the wilderness:

> There were cases of vintage wines and champagne, as well as boxes of brandies, sherries and burgundies. Everything that Europe could transport, the expedition carried: brandied peaches, maraschino cherries, fine cheeses, tins of truffles, hearts of palm, and cans of lobster, shrimp and oysters. The count actually wept when told that most all these things would have to be left on the beach.[264]

The "Count" actually soldiered on to the Klondike, although many of his entourage withered at the challenge and went home.

Frank Hahnenberg was another man on the trail in the early spring who had little knowledge of where he was going but who demonstrated astonishing tenacity. He was a member of a party whose leaking vessel came aground at Haines. Hahnenberg had been one of the dupes who had bought a ticket for Glover's steam-powered snow trains to the Klondike, but upon arriving in Seattle, he discovered that the snow trains were a bust, and he had lost his four hundred dollar passage. Shopping around for another way to get to the

Klondike, he and a partner bought tickets on a converted coal ship named the *Alice Blanchard*. Aboard the vessel were 215 men and 7 women plus assorted horses, cows, dogs, pigs and mules.

The voyage was a nightmare. There was only one toilet for the men to share, while the women used a facility in the captain's quarters. Five days after leaving Seattle, the passengers were in revolt. There was not enough food or water, and after several meetings with the crew, they forced the boat to dock in Wrangell and Ketchikan to pick up supplies. The *Alice Blanchard* continued on its voyage to the Lynn Canal until one morning at three o'clock it hit an iceberg and started taking on water.

Utter confusion reigned as the boat settled into the water at the rate of one foot per minute. The lifeboats sank after being lowered into the water, and the terrified passengers manned the pumps as the ship was run aground at high tide. Once they had patched a ten-foot hole in the bow, they were seaworthy after a fashion, and the leaky ship continued north. Reaching Haines, the ship anchored as close to shore as possible, and most of the men went ashore to help gather timber so the ship could be propped up at low tide.

Fed up with their experience, more than fifty passengers left the ship at Haines with all their supplies and decided to sled their outfits up the Chilkat River. They reached Dalton House over the rapidly melting snow. After a futile attempt at prospecting in the vicinity, most of the dispirited party turned back, although some reached the White River region before running out of food.[265] Hahnenberg and a new-found partner returned to Haines after their Dalton Trail experience and carried on to Skagway, from where they made their way to Dyea and tackled the Chilkoot.[266]

Syndicated Madness

The Klondike stirred more than a little madness in the minds of thousands of eager but naïve investors who dreamed of making big money in a hurry. More money was spent by people going to the Klondike than they ever recovered from the ground once they got there.[267] Much of that money went into the pockets of businessmen eager to sell merchandise to gold-obsessed customers, while some of it ended up in the hands of crooked schemers.

Many eager stampeders formed collectives or syndicates, in which they pooled their resources in the belief that the investment of a group would yield a better chance of finding gold than they would have as individuals. Several of these groups made it all the way to the Yukon and some did find gold, but many more were flash-in-the-pan enterprises spawned in the hoopla and mania surrounding "Klondicitis." Hucksters and confidence men eagerly took advantage of unsuspecting Klondike maniacs.

One of the worst fraudsters was George Rennick, and the most ill-fated of all those heading for the Klondike were the dreamers who followed Rennick's scheme to reach the Klondike by crossing over the glaciers of Yakutat Bay to reach the Dalton Trail. Because the interior above Yakutat was almost unexplored, it was an ideal route for the cunning and devious con man to promote to his customers.

At the same time as Rennick began floating his scheme, the newspapers were, knowingly or not, helping him by misinforming readers about the Yakutat and its environs. The Sitka *Alaskan* described the Yakutat route to the Klondike as:

> an entirely new and easy route that has already been surveyed from the extreme northeastern point of Disenchantment Bay nearly straight to Allsek [*sic*] River over about 40 miles of glacier which when covered with snow furnishes an easy and safe route for transporting supplies on sledges.[268]

In another article, the newspaper proclaimed the route to be one of the best for getting to the Klondike:

> Regarding the new inlet as will be seen in our table of distances given below, the journey is only 425 miles to the mines, and that, too, over rolling grassland! No mountains to ascend, no passes to plod through, probably no mud fields to wade across, and most certainly, no great extremes of cold to endure.[269]

Rennick secured financial support from a number of investors, including some executives of Standard Oil. To protect their interests they engaged a man by the name of Edwards to shadow Rennick's activities. Wanting to escape the scrutiny of Edwards and continue his con, Rennick contrived to get Edwards out of the way and out of touch. To that end he hired ten men to undertake an expedition in search of an allegedly rich but actually non-existent mine somewhere in the far north, and he arranged for Edwards to join the party. Rennick's agent on this expedition, George Stinson, was under instructions to take the expedition to the most isolated place possible in Alaska.

Stinson and Edwards set off from Seattle in the seventy-ton steam schooner *Augusta* with a motley party of inexperienced misfits. Several hundred onlookers were at the wharf when the *Augusta* departed with much fanfare from a brass band. The ship had barely pulled away from the dock when a brawl broke out between members of the party and the ship's crew. The dogs they had with them joined the melee, tearing each other apart. When the *Augusta* reached the nearby town of Port Townsend, two members of the party deserted.

Though a comfortable vessel for the passengers, the old ship purposely chugged along, in compliance with Rennick's plotting, at a sluggish five knots, and to slow things down even more, Stinson had the *Augusta* stop at as many ports along the way as he could manage—Bella Bella, Metlakatla, Prince Rupert, Mary Island, Ketchikan and Sitka. In Sitka, Stinson met an old friend who steered him to the most isolated place he knew: Yakutat. Upon departing from Sitka, Stinson told the exploration party and ship's crew that they were going to the Tatshenshini River via the Yakutat Glaciers. They anchored near the village of Yakutat, which consisted of a Swedish Church mission, a couple of trading posts and a cluster of fifty Native shacks spread out along the shoreline.

After Stinson and an advance party returned to the anchored ship from a reconnaissance of the area, they set off to the far end of Disenchantment Bay, where they unloaded their ten tons of supplies. The *Augusta* sailed away and the remaining members of the expedition made their way inland, setting up a camp on the glacier away from the sea. There they lay idle, both because of inclement weather and because Stinson knew there was no gold at the end of their trail and had no idea where to go next. Tensions among the members were high as the winter set in. Three members of the party became so enraged that their fellows feared they were capable of committing murder. One man fled to Yakutat, arriving snowblind and disoriented after being rescued by a group of Natives who found him wandering on the glacier. Back in the camp, the party split into two factions in a dispute over the best way to go forward, but in the end they reached a détente, with Edwards, the Standard Oil man, remaining diplomatically neutral, caught in the middle.

As spring approached the campers maintained a tense stand-off. Nobody was willing to say out loud what everybody knew—that the whole enterprise was a fraud. The party broke up in the spring and some members trudged back to Yakutat. On their way they encountered hundreds of other hopeful immigrants from the south struggling across the glacier in search of Rennick's mythical mine. Rennick had been busy back in the States over the winter. With the advance party well isolated from the outside world at Yakutat and unable to tell the tale of Rennick's duplicity, Rennick had continued to rustle up money from more syndicated ventures.

One party headed for Yakutat, totalling one hundred men and one woman, came from New York and Minnesota. In Seattle, this syndicate secured an old rustbucket called the *Blakely* and modified the vessel to accommodate the large group of hopeful Argonauts. The members of this large contingent left Seattle full of confidence about the successful outcome of their venture, but it didn't take long for all of that to change.

The overcrowded *Blakely* left port February 24, 1898. As the weather deteriorated and the sea became rough, everyone suffered from seasickness. The captain remained locked in his cabin drinking whiskey until he had consumed his supply. Useless while drunk, the captain proved to be an able seaman once he sobered up. The pumps on the little wave-tossed vessel worked full time to keep ahead of the leaks. One of the deck hands was swept to his death in the Gulf of Alaska, but finally the waters calmed on March 9, and for the first time in nearly a week, those who were able to eat were treated to a warm meal. They reached Yakutat March 24.

By this time the party was not in good shape. The supplies had become sodden with salt water and much was ruined. Some members chose to ascend the Malaspina Glacier, and the decision led to tragedy. Of the eighteen original individuals in this party, only three survived, and two of them were left blind by the ordeal. Others from the syndicate chose to go over the Nunatuk Glacier, making numerous trips back and forth to ferry their supplies forty miles to the Tatshenshini River, facing brutal storms, ice, mushy snow, fog and exhaustion. They made their way up the river to the confluence of the Alsek and the Tatshenshini rivers and established a camp they called New Denmark.

Unable to see a way forward, some of the once-confident stampeders threw in the towel and retreated to Yakutat, leaving a trail of abandoned gear along the way. Of those who continued toward the Yukon, some went up the Alsek River, headed for the rumoured copper in the White River region. Others made it to the Kluane region.[270] Another group decided to travel up the Tatshenshini River in the hope of connecting with the Dalton Trail. They stumbled onto the Dalton Trail some eighteen months later in August of 1899, exhausted, starving and suffering from scurvy and disease. Some required assistance from the Mounties to leave the country.[271]

Only twenty members of the syndicate made it to the trail, which, ironically, they could have reached in a few days if only they had set out from Pyramid Harbor rather than Yakutat. Of one party with 101 syndicate members who started out, 41 are said to have perished. Theirs was one of the most tragic of all the gold pilgrimages attempting to reach the Klondike.[272]

Rennick, the mastermind behind the Yakutat enterprise, paid the price for his malevolent deception. One survivor, his life ruined by Rennick's mendacious scheme, returned from the north and tracked down the con man in Seattle. He finished Rennick off with a bullet.[273]

The Mysterious Mission

While Rennick's doomed investors were struggling toward the Yukon interior from Yakutat, a better-prepared and informed party of gold seekers was heading for the Dalton Trail by way of Pyramid Harbor. Like Rennick's syndicate, its members had backing from the Standard Oil Company. Unlike Rennick, they were founding their endeavour on fact rather than deception: they knew where there was real gold.

In the fall of 1897 gold had been discovered in the southwest corner of the Yukon territory, but the extent of the find was still not known.[274] Some mining had been attempted the winter of 1897–98, and small prospecting parties had entered the area before the snow melted in the spring, but this party with oil company backing was by far the most well-organized group. It was comprised of thirty-six men recruited mainly from New England,

and because they were sworn to secrecy about the purpose of their mission and their destination in the interior, they became known as "The Mysterious Thirty-Six."[275]

The group was led by Lieutenant S. Adair, who had passed through this region on his way out of the Yukon in the fall of 1897. Howard C. Scott was the second in command. The party had only one member who had any practical experience in mining, a man named Moran. The others came from all parts of the United States, but predominantly from New England, and from several walks of life. They included a railroad brakeman, a clerk, an ice man, a travelling salesman, a farmer, a steamboat man, a grocer, a gas company foreman and a journalist. The one thing that united them was their determination to look for gold.

The group arrived in Seattle in early February 1898, where they remained until they departed on the *Farallon* March 9. The *Farallon* stopped in Victoria, where the members of the party picked up their mining licenses, then sailed for Pyramid Harbor, arriving there on March 16. Nine days later the party reached the Klehini River.

On foot, the party of thirty-six pulled their supplies along on large sleds, over snowdrifts, through rivers and up and down hills. The work was hard and at least one member suffered from varicose veins for the rest of his life, brought on, he claimed, by the strain of dragging a sled through the mud and snow of the spring melt. They developed an expert technique with the sleds: one person, who was strapped into a harness attached to a rope, dragged the sled with a load weighing up to 450 pounds, while a second steered the load with the gee pole. As one of them described their method:

> If you should try to guide your sled with the drag-rope alone, you would find that it would swerve on every uneven spot, and slip sideways on a slope, and dig its nose into the sides of the trail where the snow is soft; but with your right hand on a firm-set gee-pole, you will be able to steady your sled and guide it accurately where the trail is rough and rutty.[276]

When they reached open water, everyone lent a hand and the sleds were lifted and carried across to the other side. They got caught in a blizzard on

Members of the Mysterious Thirty-Six packed their own supplies over the snow to Dalton Post in the spring of 1898. ELIZABETH BANKS NICHOLS COLLECTION, MACBRIDE MUSEUM OF YUKON HISTORY, 1989-30-046

Hiking along the shore of Dezadeash Lake, with the Dalton Range in the background. ELIZABETH BANKS NICHOLS COLLECTION, MACBRIDE MUSEUM OF YUKON HISTORY, 1989-30-077

the barren lands beyond the summit on April 9. As the party progressed, so did the weather. A month after arriving in Pyramid Harbor they had reached Neskatahéen. With the snow gone, they carried their loads on their backs.

Once into the interior the party broke into smaller groups that spread out across the countryside. One group set up its base of operations on the Dalton Trail along the Dezadeash River and built a small windowless shack that they named "Pennock's Post." Others built a small cache at the northernmost point of the Dezadeash River known as Champlain's Landing and later, Champagne. It was named after Paul Champlain, an associate of the Mysterious Thirty-Six (Champlain also worked briefly for the famous Canadian geologist, J.B. Tyrrell, when the scientist travelled through the region).[277] Another cache, named "Camp Storey," was established by members of the Mysterious Thirty-Six between Champlain's Landing and Hutchi. Another camp was called Cannon Creek. These shacks, which were named after members of the party, served as base camps and storage depots for food and equipment. From the camps, the mysterians spread out and prospected adjacent creeks.

They rafted supplies down the river to Champlain's Landing, and they hiked back and forth along Dalton's trail from one camp to another, becoming well-known to the Mounties. When none of the prospects in this vicinity turned up any gold, they concentrated their efforts at Moran's Camp on Alder Creek, a spot now within the boundaries of Kluane National Park, in the front ranges of the St. Elias Mountains to the west of Dalton's trail.

As the party at Moran's Camp grew in size, their facilities expanded. They built a storehouse, a kitchen and a dining hall. They set up half a dozen tents as sleeping quarters. Under Moran's guidance, they ran tunnels into the gravel banks along Kah-Sha Creek looking for the pay streak.

Life in the camp was hard for the Mysterious Thirty-Six. Lieutenant Adair, a former army man, ran the operation along military lines, with a chain of command and strict discipline, but most of the members were unaccustomed to such rigid regulation. The operation had other problems, according to the recollections of an observer:

> The men were put on rations, which was a new and unpleasant experience for them. They grumbled, although they had to admit

that Adair shared equally with them. It wasn't safe to stow a cracker under one's blanket for morning—someone would steal it.

[Arthur]Thompson . . . was so hungry he could have eaten the bacon rind they used to grease the whipsaw with! And he's a Harvard graduate![278]

Adair sent a party of six men back to Dalton Post for supplies and stationed party members Reitz and Johnson in a camp at Klukshu to fish the salmon run and wait for supplies from the coast. The six returned footsore and lame, each carrying fifty to eighty pounds of supplies they had purchased from several discouraged prospectors. Finally, the first of Dalton's pack trains for Kah-Sha Creek arrived in mid-July, bringing much-needed provisions, and more followed in August.[279]

Alder Creek and nearby Shorty Creek turned out to be a paying claim area. Some of the prospectors were taking out fifteen dollars of gold per day, a decent rate of pay, and Lieutenant Adair bought them out to gain control of the entire creek. A mining expert named Dunn inspected a four-mile-long quartz reef and took samples to analyze back in the States.[280] Not everyone found gold in those hills; some disappointed men left Shorty Creek

Moran's Tunnel on Kah-Sha Creek. ELIZABETH BANKS NICHOLS COLLECTION, MACBRIDE MUSEUM OF YUKON HISTORY, 1989-30-118

empty-handed and departed the country.[281] Adair, however, appeared to be well-financed personally and was planning to bring in seventy-five thousand dollars worth of mining equipment during the winter for hydraulic mining the following year. But as with many Klondike-inspired schemes, it all came to nothing. The party left the region at the end of the summer.[282] None of the claims staked on Alder and Shorty creeks and assigned to Adair was renewed and the claims were forfeited October 1, 1899.[283]

All summer long the traffic passing back and forth along the Dalton Trail was not heavy, but it was constant. There were Mounties on patrol, gold seekers coming to and from the Klondike and other would-be miners going to the Last Chance district or the White River. J.B. Tyrrell, the Canadian geologist, studied the trail for the Canadian government, both coming to and returning from Dawson City. On the return journey Tyrrell had a traveling companion: Arthur N.C. Treadgold, a British correspondent for the *Mining Journal*. Treadgold liked the opportunity he saw in the Klondike and left filled with ideas. In a short time he would return to run one of the biggest dredging companies in the Yukon.[284]

After his exploratory trip over the trail with Onderdonk, Henry Bratnober next took a journey into the White River with Jack Dalton by horse in July. Bratnober had hired two men to prospect in that area during the winter, and they succeeded in sinking a forty-foot shaft and finding copper. Bratnober and Dalton found copper, too, bringing out a sample of a hundred pounds of nuggets.[285] "When I was there . . ." said Bratnober, "the water was low, and the copper could easily be picked out of the streams and placed in sacks. Yes, that country has a wonderful copper future."[286]

Women on the Dalton Trail

The ratio of men to women on the Dalton Trail that summer was about 140 to 1. Few women tried to challenge the Klondike, for North American society did not deem the wild life of the frontier to be appropriate for proper Victorian ladies. The general social attitude found expression in the words of Mrs. Frederick Schwatka, wife of the veteran Yukon explorer, who remarked, "The average woman would find it more to her interests to leave the hardships . . . and dangers to men . . . who are better able naturally to support what will have to be undergone."[287] Yet women were well aware of the excitement brought on by the stampede. They were affected profoundly when their lovers, sweethearts, husbands, brothers and fathers set off for the Klondike seeking opportunity, fortune and adventure.

A few female romantics made grand plans to go north themselves. One group of socialites from New York, for example, created the Women's Klondike Expedition. Forty of them banded together to hire two Pullman sleeping cars to carry them across the continent in comfort by rail. They planned to sail up the west coast by boat to Sitka. They imagined themselves continuing from there to Dawson in luxury in self-contained horse-drawn caravans consisting of six vans equipped with sleeping quarters, with four more to carry their provisions.

Their plan made the newspapers, but the women eventually abandoned their idea. Another enterprise initiated on the east coast, The Women's Clondyke Expedition, managed to collect five hundred women into a syndicate and hired a ship to take them around South America into the Pacific Ocean and up the west coast. The voyage proved hazardous and the women endured being shipwrecked in the Straits of Magellan. By the time their repaired vessel limped into the port of Seattle, they all called it quits and headed home—by land.

In another case of feminine entrepreneurship, three women in Seattle planned to incorporate the Women's Yukon Alaska Mining and Investment Company, using the capital to hire men to go to the Klondike and do the work of mining for a share of the gold they would

EN ROUTE FOR CHILKOOT.
Newspapers provided fashion tips for women planning to make the trek to the Klondike. *CHICAGO TRIBUNE*, FEBRUARY 21, 1898

recover. These female investors, however, had no thought of going to the gold fields themselves.

Only a few independent-minded women had the temerity to join the tens of thousands of men who passed over the Chilkoot and White passes at the height of the gold rush.[288] These few women who did head for the Klondike had their job cut out for them.

The first two white women known to have travelled over the Dalton Trail may have had the toughest time of any who attempted it. In late August of 1897 Mrs. George Bounds and Mary Ellen Galvin, wife of Pat Galvin, left Dawson City with their husbands, headed for the Dalton Trail. The two couples hoped to reach the coast before winter set in, but the weather turned cold, the snow fell and the wind blew. The clothing of the women was in tatters when they finally reached Juneau. The women had begun their trek on horseback, with the men walking, yet Mary Ellen ended up walking most of the distance because the harsh conditions were too much for her horse, and it died. "I walked about one hundred miles of the way," she said when she had completed the trip. "One of the men nearly played out, but he said he was bound to stick to it, he wasn't going to be outdone by a woman."[289] Mrs. Bounds also seemed to survive the trail well. According to a report in a newspaper, "she had never had less of what she wanted to eat in her life, but at the same time her health was never better. She said that she felt like a woman new born."[290]

When the Dalton Trail became busier in 1898, a few other women appeared in the records of those travelling along it. A young woman believed to be a journalist named Miss MacIntosh was seen by the Mounties at Pleasant Camp with saddle horse and pack horse, travelling alone to Dawson. She said that because of the lateness of the season (it was mid-August), she planned to spend the winter at Dalton House. Another party consisting of a Mrs. Shirley, two nephews and a niece headed up the Dalton Trail for the White River. They had the tedious work of double-tracking to move their supplies slowly along the trail. Mrs. Shirley and her niece eventually decided to remain at Pleasant Camp while the two nephews proceeded to Dalton House.[291] Another woman was noted travelling on the Dalton Trail in farmers' overalls, wearing a fancy hat and carrying a canary in a cage. She said the canary was a precaution against mine gas.[292]

One able woman to tackle the Dalton Trail in the summer of 1898 was a twenty-two-year-old newlywed from Arizona, Mrs. C.J. Dunbarton. Her husband, Charlie, at six feet six inches, was one of the tallest men on the trail to Dawson that year. She and her husband were bringing in sixty-five head of cattle for the Dawson market. She was a good-looking woman, but after six or seven weeks on the trail, she was, by one account, "the raggedest woman you ever saw."[293] One seasoned herder who watched her work said that she must have been brought up on a ranch as she was a more able hand than her husband.[294]

The summer of 1898 brought to the Dalton Trail a unique woman, a veteran of the north who had been to Alaska twice before and knew exactly what she was getting into: Della Murray Banks. Accompanying her husband, Austin, and a party of nine others in search of gold, she knew about the dangers of frontier life. During an earlier trip north, she had burned her hand badly and lost two fingers. Mrs. Banks, her husband and their companions gathered at Pyramid Harbor before starting off for Dawson.

Mrs. Banks met two ladies at Pyramid Harbor who were planning to accompany the party. One regarded the trip as a lark, and naturally didn't expect to do any work. She wouldn't think of going if there was any possibility of getting her feet wet! She wouldn't eat off a tin plate, drink from a tin cup or eat beans or bacon. She would live on cream, milk and eggs. She couldn't even ride a horse! Della decided she wouldn't go if those women went. "I was willing to do my share," she said later, "but that didn't include waiting on Mrs. Tucker." The two other ladies finally decided instead to spend the summer in Seattle, where they could keep their feet dry. Della smiled when she heard that; she said, "They didn't know Seattle!"

Mrs. Banks hired on at fifty dollars a month to cook for the travelling party. Every evening regardless of the weather or location, under the open sky, she prepared meals for the hungry men that included ninety biscuits, baked fifteen at a time in a simple sheet-metal stove. More often than not, she did this while kneeling on the ground.

At the end of one hard day, one of the men told her that if it were up to him, there would have been no meal prepared that night. She responded simply by observing that she had covered the same distance that he had.[295]

She rode a durable, steady pack horse named Polly and used only a rope halter and a blanket folded over Polly's back and lashed in place with a leather band. She could adjust herself to any situation, an admirable trait that helped her cope with difficult conditions better than some of the men on the trail with her. Fifty years later, in an account published in the *Alaska Sportsman*, she wryly commented on some of the men in her party: "It wasn't the man who didn't know, but the man who wouldn't learn, that made it hard."[296]

By the time her party reached the Yukon River, it was too late in the season for her to continue. Tired and worn out by the overland trip, she booked

Every day, Della Murray Banks baked 90 biscuits, 15 at a time, in a simple sheet-iron stove for her hungry crew. DELLA MURRAY BANKS, FROM *ALASKA SPORTSMAN*

passage on a steamer and returned to the coast, while her husband continued to Dawson City.

A Last Resting Place

A few weary men and many beasts ended up making the Dalton Trail their tragic final home. "There's never so lonesome a grave as one beside a trail," said Della Banks. "We passed one with a square post at head and foot while a blazed tree carried the name of the dead man and the names of the comrades who buried him. 'Frank Goodman died July 20, 1898.' Long afterward I learned that he had belonged to the Thibault [Thebo] cattle outfit, and had died of typhoid fever."[297]

River crossings were the most dangerous points on the trail. One German drowned on the Alaskan side of the border while crossing the Salmon River in June 1898. Ernest Amos, a cattleman, drowned in the same river a month later. Both were buried nearby.[298] Some gold seekers going in on the trail became lost and suffered deprivation. They completed the trail if they were lucky. Some going out, desperate to escape the Yukon, fled over the trail with insufficient supplies and simply ran short. The trail was a hardship to many who travelled it that year, and occasionally it was deadly.[299]

Although the trail presented many physical challenges, there was no major catastrophe or act of violence, no avalanche, no marine disaster or fire to afflict those using it in 1898. There was, however, one mysterious apparent fatality that greatly troubled both Jack Dalton and the Mounties. From the time of its establishment, Dalton's trusted agent at his trading post near Neskatahéen had been Ike Martin, a middle-aged man, short and wiry, with a sprinkling of grey in his black hair. Martin reported to Sergeant Major Barker on August 22 that he had been robbed of $860. Suspecting some men who had passed through earlier in the day, he and Barker set out in pursuit. While they were camped that night en route to Rainy Hollow, their horses wandered off. Barker recovered his mount, but Martin could not find his and told the Mountie to carry on without him while he would walk the eleven miles to Dalton Trail Post. He never arrived. The mystery of Martin's disappearance was never explained. Dalton dismissed out of hand any suggestion that Martin had been dishonest.[300]

While the Dalton Trail brought tragedy to a few of the men on it, the travellers faring the worst were the horses. As everywhere else during the gold rush, the treatment of these beasts of burden was cruel and heartless.

Like the Chilkoot and White Pass trails—though not to the same extent—the Dalton Trail in the summer of 1898 was filled with the corpses of horses. Many of them had died the previous autumn from hunger, cold and snow-blindness while bearing the burdens of those people making their way out over the trail and those attempting to make their way in. The autumn toll had been merciless. The Brauer party started with twelve horses, but their progress through the deep snows was brutal on the worn-out animals; they shot the last of the horses when they reached Dalton House.[301] Israel Lee lost ten in the Chilkat Pass before reaching Dalton House, and the Galvin contingent lost all eleven of theirs. Similarly, W.P Wood and J.S. Dickerson of Sumner, Washington, lost all of their horses and turned back.[302] Jack Dalton was more experienced and had more at stake. He lost only two horses en route from Fort Selkirk to his post on the Tatshenshini River. Most terrible of all, however, was the story of Willis Thorp, who made a fruitless attempt to cross the Chilkat Pass late in the year and had to turn back for the coast. He encountered a fall storm on the way and lost eighty-four horses.[303]

By 1898 the trail was littered with the rotting corpses and the packs that the horses had been carrying. One beneficiary of the Thorp tragedy was Della Murray Banks, who started from Pyramid Harbor with only a rope around her horse's neck and a blanket to sit on. First, she found a mule bit for her horse, then, when she arrived at Glacier Camp near the summit of the Chilkat Pass, she traded that bit for a regular bridle she found hanging in a tree. By the time the party arrived at Dalton Post, she was riding on a fine saddle and with a good bridle, both acquired from the dead animals they had passed along the way.[304]

While it was the bitter cold and starvation that killed off the horses in the winter, it was the swamp that got them in the summer, if the mosquitoes didn't drive them mad first. When it came to horses, men's hearts turned to stone. Cattle were money on the hoof, and every effort was made to care for them and deliver them to market in good condition, but it seemed as though those using horses as pack animals saw no other value in them. They worked the poor creatures to death and then moved on.

Della Murray Banks mounted on her horse, Polly. By the time she reached Dalton House, she had found a good bridle and pack saddle along the trail.
DELLA MURRAY BANKS, FROM *ALASKA SPORTSMAN*

A typical story of horse abuse was that of William Shape, one of the many stampeders on the Dalton Trail. Shape was no shining example of human compassion, but he did stop with his partner to help two men whose pack horse had become bogged down in one of the awful swamps. The four of them were able to get the poor animal out of the mire, but it was shaking, exhausted and unwilling to move on. With a single shot from a revolver, they disposed of the spent beast. Shape and his partner purchased a mare and a little sorrel for their own use from a cattle drive camped near Fort Selkirk to carry their supplies out of the Yukon over the Dalton Trail. Day after day they pressed on. They showed little regard for the condition of the animals. The faithful little mare weakened, but they hurried on toward the coast, not willing to stop to allow her to regain her strength. Nearing their goal, Shape noted that the mare had collapsed several times during the day, "but was doing nicely." Two days later, she could go no further, so they shot her.

While his horses collapsed from exhaustion, Shape certainly did not. Ironically, Shape, who in the past fourteen months had walked more than a thousand miles, over all kinds of terrain, through all kinds of weather, had gained fifteen pounds.[305]

"Bogged": It was the horses which suffered the most from the conditions on the trail. THE BANCROFT LIBRARY, UNIVERSITY OF CALIFORNIA, BERKELEY

Slaughter on the Yukon

In the summer of 2009 I gave an illustrated talk on the Dalton Trail at the Sheldon Museum in Haines, Alaska, in which I described the cattle drives over the trail in the early days. I told the audience that supplying cattle to Dawson City during the Klondike gold rush was big business, and that hungry miners with pokes full of gold paid premium prices for a steak or a good roast. After I had concluded, I was approached by a gentleman who at one time lived near Fort Selkirk. I don't recall his name, but I hope we meet again because I am infinitely grateful for what he told me.

One of the archival photographs in my presentation was of a place that he referred to as Slaughterhouse Slough. He told me that it was near Fort Selkirk, a location confirmed by a hand-written inscription on the original photograph that stated, simply, "Killing Pens Near Selkirk." I was intrigued by the possibility that this site was closer to Fort Selkirk than I had imagined. I had always assumed that no one would have driven a herd all the way to Fort Selkirk if it was possible to stop upstream and let the current carry a shipment to Dawson City. Further research produced a few tantalizing references to the continuation of the Dalton Trail that followed the eastern bank of the Yukon River from Five Finger Rapid to Fort Selkirk.

When I returned to Whitehorse I approached Bruce Barrett of the Historic Sites division of the Yukon Department of Tourism and Culture.

We talked about the possibility of locating Slaughterhouse Slough and planned to make the trip in early August of 2010.

Fort Selkirk is accessible only by air, or by boat from either the Pelly or Yukon rivers. For my visit the approach was to be by boat. Before taking to the water, I drove thirty miles on the hottest day of the summer from the tiny settlement of Pelly Crossing along a dusty serpentine dirt road to Pelly Farm. There I met Bruce and a crew loading lumber into a boat and preparing to set off for the downstream junction of the Pelly with the Yukon. Twenty minutes later we arrived at Fort Selkirk. That afternoon Bruce and I linked up with Don Trudeau, the manager of the restoration work at the historic village of Fort Selkirk, who took over as skipper of our small riverboat. We pushed off from Selkirk and headed up the Yukon River.

Don had already consulted with Franklin Roberts, a long-time resident of Pelly, who knows the area well. He and Franklin had visited the suspected slaughtering site a couple of days before my arrival, so that is where we headed first. As we approached the site I compared the skyline beyond the river bank to that in an old gold rush photo that I held in front of me. They were a match. While Don held his boat in a stable position in the shallow water, I excitedly snapped off a dozen photos of the view of the shore with the hills in the background, and then we eased the boat into shore.

The terrain above the beach where we landed was filled with deadfalls, young aspen, wild rose bushes and fireweed. The brambles could easily trip you if you weren't alert and agile on your feet. The landscape had changed during the last century, and a recent forest fire had swept through the area, eradicating some of the old aspect. We began to think it would be difficult to recognize the site.

Then, as we climbed the bank, we started to notice flashes of white partially hidden in the juvenile undergrowth all around us. The white, upon closer examination, became bones: jawbones, skulls and foot bones—all distinctively belonging to long-dead cattle. After my year of anticipation, finding this place was almost too easy, and the bones gave verity to the image captured in the old photograph. Without the photograph, the reports of local residents, the details from old newspapers and the boat to take us to the site where the bones lay scattered, I would not have been able to find Slaughterhouse Slough. The story of this place might have become ever more obscured as years passed, fading as the bones decayed and the photograph yellowed.

Don suggested that we walk down the shoreline a hundred yards or so. Here, as the old photograph revealed, was where the men had camped. As we moved toward this target the bones thinned and disappeared, and other old relics began appearing: tin cans, a piece of chimney pipe and fragments of sheet metal lay partially hidden in the thickening undergrowth. Together, the photograph, the bones and the other relics revealed an interesting story about what had happened at this site in the fall of 1898. It was here, after a journey of more than two thousand miles, that a herd of cattle belonging to Charlie Thebo was corralled, systematically slaughtered and butchered, and then loaded aboard large, hand-made scows for the trip to Dawson City. Charlie Thebo, as I learned later, was an American cattleman who established and operated a meat business in Dawson City for several years after the gold rush was over.

I needed to understand more of the butchering process. Despite growing up on a farm where we had raised Herefords, I was never involved in the slaughtering or butchering of our herd. When I returned to Whitehorse I

Slaughterhouse Slough. Charlie Thebo's slaughtering pens on the bank of the Yukon River near Fort Selkirk. Two large scows awaited the beef that was to be hauled to Dawson City. THE BANCROFT LIBRARY, UNIVERSITY OF CALIFORNIA, BERKELEY

Slaughterhouse Slough, August 2, 2010. MICHAEL GATES COLLECTION

sought some practical insights into the remains that I had seen during our brief visit to Slaughterhouse Slough. I spoke to Stacey, the proprietor of Stacey's Butcher Block, our neighbourhood meat supplier, about what we had seen. He referred me to diagrams that illustrated butchering. The portions of the carcass normally discarded during butchering matched the remains that were left beside the Yukon River.

Too late, I realized that I had overlooked a tiny detail. The only bones left behind at Slaughterhouse Slough were those of no value. Yet tongue is highly prized and would never have been discarded. Did the jaw bones left at the site show any cut marks or other indications that the tongues had been cut out when the cattle were butchered? In the excitement of the moment, I had neglected to think of this question or examine the abandoned jaw bones for the evidence.

A year later I learned even more about the cattle drives over the Dalton Trail. I had unearthed a lengthy account of a cattle drive over the trail in 1898 written by George Tuxford, a Welsh immigrant farmer from Moose Jaw, Saskatchewan. Tuxford, his brother Alan and a neighbour, John Thomson, moved their herd as far as Rink Rapid, which is located just a few miles farther down river from the more infamous Five Finger Rapid. There they set up camp, and when the autumn weather was cool enough, slaughtered and butchered their sixty-six head of cattle and oxen and then rafted the meat to Dawson City just before freeze-up.

In his account, Tuxford stated that they resorted to killing each animal by shooting it in the head before butchering it. Finding evidence of this method of killing should confirm the site of the Tuxford slaughter.

In late July of 2011, again in hot, sunny weather, Bruce Barrett and I, accompanied by Yukon linguist Doug Hitch, took a day trip to the site. Early in the morning we had driven 125 miles north from Whitehorse along the Klondike Highway, parked and hiked approximately three miles through dense underbrush along the banks of the Yukon River to get to the site. In as systematic a manner as we could manage in the thick vegetation, we spread out and followed three parallel lines along the shore. We were intent on intercepting the remains of the Tuxford party encampment. Eventually the terrain levelled and the vegetation thinned to a scattering of spruce trees on a thick ground cover of moss.

We located a few isolated items, including a set of old sled runners, some tin cans and a blue enamelware coffee pot. Then Bruce whooped and announced that he had found what we were looking for. Spread out where he stood was a thin scattering of bone, including jaw fragments, teeth and a moss-covered skull. I raised the skull from its resting place and brushed aside the moss, revealing the gaping hole in the forehead. This was the evidence of the Tuxford party we were looking for. We spread out and circled the discovery area and found more remains scattered widely, though thinly, in the area closer to the river bank. Included in these finds were a foot bone, more jaw fragments

Bruce Barrett found the first skull with a bullet hole in the forehead. MICHAEL GATES COLLECTION

and teeth, complete jawbones and a second skull with a similar hole in the forehead.

With time running out, and the primary objective of this trip confirmed, we turned our backs to the river and fought our way through the thick branches and deadfalls to our cars. Discussing the finds later, I concluded that we had confirmed the location where the party had camped, but the remains of more than sixty cows and oxen had eluded us. According to Tuxford, they had carried the waste material some distance away from the site of the butchering. Perhaps a more intensive future examination of the site would locate the dump site? We never located the pile of cast-away tins and bottles that characterize almost every old campsite I have ever seen in the back woods. As with the cut marks on the jawbones at Slaughterhouse Slough, I now have a good excuse to return to the site to uncover more remains and unravel more details of the Tuxford party encampment of 114 years ago.

CHAPTER 8

Cattle Drives on the Dalton Trail

By the middle of the summer of 1898 it was clear that the Dalton Trail was not going to be the main route to the Klondike. Most of the stampeders were choosing other entrances to the gold fields. Although there was a steady stream of gold-seekers using the trail to get into the Last Chance district or the White River region in the southwest Yukon, the number using the trail to get all the way to the Klondike was relatively small. Thousands of people were filing into the Yukon over the Chilkoot and White passes while only hundreds were using Dalton's Chilkat route. Mail was reaching Dawson through Dyea or Skagway more quickly than it could move overland by Dalton's route. There was yet another drawback to development of Dalton's trail: the railroad being constructed from Skagway to the White Pass and beyond was eclipsing the potential for a rail link from Pyramid Harbor to the Yukon River.

There was, however, one use for which Dalton's trail was best suited—moving livestock. The Chilkoot Trail was an almost impossible route for moving livestock because of the precipitous final ascent at the summit. While the White Pass was an easier route than the Chilkoot to move cattle into the interior, it presented herders with a series of daunting obstacles: the chain of lakes on which they could be becalmed or torn apart in tempestuous storms, and the turbulent waters of Miles Canyon, Squaw, Whitehorse, Five Finger and Rink rapids.[306] To transport livestock over these stretches of treacherous water, trail crews had to construct scows and section them into compartments to prevent the live animals from shifting dangerously to one side or the other. Otherwise, a sudden movement of the herd could cause the crude boats to capsize. During the long days aboard the scows, the cattle would become anxious and would lose weight. If the makeshift vessels encountered bad weather it meant they would meet even worse water. Entire scow loads of livestock perished in the foaming waters of Whitehorse Rapid and the dangerous shoals at Five Finger Rapid. [307]

Some British Columbia ranchers attempted to trail their livestock north from Ashcroft over the all-Canadian route, following the Telegraph Trail line that had been proposed for the intercontinental telegraph of three decades before. Because of the long distance over tough terrain, very few, if any, animals ever reached Dawson City from this route.[308]

The Dalton Trail, by comparison, was ideal. The climb to the Chilkat Pass was easy enough, and once over the summit the trail was relatively flat and the grazing was good. A herd could eat along the way and maintain or gain weight. The trail came out at the Yukon River near the site of present-day Carmacks, and branches followed either bank of the Yukon River to points below Five Finger and Rink rapids. From there, the river was clear of rapids and it was relatively easy floating by raft or scow to Dawson City.[309] If a herd of animals left Pyramid Harbor in June after the snows melted, they could reach the Yukon River below all of the lakes and rapids before freeze-up and arrive in Dawson plump and ready for market.

The cattle that ended up in Dawson were moved to rail shipping points from ranches all over western North America. Canadian cattle came from British Columbia, Alberta, Saskatchewan and Manitoba. American herds originated in Montana, Washington, Oregon and California. Some animals came from as far away as New Mexico, a distance of thirty-five hundred miles. The cattle drives to the Klondike and Alaska were the longest ever seen in the American West.

When the cattle reached steel, they were herded into box cars and shipped to western American and Canadian ports where they were transferred to freighters or barges, many of which had to be towed up the Inside Passage to Pyramid Harbor. These craft were often abandoned hulks, resurrected to cash in on the Klondike frenzy and hastily made over to accommodate livestock.

Often, more care was given to maximizing profit than to the welfare of the animals. The bark *Colorado*, for example, was towed out of Seattle harbour with 160 cattle and horses crammed into the after hold. Almost immediately after departure it had to make an emergency stop at Port Townsend because the animals were in distress. Two steers and two horses had died from suffocation in the short sailing time. The ship was so overloaded that it was impossible to provide adequate ventilation. The temperature in the animal pen had reached 120°F and even the men caring for the animals could not go down into the hold. The ship waited in port until forty horses could be removed and held for another ship to transport them. [310]

Cattlemen who landed their animals at Pyramid Harbor could hold the livestock in Jack Dalton's huge corrals along the shore until they were ready to move them along the trail. Some cattle shippers kept the number of drovers to a minimum to reduce costs; some brought in oxen because they could be used as pack animals before being sold for meat; some shod the hooves of the beef cattle to protect their feet against the rough rock of the route. Most chose older, larger animals, up to seventeen hundred pounds in weight, on the premise that they could maximize the poundage they would deliver to market in Dawson.

Cattle pens at Pyramid Harbor, the beginning of the trail. COURTESY OF CANDY WAUGAMAN

During the winter of 1897–98 several shipments of animals went north to the starting point of the Dalton Trail. One of the largest belonged to Charles Peabody, the manager of the Washington and Alaska Steamship Line, who arranged to send in 425 head of hogs and cattle, with sleds, saddles and wagons under the control of fifty stockmen. His enterprise was praised in the press as a practical solution to the famine that was thought to be afflicting the Klondike.[311]

Early in the spring of 1898 a report surfaced that Charlie Thebo was assembling a herd of two thousand steers in Montana to ship in over the Dalton Trail in June.[312] Thebo planned to break the herd into smaller groups, each consisting of one hundred animals. Every group would have six cowboys herding it, each man equipped with a packhorse and a saddle horse. In the end, Thebo took in a smaller herd, probably no more than one thousand head.[313] For transport from the north end of the trail at the Yukon River, he made a deal with Pat Galvin who said he could meet Thebo with his sternwheel river boat. Galvin, who had come out over the Dalton Trail with his wife and a sack full of gold a few months earlier, had plenty of money to burn and was going into the riverboat business.

The Incredible Meat Race

The trail was crowded in 1898 as numerous herds landed and trekked over the trail.[314] According to the Mounted Police, a total of 2,172 cattle, 722 horses and 377 sheep used the Dalton Trail during the brief summer.[315] For all the meat shippers the trip was a gamble, and for some it ended in disaster. Captain Elkyor from Manitoba tried to bring in a combined herd of cattle and sheep over the Dalton Trail. On July 18 one of his employees, Ernest Amos from Winnipeg, drowned while trying to save a couple of horses that were caught in the fast current of the Salmon (Tsirku) River. Some of Elkyor's sheep were swept away to an island in the middle of the river, where they were shot by Chilkats and carried off.[316]

Every one of the cattlemen was in a hurry to get to Dawson because whoever arrived at the head of the pack would make windfall profits. Timing was everything—that and making the right decisions along the way. Some decided to slaughter their animals once the herd reached the Yukon and boat the meat downriver to Dawson. To do this, they would have to wait until the temperatures were at or below freezing so that the meat wouldn't spoil.

Others chose to build scows when they reached the Yukon River and then ship their animals live. Bringing a scow to shore to let the animals graze each evening was a challenging and time-consuming task that some skippers failed to master. If they did not do this, the animals lost weight on the way to Dawson, losing profits for the herder, as well. And if they waited too long to set off, they risked being frozen in for the winter and not reaching market at all.

Pat Burns, the well-known Calgary rancher who already had achieved success in the north with the herd driven to Dawson by Billy Perdue in 1897, planned a second cattle drive. This time his beasts would be under the supervision of another Billy: Billy Henry, an Englishman and a seasoned veteran of the range. Henry started from southern Alberta with 250 head, but a train accident near Calgary reduced the herd to 185. He shipped the remaining cattle to Vancouver by rail, and by steamer to Pyramid Harbor, where he found himself and his livestock lining up with a number of other parties, all with the same intention: to move their meat to Dawson City.

Trailing cattle over the Dalton route was a job that started out easily enough as the herds moved up the Chilkat Valley, but crossing the Klehini River could be hazardous to both man and beast. Henry made this portion of the trip with difficulty. Another challenge came thirteen miles up the trail, when he had to pay Jack Dalton for the pleasure of using it. Encountering a party of rough-looking armed men who demanded a toll for the cattle, he decided it would be wise to pay up without protest. About thirty miles farther, he arrived at the Canadian border.

At this point he learned some alarming news: Charlie Thebo's cattle were just ahead of him. Right behind him was Charlie Dunbarton and his Arizona herd and more of Thebo's livestock. It would be a race to see who would get their cattle to Dawson City first. The winner would get top dollar for his beef from the twenty-five thousand hungry stampeders waiting in the Klondike, but meat arriving later would fetch a lower price.

Departing Pyramid Harbor July 1, the Burns herd moved slowly and uneventfully over the 250 miles to the Yukon River, arriving there September 20. Henry moved the herd along the western shore of the river to a point below Fiver Finger Rapid where mountain cliffs met the water and no more overland travel was possible. After gathering all the strays, he moved the herd

A small herd moving up the Klehini River near Pleasant Camp. YUKON ARCHIVES, J.B. TYRRELL FONDS, 82/15, 6

back upriver to a place where his crew had room to build some corrals and two killing pens, each with a "Spanish Wheel" for lifting and hanging the butchered cattle.[317]

By the middle of October it became cold enough to start the killing. Jack Collins, the butcher on Henry's crew, began slaughtering and worked up from ten to twenty-five animals every day. By the time the cattle and horses were butchered, ice was forming along the banks of the Yukon River. Meanwhile, Billy Henry made a deal with Charlie Thebo's small sawmill at Five Fingers to cut six-by-six timbers so he could build two scows. Henry then caught a ride into Dawson City where he hired four lumberjacks to return to the rapids with him to construct the scows, each seventy-two feet long and thirty-two feet wide. By the time the scows were finished, the livestock had been butchered and the meat was frozen, ready to be loaded on the scows for shipping to Dawson.[318] Again, time was of the essence. Henry knew that Charlie Thebo, with his load of beef, was already well on his way to market.

Pat Burns' herd wasn't the only Canadian meat on the move. Back in May, another prairie herd had been assembled, but its owners had a different plan of attack. George Tuxford and his brother Alan banded together with their soon-to-be-brother-in law, James Thomson, to move a herd from Moose Jaw, Saskatchewan, to the Dawson market.[319] The Tuxford brothers were Welshmen. George had immigrated to Canada in 1886 and home-steaded north of Moose Jaw the following year. James Thomson was a veteran of the North West Rebellion. Instead of stampeding to the north in search of gold, they decided to follow in the footsteps of Ed Fearon, the Saskatchewan rancher from Maple Creek who had done so well with cattle in Dawson in 1897.

The Tuxfords and Thomson purchased seventy Saskatchewan animals, mainly four-year-old steers together with some pack-broken oxen, and load-ed them onto CPR cattle cars for the trip to Vancouver. En route, they passed the boxcars that were carrying the herd belonging to Burchell and Howey from Brandon, Manitoba. The two parties raced neck and neck toward their ultimate goal in the Klondike.

After an annoying delay in Vancouver, they loaded their animals and supplies onto the boat *Coquitlam* and departed Vancouver on June 8, ar-riving at Pyramid Harbor six days later. The harbour was hectic, with many herds being tended in Dalton's corrals until the Chilkat Pass was free of snow. Billy Henry was there with the Burns cattle, as were Colonel F.G.O. Sissons and Charlie Thebo, who had the largest herd. The cattlemen were friendly with each other while they waited to start, but once they hit the trail it would be strictly business and every team for itself.

The Tuxford–Thomson strategy, once they started over the trail, was to use the oxen as pack animals, so each rider had only one horse. Each ox car-ried two fifty-pound panniers, carefully hitched to their backs. The feed was not plentiful, and the rock-filled river bottoms damaged the cattle's feet. The herders learned that even rest did not allow two of the animals to recover from their injuries. The lame beasts slowed down the progress of the herd, so with regret the men decided to shoot them, at a loss of a thousand dollars.

By the time the footsore herd arrived at Rink Rapid on the Yukon River, the Tuxford party had lost two more steers and one of the horses. The horse had died a gruesome death when it was impaled on the branch of a fallen tree not far from Carmack's Post. The remaining two horses were emaciated and worn out. Here on the banks of the Yukon River, the three-man party realized their small number put them at a disadvantage. One had to keep the herd together while the other two got to work constructing rafts to convey the meat to Dawson. Then they had to erect corrals and slaughter pens and butcher all of the animals by themselves.

Their progress was slow, and it was heartbreaking to know that others were gaining time on them. The Burns herd under Billy Henry was a week ahead of them. They also saw Charlie Thebo go by them on rafts his team had constructed upstream from their camp. Rudio and Kaufman, a partnership from Walla Walla, Washington, successfully ran the Rink Rapid with their herd. The partners watched others float by while they laboriously constructed their rafts and pens and butchered the animals one at a time.

Sissons, with his shod cattle, passed their camp en route to the mouth of the Pelly River; after that, Burchell and Howey, running three large scows, also passed by. They saw a few sheep: a flock of two hundred went by on the river, and some unclaimed sheep browsed nearby, survivors of a tragic accident that had occurred when one party attempted unsuccessfully to run the Rink Rapid some weeks earlier, and the owner had drowned together with most of his animals.

It was October before the Saskatchewan men were ready to push off into the icy waters of the Yukon. They set the two remaining horses free to forage

Oxen were useful for packing supplies over the trail. They also produced a large quantity of meat at the end of the journey. MACBRIDE MUSEUM OF YUKON HISTORY COLLECTION, 1989-30-140

for themselves, rather than butcher them with the cattle and oxen. They loaded twenty tons of meat onto three rafts: two large ones that were sixty feet long by twenty four feet wide, and a third, smaller craft. In company with four stampeders they met at Rink Rapid, they shoved off into the strong current and let the river carry them on to their destination. Below Fort Selkirk, they caught sight of the Sissons party, also floating a load of meat to Dawson City.[320]

The Tuxford rafts made slow progress through the ice-clogged Yukon River in sub-zero temperatures, catching up on sandbars in the rapidly falling water level. Only one raft made it safely to the shore at Dawson; a second one, caught in the strong wind and river current, floated helplessly past the booming gold rush town, and the third froze into the ice up river before landing.

As the hungry miners in Dawson waited impatiently for the shipments of meat to arrive, the various outfits bringing in meat raced for the finish. Like his rivals, Charlie Thebo encountered trouble. His venture partner, Pat Galvin, was to have sent the sternwheeler *Yukoner* to meet the trail crew and transport their load to Dawson. Unfortunately, the *Yukoner* became stranded one thousand miles downstream and never made it to the rendezvous point.

River scows had to be partitioned to carry cattle on the Yukon River in order to prevent the vessel from capsizing. PRINTS AND PHOTOGRAPHS DIVISION, LIBRARY OF CONGRESS

Thebo had to improvise. Using lumber from a portable sawmill he had erected below Five Finger Rapid, he built scows like those of the other cattlemen to get the meat to market.[321] Eager to process his animals, he sent his first shipments too early in the season; in the warm weather, much of the beef was rotten by the time it arrived in Dawson. One estimate was that seven hundred of a thousand head were spoiled by the time their meat got to market.[322] Holding back the remainder of his shipment, Thebo found that delivering it was not easy. The *Klondike Nugget* newspaper ran a story about it:

> Tuesday last found one of Pat Galvin's immense scows badly [stranded] on a bar in the centre of the river, somewhere above the Stewart. The floating ice was in immense cakes and endangered the barge. Mr. Thebold [*sic*] was in charge and at once decided that prompt measures alone could save the craft and any of its contents. The water was shallow and the ice was administering crushing blows behind. A small boat to transfer the cargo of meat was not to be thought of as it could not live a minute, and it would take days to transfer. Orders were given to lighten the cargo and reluctantly the precious quarters of beef were raised to the level of the gunwhale [*sic*] and slid into the water. Twenty or thirty quarters and still the craft wouldn't budge and thump! thump! went the ice on her stern. Fifty, sixty quarters but pike poles were still useless. Eighty, ninety, a hundred quarters of succulent beef was lost to Dawson, but the barge would not budge. At last, when the hundred and twenty eighth quarter had vanished amongst the floating ice, by a Herculean effort the boat was floated into deeper water and proceded [*sic*] on her way. [323]

By the time his ambitious project was complete, Thebo may have wished that he had stayed home. He was not the only entrepreneur who had a hard time delivering his meat. The same article in the newspaper reported that another scow loaded with meat was wrecked and lost at the mouth of the Indian River.[324] A third shipment was lost about the same time in the stormy waters of Teslin Lake.[325]

Thebo's fortunes eventually improved. Galvin went out of business permanently, so Thebo took over the Galvin Syndicate the following year. By

September of 1899 Thebo was advertising the largest supply of freshly slaughtered beef, pork and mutton in the Yukon.

Of all the cattlemen who brought beef into Dawson City in the fall of 1898, it was Billy Henry, bringing the Burns beef, who came out on top. He sold seventy-five thousand pounds of beef to the NWMP for seventy-five cents a pound, with the balance going to hotels and other customers for a dollar a pound.[326] Even the hides were sold at fifty cents a pound.[327]

Every part of the animal had some value for the Dawson market. According to one meat seller:

Billy Henry brought a large herd over the Dalton Trail to Dawson for Pat Burns in 1898. MICHAEL GATES COLLECTION

> With meat so highly priced you can well imagine nothing was wasted. All meat was readily sold, all bones were sold for soup, and the offal and hides were cooked in a huge stew kettle constantly boiling at the back of the slaughter house. During the summer months when dogs were not in use we would board them; we had as many as 160 dogs at one time. Their rations were taken from the stew kettle. For winter feed we prepared boiled hides, tallow and corn or oat meal; this was pressed into a concentrated cake and thrown to the dogs on the trail.[328]

Henry fared very well from the enterprise; in addition to his base pay of one hundred dollars a month, he received 12.5 percent of the profits.[329]

The Tuxford party was not so fortunate. Although their meat did not spoil on the trip downriver, they did not get the best price they could have hoped for. They had to settle for forty cents a pound for the first raft load that arrived in Dawson. After six months in transit to the Klondike, Tuxford and

Thomson headed back to Moose Jaw the following summer. Many years later, James Thomson remembered how he felt when he returned home from the north: "Moose Jaw looked awfully good. It looked like a place I never wanted to leave again."[330]

The herd being run by Charlie Dunbarton, the lanky American newly-wed, put into the Yukon River at a point above Fort Selkirk, but his raft became stranded on a river bar as ice formed around it. Things didn't look good for his investment, but luckily an empty scow came by, and his men transferred their meat to it. Nevertheless, the final hundred miles of their journey took nine days amid dense ice floes. When they arrived at the Dawson waterfront, it looked as though an unfavourable wind would prevent them from landing. At the last minute, a large crowd of meat lovers assembled on the shore and used a dozen rope lines to haul the rafts ashore safely. [331]

The Sissons herd from Medicine Hat almost didn't make it to Dawson. When they finally did arrive, having lost the race with the Tuxfords, they sold to a market that was almost saturated with beef; they received twenty-five cents a pound. They could console themselves with the thought that had they been one day later, they probably would have been frozen into the Yukon ice several miles above Dawson City.[332]

By the time the Yukon River froze up completely in 1898, there was plenty of meat in Dawson City. Nearly a dozen scows loaded with slaughtered cattle were anchored along the Dawson City waterfront. The price fell accordingly: by February beef was selling for only 25¢ a pound, while mutton, being a rare commodity in the city of gold, sold at $1.25, and pork, which was even rarer, went for $1.50.

INTERLUDE

Looking Back

During a visit to Haines, Alaska, in 2009, my wife Kathy and I decided to look for the site of the gold rush town of Porcupine. Porcupine was located near the mouth of Porcupine Creek, a tributary on the west side of the Klehini River, about thirty-five miles from Pyramid Harbor. For a short period after the peak of the Klondike gold rush, it looked like Porcupine Creek would become the next Klondike, but events didn't turn out that way. On the day of our search, the temperatures were the hottest of the summer and the rocky floodplain of the Klehini River shimmered in the sun. We might have expected weather more typical of the area: a strong wind blowing up the valley from the Lynn Canal, or even rain or fog.

We turned off the Haines Highway and crossed the Klehini River Bridge. A sign pointed the way to Porcupine. The road was paved for a short distance, and then it turned to rock and finally to dirt. Dust filled the air behind us, and I used the wiper to remove the dense film that quickly accumulated on the rear window.

We travelled along a narrow road shaded by tall trees. An opening in the canopy ahead of us revealed the glacier-filled mountains that bracketed the river valley at this point. Finally, the road broke out of the forest, skirted the rocky flood plain and then descended to the gravel bed of the Klehini River. We followed the track for several miles until it swung back up into the trees bordering the river valley. We continued until we reached a fork in the road.

A party of gold-seekers crossing the Klehini River near Porcupine Creek, 1898.
DELLA MURRAY BANKS, FROM *ALASKA SPORTSMAN*

Beyond this point each branch of the road was nothing more than a rough dirt track. One crossed Porcupine Creek, which at the time was a churning torrent of greyish-brown, silt-laden water. Was this a sign of mining activity beyond? In the distance was a large log house with a steep, sloped metal roof. Was it a miner's camp? On that day, we weren't inclined to drop in unannounced on strangers, so we opted to turn around.

On the return trip down the barren Klehini River flood plain, we stopped to look at the view and take some photographs. I had brought a selection of century-old photographs with me, and it was Kathy who noticed that one of them corresponded with the vista that lay before us. From this point looking down the river toward the coast, we saw that the profile of the hills tallied perfectly with a view in one of the photographs taken by Della Murray Banks during her trip over the trail with her husband in 1898. It was one of several images snapped during her journey; another showed her atop her horse Polly with only a rope attached to a halter and some blankets placed on Polly's back to soften the ride.

Matching one of her early photos with the actual place where the photo was taken 110 years before softened my disappointment at not finding the remains of Porcupine. Still, I wondered if we had reached the right spot before

The Klehini River near Porcupine Creek as it looks today. MICHAEL GATES COLLECTION

we turned around, and mentally I added a return visit to that fork in the trail to my list of journeys for the future. With elevated spirits, we climbed back into the air-conditioned comfort of our minivan, returned to the highway and continued on our way north to Haines Junction.

CHAPTER 9

•

1899–1902: The Porcupine Years

In 1898 the amount of gold being taken out of the Last Chance mining district, which included Alder Creek and Shorty Creek, did not measure up to expectations. Other promising mineral showings, however, were stirring speculative interest in the vicinity of the Dalton Trail. Jack Dalton was at the centre of the action, promoting the region's potential and cashing in on the business being generated.

"About the latter part of September," reported Inspector Jarvis of the North-West Mounted Police, "a very rich strike of copper was made about 15 miles to the westward of the Dalton Trail Post, about three miles from Rainy Hollow in British Columbia. Fifteen claims were staked and then recorded in Bennett. The samples were tested at the Treadwell mine and assayed out at 38 percent copper."[333] Jarvis judged that news of copper deposits in the White River area might draw a new stampede of prospectors to various locations along or near the Dalton Trail.[334]

In late August a new gold strike was reported at Boulder Creek, just south of Pleasant Camp. This discovery raised some issues for Inspector Jarvis because he needed to ascertain whether the gold strike occurred on Canadian soil or in American territory. Superintendent Wood echoed his concern, stating that until the location of the boundary was determined, it would be impossible to know which mining laws were to be enforced.[335]

Early mining on Porcupine Creek was done by hand. YUKON ARCHIVES, H.C. BARLEY FONDS, #4854

Nevertheless Jarvis gave leave to some of his men to take a day to go and investigate the creek for themselves.[336]

The Klehini–Porcupine watershed had shown earlier signs of gold. In late summer of 1897, Sylva W. Mix had passed through this country as a trail hand in the Waechter party herding cattle on the route to Dawson. Prospecting along the way, Mix found promising indications of gold in the vicinity of Pleasant Camp, and returned early in May of 1898 with partners Ed Fenley and Perry Wiley. That summer they looked for gold along Boulder Creek, and when that didn't yield anything of interest, they crossed the valley and tried Porcupine Creek. Finding good prospects there, they built a rocker and soon were each taking ten dollars daily.[337] When it started to get cold, Wiley left for the Outside. Mix and Fenley stayed behind and kept prospecting along Porcupine Creek. One afternoon while they were working a small shelf of gravel, Mix picked up five dollars in nuggets, then scraped up a pan full of dirt and recovered another six dollars worth. Having found this promising location, he returned with Fenley the next morning armed with a pick and a shovel. According to Mix:

[I told Fenley] I would show him something that would gladden his heart, and I did. When we reached the spot—a little point that jutted out—I put the pan against the bank, scraped it full, and we got $7 from this. Fenley's eyes stuck out of his head and he jumped up and down with glee. Then he took the pick, scrambled up on the shelf and picked down about a barrel of dirt and as it fell I could see the coarse gold all through it and some nuggets. He saw them and jumped down exclaiming in a most excited manner, "See, see! see!" pointing at and picking up the gold as fast as he could. I could not help laughing at him, but I was amazed as he was at the rich find.[338]

The two men set about working with a crude sluice made with canvas, and in two hours had panned out seventy-five dollars. They continued to work there for another ten days until the weather got too bad to continue, but on the last day they recovered about $185. In that time they had collected nuggets and gold dust worth a total of $1,150.[339]

They went to Juneau, where they put the gold on display in the Circle City Hotel. Mix proclaimed he wouldn't sell his claim for two hundred thousand dollars. Public interest in the Porcupine ignited instantly, and a miner with another claim in the area quickly sold a quarter share for four thousand dollars.[340]

Dalton was in the thick of things as the Porcupine stampede developed. He became a partner in the discovery claim on Porcupine Creek where, on October 22, thirteen claim holders held a meeting. They appointed J.C. Nail as the chairman and Mix as the mining recorder, and agreed that the new Porcupine Mining District would be governed by the US Mining Code, and a legal claim size would be twenty acres.[341]

Soon there were fifty men prospecting in the area, but the weather quickly progressed to winter. With six feet of snow on the ground mining was impossible, and only a few men remained there. It was so isolated that several of the men wrote the *Seattle Times*, advertising for wives. Age requirements varied, and some specified they were looking for "women of means." Whether they succeeded in finding suitable mates is not known.[342] It was lonely in the winter of 1898 on Porcupine Creek. What would happen in the spring, though, would be another story.[343]

Porcupine City is Born

During the winter of 1898–99 people in Juneau and elsewhere to the south held their breath about this new find of gold. Would Porcupine Creek become the new Eldorado? People had to rely upon news that was filtering out with the prospectors who had been working in the area.

On October 30 Dick Lowe (known as a king of the Klondike for his astute participation in the staking rush there) reported positively on the new find at Porcupine and stated that he had left five thousand dollars in Juneau for Jack Dalton to use in developing the creek. On November 1 miners C.G. Lewis and Carl A. West, returning to Juneau on the *Dirigo*, sang the praise of the new discovery. Without any mining equipment, they had scraped thirty dollars of gold out of crevices on McKinley Creek before being driven out by the snow.[344] Two other men reported taking out $360 from Porcupine Creek in fourteen hours. Then there were Mix and Finley, who arrived in Juneau and proudly displayed five hundred dollars worth of the gold that they had recovered. E.A. Bloom, arriving in Juneau in January, reported that there were "promising indications" on several new creeks as good as Porcupine. He stated that the Porcupine district was another Klondike.

The most authoritative and comprehensive news came from Jack Dalton, who took a steamer from Skagway to Juneau late in 1898. Passengers who accompanied Dalton on the *Farallon* told the press that he was reporting gold recovery of $150 per pan. Dalton, who was not one to exaggerate, more likely told them that this was the daily recovery, but with the heightened level of media interest and the public desire for promising news, it was possible that his news became overstated in the retelling.[345] Although Dalton warned the newspapers that the winter was not the right time of year to attempt to enter the Porcupine district, the effect of his cautionary words was nullified by the two sacks of coarse gold that he showed reporters.[346]

Juneau was filled with busted miners from the Cook Inlet and Atlin, British Columbia. The American prospectors were simmering with rage over the treatment they had received when they tried to get in on the new gold strike in Atlin.[347] The British Columbia government had passed legislation that excluded Americans from staking claims in the province. Before the law was overturned later in the federal courts on jurisdictional grounds, a lot of political damage had been done. The Americans were eager to find gold in an area they could call their own, so they listened eagerly to the reports coming out of Porcupine. Porcupine had the advantage of being easy to get to and, unlike Atlin, it was on American soil.

Dalton returned from his business outside and ate Christmas dinner at Pleasant Camp with Inspector Jarvis of the North-West Mounted Police.[348] He learned that reports on production in the Porcupine mining district continued to be upbeat and optimistic. Mining was in full swing despite the heavy snows.[349] The Chilkat River was frozen over and suitable for hauling supplies, and a thousand tons of goods were waiting to be hauled up to Porcupine.

Despite the weather and six feet of snow on the ground, miners stampeded to Porcupine in droves, staking wildly, until the creeks were littered by a bewildering profusion of stakes placed by men who had seen neither gold, nor even the ground beneath the snowdrifts. As one eyewitness reported:

> There was a crowd in here during the winter whose prospecting outfits consisted of an ax to cut a smooth surface on a tree and a pencil to write a location notice; and it was simply a race from one

Jack Dalton diversified his business to include trading, general merchandise, transportation and milling of lumber (above) in his mill at Porcupine. YUKON ARCHIVES, H.C. BARLEY FONDS, #4691

creek to another without prospecting or even sticking a pick in the ground.[350]

Taking advantage of the frenzy, "sharpers and bunco men" haunted the creeks, ready at every turn "to fleece the unsuspecting with the sale of bogus claims."[351] The publicity around the strike tempted hundreds of men to stampede to the Dalton Trail and the Porcupine goldfields. With typical Chamber of Commerce rhetoric, one Juneau newspaper announced that the Porcupine had the world's attention and predicted that no fewer than fifteen thousand gold seekers would pass through Juneau on their way to the new field. In fact, nearly a thousand prospectors visited the region before the end of the winter and hundreds were already established on Porcupine and the adjacent creeks. One eyewitness stated that there were at least five hundred men in the district building cabins and clearing enough snow to test a few pans.[352]

To cash in on the rising demand for services, Dalton hauled in a sawmill and brought in supplies for his Porcupine store over the frozen Chilkat River in the winter and spring. As soon as the snow was off the ground, he had surveyor G.W. Garside lay out a townsite of 150 acres on the banks of the Klehini River a half mile below the mouth of Porcupine Creek. By July, lots were selling for a hundred dollars, and the price later rose to three hundred.[353]

That summer the headlines in Alaskan newspapers proclaimed the promise of Porcupine. "Sluicing $500 Per Day," shouted one headline; "$1,200 Taken Out in One Day by Two Men—$36 from a Single Pan," announced another. Gold nuggets as large as filberts were being recovered and Perry Wiley, one of the original locators, took out $15,000.[354] With news like that and the influx of prospectors into the region, there was reason for Dalton and his partners to be optimistic about the potential of the Porcupine.

After Dalton's disappointment of 1898 when his plans of a pony express had gone bust, business seemed to be booming for him in 1899. In partnership with friend Ed Hanley and lawyer John Malony, he incorporated the Porcupine Trading Company, which encompassed mining, cutting lumber, retail sales, transportation and the operation of the Dalton Trail to the interior. In a separate investment, Dalton and Hanley paid twelve thousand

Porcupine became a tent city when gold was first discovered nearby. COURTESY
OF M.J. KIRCHHOFF

dollars to Mix, Fenley and Wiley to buy a controlling interest in the discovery claim on Porcupine Creek. By late 1899 the claim had produced forty thousand dollars in gold. The district as a whole had produced fifty thousand dollars.[355]

The town site of Porcupine developed almost overnight. By May, it consisted of "several substantial buildings," including two stores and a sawmill.[356] Soon, two hotels were added to the community: the Lindsay (owned by Dalton and operated by John Lindsay and his wife, Irene) and the Burkhardt (operated by F.F. Clark, formerly of Skagway).[357] The Lindsay started out as a canvas tent structure and evolved into a substantial wooden building of two and a half storeys. Many of the other winter tents of Porcupine were replaced by more permanent structures during the summer months. By September the Dalton Company's big store and warehouse were complete and several other buildings were going up. Jack Dalton also built a handsome residence for himself, his wife, Estella, and son, Jack Jr.[358] To support his blossoming businesses, Dalton ordered in hundreds of tons of goods and constructed a warehouse in Haines to house them.[359] The gold production around Porcupine did not rise to the levels seen in the Klondike, but it was still respectable enough to support a boom.

The new town of Porcupine was not the only settlement to be born on the Dalton Trail during the excitement of 1899. Signs of gold were found on the Salmon River about thirty miles northwest of Pyramid Harbor, so a small community consisting of two log buildings and a cluster of tents sprang up on the trail nearby. Dan Walker, a tinsmith from Juneau, had gone back to his hometown in January to secure provisions and equipment to establish a restaurant and store. Soon a sawmill was set up at the site as well, and the place became known as Walkerville.[360] The settlement had a short life. Only a small amount of gold was recovered in this area, and eventually everyone in Walkerville migrated to Porcupine or left the region entirely.

Three miles farther along the trail on the opposite side of the Klehini River was Camp Sunshine, a small stopping point named ironically because the sun's rays did not fall upon the site in the winter. Sunshine (also referred to as Sunrise) consisted of a cluster of tents and a single log barn maintained by Jack Dalton for his transportation business.[361]

The community that seemed to benefit the most from the flurry of prospecting, investment and speculation in the Porcupine District was Haines. Transformed by the Dalton Trail and the gold rushes, what had been

Walkerville was one of the temporary communities that sprouted on the trail when gold was found nearby. YUKON ARCHIVES, H.C. BARLEY FONDS, #4697

previously little more than a church mission became a thriving commercial hub. Realizing its potential, Jack Dalton and his wife Estella had purchased an acre of waterfront land some years before from the mission to use as a landing place for supplies. By May of 1899 there were between twenty and thirty houses and tents in Haines. The town boasted eight barrooms and five or six restaurants, as well as hotels and stores strung out along the waterfront. Haines now had a post office, as had Chilkat and Pyramid Harbor, and a good wagon road crossed the peninsula and linked it to Chilkat. Haines had a sheltered anchorage, so it was a regular stop for ocean-going steamers coming to Skagway.[362] There was, in addition, daily steamer service between Haines and Skagway. A wharf was under construction and a sawmill was operating.[363]

Inland at Porcupine, the miners began grumbling about the steep rates charged by Dalton for use of his trail. Shorty Bigelow, the prospector whose name adorned Shorty Creek farther inland, spearheaded efforts to establish an alternate route, but the idea ran into big trouble, and not just from Jack Dalton. A work crew of people interested in constructing a road up the northeast side of Chilkat Inlet marked a trail that passed through the village of Klukwan. When the Chilkats of Klukwan saw the road work beginning, they became angry and took up arms, driving away the party working on the trail. As a result, Chief Kudawat and several Chilkat men were arrested and taken to Sitka for trial. The court determined that the Chilkats had a right to prevent people building a road through their village, but cautioned that they had no right to resort to arms to enforce it. They were released after the trial.[364] Thanks to his old enemies, the Chilkats, Dalton was able to hold on to his trail monopoly for a little while longer.

The Mounties Hold the Line

While the boundary line between Canada and the United States remained unconfirmed the uncertainties surrounding its location continued to be an irritant for the two nations. Tension over the boundary was the main reason for the large detachment of Mounted Police at Pleasant Camp. Britain, Canada and the United States proceeded with negotiations. Late in 1898, after the federal elections were over, the United States consented to a Canadian proposal for a port at Pyramid Harbor. It was agreed that America would retain nominal ownership over the land, but this proposal resulted in a storm of protests in the Western States, where citizens objected to anything resembling the surrender of sovereignty over soil claimed by America. The proposal was withdrawn as a result of the furor, but it surfaced again a few months later in July 1899, when a scheme was devised to give Canada a perpetual lease of a half square mile at Pyramid Harbor for a docking place where goods could be transferred to a railroad that connected with the Yukon. The lease arrangement recognized American sovereignty, and now it was Canada's turn to reject the proposal.[365] As hope died for a port and rail terminal at Pyramid Harbor, all plans for a railroad over the Chilkat Pass dropped into no man's land.

Rumours of hostility and infringements along the still undefined boundary muddied the waters of negotiations. On March 17, 1899, articles in newspapers across the United States reported an armed conflict had occurred between American and Canadian miners. In an account that would have been more appropriate in the pages of a dime novel, the Mounted Police were said to have moved the Canadian flag farther into American territory to enable them and forty Canadian miners to stake claims in the Porcupine district. According to the account, when a deputation of Americans confronted the Canadians, a gunfight ensued that resulted in four deaths and many serious wounds.[366] The story was all a hoax. The perpetrator was never identified, but several American residents in Haines, Chilkat and Pyramid Harbor continued to stir the pot, claiming there was conflict and attempting to induce the US government to station troops in the vicinity.[367] Canadian authorities were quick to issue denials to quell the alarm of American readers.

Soon after the false news report appeared, British and American officials agreed in early August to establish an interim boundary line, a *modus vivendi*, until the final line could be determined.[368] This interim boundary line came into force on October 20, 1899. It ran down the Klehini River to the Chilkat River, then continued east to the Chilkat River mouth, thus placing Porcupine Creek and its tributaries in American territory, but nearby Boulder Creek on the Canadian side.[369]

Once this temporary line was established, the Mounted Police had to deal with a changed reality. They set up a new detachment named Wells at the new boundary line on the Chilkat River to intercept the miners entering

Canadian territory between there and Pleasant Camp, and to collect customs duty. While two constables began working from a temporary station under canvas, they constructed a two-storey frame structure with a footprint of 250 square feet. They made plans to build additional structures at what might become the final boundary line.[370] The British Columbia government had dispatched Captain Rant to establish a mining recorder's office at Pleasant Camp, and in November he also moved to Wells.

The Mounted Police settled into their new routine during 1899. They watched as use of the trail declined except for local traffic and the activity in the Last Chance mining district dwindled. Interest in other mineral finds still generated some traffic. Alfred Brooks, working for the United States Geological Survey, led an expedition in 1899 from Pyramid Harbor to the rumoured copper deposits of the White River and beyond. Another pack train travelled in the opposite direction. It had departed from Copper River, Alaska, and passed through the White River district, arriving at Pleasant

The Dalton Trail was relatively quiet. The Mounted Police spent most of their time attending to routine activities and little on investigating crime. MACBRIDE MUSEUM OF YUKON HISTORY COLLECTION, MBM 95-213

Camp on September 11, laden with copper samples. Prospectors also flocked into the Rainy Hollow district looking for copper. Porcupine Creek and adjacent tributaries—McKinley, Glacier, Calhoone, and Nugget creeks—remained a focus of mining interest. In one day, two men on Porcupine Creek took out almost one hundred ounces, and the biggest pan reported was $116.

Life began to get even quieter for the Mounties. With all the activity on the Dalton Trail becoming concentrated in American territory near the coast, in late August of 1899 the police reduced their patrols over the trail to Five Fingers. They maintained a twice-monthly mail service for the interior settlements, carrying out shipments and collecting incoming mail from the coastal post offices. Crime on the trail was virtually non-existent.

During the summer, the detachment in the interior at Dalton House expanded. One non-commissioned officer, three constables and a special constable were posted there and began constructing a stable and buildings to accommodate six men. In October, however, all but Constable Pringle and a special constable were recalled to Pleasant Camp, experiencing hardship because of the poor weather at that time of year.

The commander's reports indicated discipline was good among the Mounties, with Constable J.A. Pringle, in charge of Dalton House, singled out for recognition along with Constable Hoskens. Corporal Spreadbury was praised for being efficient and hard-working.[371] Sergeants Barker and Lasswitz, however, whose service had been praised in the previous year, were demoted and fined for insubordination early in 1899.[372]

In sum, nothing earth-shaking happened on the Canadian side of the Dalton Trail during 1899, with the exception of a real earthquake and aftershocks that were felt between September 10 and 15.

The Turn of the Century

1900 would prove to be an undemanding year for the Mounties on the Dalton Trail, with little crime happening and most of the traffic staying on the coastal side of the mountains. They provided assistance to surveyor G. White-Fraser when the British Columbia government dispatched him to determine the provincial boundary line shared with the Yukon territory. They were on hand when a provincial government commission went to the Dalton Trail to confirm titles to claims on creeks, such as Glacier, Slate and Boulder, which the *modus vivendi* boundary now placed in Canada.[373] The Americans who were on a stampede to Bear Creek refused to cooperate with the commission, holding to a hope that the disputed territory eventually would be determined to be American ground, so the results of the commission were unsatisfactory.[374]

The Mounties patrolled between Wells and Rainy Hollow on a regular basis, they made trail improvements between Porcupine and Pleasant Camp and they collected $1,954.02 in customs and mining duty. In 1900 there were still a few passing cattle drives for them to monitor. These occurred less frequently after the completion of the White Pass and Yukon Route Railway from Skagway to Whitehorse, although herders still found it expedient to herd the livestock overland from Whitehorse on the northern segment of Dalton's trail to avoid the lakes and rapids. Thebo and Gallagher, Charlie Dunbarton, McKay Brothers, Senator Mayfield and a man named Nichols had all brought herds over the trail in 1899. In summer of 1900, however, only 431 animals were taken over the trail; nearly half of them were Dalton's own herds under the name of the Dalton Trading Company. The cattle were under contract to the American army, headed for delivery in Alaska at points far down the Yukon River below Dawson City.

The main focus of attention for the NWMP detachment in 1900 was their watching brief on the population boom at the border. Mining activity was exploding in the Porcupine district. Despite the five to six feet of snow still on the ground at the creek in the spring, the stampede to Porcupine was big enough to drain the population from the town of Haines. Porcupine now had four saloons, two hotels and two dance halls with ladies euphemistically known as "petticoat attachments." Blackjack and poker games were running high, and tents and cabins sprouted at Porcupine faster than spring wildflowers. There were five sawmills running full time.[375]

Everybody was convinced that Porcupine would be another Klondike. One account described a thousand dollars in gold being taken from a mine working of four square feet, while another reported two partners taking out forty to one hundred ounces a day from a square of bedrock between six and eight feet on a side.[376] Perry Wiley and Ed Fenley, two of the original gold discoverers at Porcupine, were still operating claims 2 and 3 on Porcupine

Porcupine became a tent city when gold was first discovered nearby. YUKON ARCHIVES, H.C. BARLEY FONDS, #4690

Creek. They predicted fifteen hundred men would be mining in the district by 1901 and that production would jump as a result.

The residents of Porcupine had some complaints about their new home in the wilderness: they did not have a regular boat from Juneau to Haines, they had to rely on the Mounted Police to bring in the mail and they were isolated from the world outside. For news, they depended upon anyone generous enough to bring a newspaper.[377] There were problems with transportation, too. Jack Dalton had seventy-five horses and mules busy with the hauling into Porcupine and he was still collecting tolls. He charged one and a half cents per pound on anything brought in over his trail and four cents a pound to do the shipping. Discontent grew over Dalton's monopoly, and residents began calling on the government to rescind Dalton's trail license because he was charging more than the permitted government rate.[378]

Jack Dalton Adapts

The completion of the White Pass and Yukon Route railway reduced the value of Dalton's trail as a means to transport goods to the interior.[379] In

1900, however, Dalton was doing booming business in other directions. His Porcupine Trading Company had bought out the other owners on the discovery claim at Porcupine, and that claim had become the biggest gold producer in the district. Dalton's store was providing goods to the miners. His sawmill couldn't keep up with the demand for lumber, while his freighting business was hauling goods to the creeks over his trail. He also had lucrative contracts to supply goods to the Mounted Police. In addition, he had landed a contract worth $100,000 to supply beef to the US Army posts at Eagle, Fort Yukon and Rampart, and he was busy taking the cattle over the trail to the Yukon River in the early part of the summer.[380]

Along with his many business successes Dalton also had his frustrations, and he let his mercurial, often combative temperament find expression more than once in 1900. In early March he and two associates removed lumber from a strip of land along the shore in Haines where the Haines Wharf Company was constructing an additional building. Dalton insisted the land was his. This dispute ended up in court. He waged another battle in Haines that ended in violence. Dalton warned Tim Vogel, a Haines saloon keeper, against supplying liquor to the workers mining Dalton's claims. When Vogel ignored the warning, Dalton beat him nearly to death.[381]

Dalton's endeavours kept on growing in the year following. Optimism was high in the Porcupine district in the spring of 1901. Over the winter 350 tons of supplies and mining equipment were brought in and plans were afoot to work the tributaries. On Porcupine Creek, Dalton had a crew of forty men constructing a flume to carry the creek water around his claims so that they could scour the bottom of the stream.[382] The town of Porcupine expanded rapidly and by the summer of 1901 it contained at least three stores, two laundries and a bath house. John Lindsay was expanding his hotel to include card rooms and a bar. Perhaps the addition most welcome to residents was the new post office. In August Thomas. G. Woodruff was appointed the first postmaster. The Mounted Police appreciated the post office because it relieved them of responsibility for making a special trip twice a month to Haines for mail.[383]

At the end of the year enthusiasm for the future of Porcupine was still high. In Seattle in December, expressing the opinion typical of generations of miners that next season would be the best ever, Jack Dalton pronounced:

Porcupine is now past the stage of uncertainty. There is no longer a question as to the richness of the district. It is most manifest to the miners that it is destined to be a great gold producer. The past season we had too much water, the floods destroying much that had been accomplished in the way of development work. But such a visitation will not, I think, be witnessed again soon, and if it should we will be much better prepared to withstand the flood. Next season we will send many men, practical miners, into Porcupine. There will be a very general development of the district and a consequent large gold yield. It will prove far larger than any output in the history of the camp.[384]

There were some signs of trouble ahead. The Porcupine gold diggings were not easy to work. The depth of the deposits, the abundance of boulders and the absence of permafrost compelled miners to employ expensive equipment that raised their capital costs substantially. A flash flood late in August demolished woodwork and machinery on the claims, and a second devastating inundation followed in October. Despite the damage, the miners were still confident of the

The early hand mining was later replaced with large scale ventures that require major investment. Despite the construction of massive flumes, Porcupine Creek could quickly swell and wash everything away. COURTESY OF THE SHELDON MUSEUM & CULTURAL CENTER, HAINES, ALASKA

Porcupine potential, although many claim owners sold out at the end of the season and the mining became consolidated into fewer hands.

The Mounted Police continued to patrol the Dalton Trail and they increased the number of patrols between Wells and Rainy Hollow, now an area of intense interest to miners. Their trips to Haines, however, became less frequent. The British Columbia government invested some money in road construction that resulted in passable horse trails from Wells to Rainy Hollow and from Wells to Bear Creek.[385] Beyond Bear Creek, little mining was going on in the interior. Many of the miners working in the area protested the Mounties' imposition of duty on goods that were being taken into what the miners saw as disputed territory. For the same reason, several American miners refused to register their claims with the British Columbia mining recorder stationed at Wells.

The Mounties encountered similar objections from the Chilkats when Inspector of Customs Busby instructed that Canadian duty be collected from any "boats, canoes and skiffs" passing Wells on the Chilkat River. When the commanding officer visited the Wells detachment, a large and resentful deputation of Chilkats greeted him. The result was that Busby rescinded his instructions and refunded all of the money collected from them earlier.[386]

At this time, Jack Dalton again became the focal point of conflict with the Chilkat people in Klukwan. In the winter of 1900–01, he and his partner John Malony were in Seattle shopping around for a small steamer that they could use to carry freight inland from Pyramid Harbor.

"Our steamer will be the first to run on the Chilkat River," said Malony:

> and we are somewhat apprehensive of trouble with the Indians, who are a warlike tribe and have already given the prospectors and miners considerable trouble. Many a man has been found dead on the trail whose death could never be explained, but was unquestionably the work of the Chilkats. All the traffic on the river in summer is now in canoes, worked by these Indians, and the prospect of a steamboat which will deprive them of that trade is expected to prove another source of irritation and trouble. We, however, expect to get the United States government to afford us the necessary protection from its military station at Skagway.[387]

Dalton had seen the failure of an earlier attempt to navigate the river with a steamer and concluded that the vessel they planned to build would have to draw less than ten inches of water and have dredging apparatus on board.[388] They refused to accept the first boat they had ordered because it was not delivered on time.

Meanwhile, a rival entrepreneur named Gardner put a small steamer called the *H.D. Gardner* into the Chilkat River to carry freight up as far as Klukwan. Shortly after coming into service, the boat caught fire and burned to the water line. When the Chilkats were accused of setting the fire because it interfered with their own river transportation business, they denied having anything to do with it.[389] Gardner immediately substituted a second boat named the *A.H. Gardner*, and Billy Dickinson, a local resident, was hired to assist its operation.[390] When Gardner subsequently received threats, an officer and thirteen men from the 24th Infantry were sent in to provide protection. Gardner's steamer had trouble navigating the river and the business was not a success. He announced a plan to replace it with a stronger vessel the following year, but the replacement never appeared.[391]

Three years later, Dalton and his partners tried the riverboat idea again, this time purchasing a light-draft, gasoline-powered launch they christened the *Chilkat*. They brought the boat to Haines in pieces aboard the *Al-Ki* and assembled it immediately. The Chilkats warned Dalton not to use it, and local residents predicted that if the Chilkats were under the influence of alcohol, they might attack and burn the small vessel. Dalton refused to change his plans and said he was prepared to ask the army for help, if necessary.[392]

The boat went into service without incident until the day Ed Hanley was operating the little vessel and noticed that his Chilkat crewman was getting nervous. They brought the boat around a bend in the river and were confronted by a shaman in full regalia invoking spirit powers against the boat. "He wore a horned headdress and clutched a magic staff and rattle," related one observer; "He crouched, he lept [*sic*] and he waved his arms. He chanted and threw ashes and dramatically pointed at the *Chilkat*."[393] At that moment the unreliable motor conked out. Hanley, struggling to get the engine started, instructed his Chilkat assistant to put on a gymnastic performance of his own. As the crewman did an imitation of the shaman's moves, the motor roared back to life and they continued on their way. Over the season they were able to make twenty-five trips in the little *Chilkat*, but the cranky little boat never performed well and was always running aground.

An Easy Life, With a Few Scares

By 1901 the work of the Mounted Police on the Dalton Trail was reduced to a dull routine. They had few local criminals to make their days interesting. Lawbreaking was no more serious than thefts from caches and evasions of customs duty at the border. The traffic over the trail dwindled to a trickle in comparison with what it had been three years before. There was still mining in the region north of Dalton House, and new discoveries of placer gold and hard rock minerals were announced often near Pleasant Camp and Rainy Hollow, but none of these discoveries came to much in the end. The police made regular patrols from their three posts on the trail: Wells at the boundary, the main detachment at Dalton Trail Post (Pleasant Camp) and Dalton House sixty miles farther into the interior. Their work was so uneventful that Superintendent Primrose, commander of the police in the territory, drew the situation to the attention of the Comptroller of the Force in Ottawa:

> Sir,
>
> With reference to the Detachments on the Dalton Trail, I beg to draw your attention to the enormous expense of these three stations.
>
> As far as I can see they are doing absolutely nothing except collecting a few dollars for the Customs Department. They are unable to do any Police duty, they being in British Columbia and that being contrary to orders.
>
> It seems to me that we could withdraw the whole Force from that country and check up anybody passing over the Dalton Trail from the Five Fingers Detachment.
>
> Unless the policy of the government has something else in view, I do not see the force of leaving a single man there.[394]

For the next few years, however, the Mounties would continue to occupy and patrol the south end of the Dalton Trail for one main reason: sovereignty. National sovereignty along the Alaskan Panhandle remained a point of dispute between Canada and the United States. Canada wanted access to salt water from British Columbia and the Yukon, while the United States argued that the boundary should be farther inland, in the area of Bennett or Tagish. In the disputed area along the Dalton Trail, many American miners still refused to abide by Canadian law or register their claims with the provincial officials located at Pleasant Camp and Wells. They also resented having to pay a royalty of 5 percent on all gold recovered in territory claimed by Canada. Animosities grew after sensational reports in American newspapers about conflict between American miners and Canadian miners and the Mounted Police. But the most bizarre expression of this tension was the almost farcical affair of the Order of the Midnight Sun.

Early in 1901 rumours started to surface about a not-so-secret organization known as the Order of the Midnight Sun. The alleged goal of this society was to take over the Yukon and establish a republic. The organization was in existence as early as December 1900. Conspirators, said to be stationed in Alaska at Skagway, Eagle and Circle City, were prepared to set their plot in motion. While the Canadian government did not give any public recognition to the threat, it took confidential measures against it, instructing officials in the north to be prepared for trouble but to deny officially that anything was going on.

Clifford Sifton, the minister who had ordered the Mounties to take possession of the northern mountain passes, sent more Mounted Police to the Yukon, bringing the total strength of the force to three hundred men. The reinforcements, including an inspector qualified to train the men in the use of their Maxim machine gun, would be posted in Whitehorse and on the Dalton Trail (the Dalton Trail detachment would be doubled in size). The police dispatched detectives to Skagway to investigate the conspiracy reports, but all the men proved to be too well known in the community to work incognito.

Things got really strange in late October when Inspector Primrose went to Skagway in person to investigate with former detective J.H. Seeley. They started drinking on the train and continued upon arriving in Skagway. The investigation turned into a pub crawl and Primrose was ultimately arrested by the American authorities and fined for drunk and disorderly conduct. Some Canadian patriots suggested that Primrose had been framed, perhaps even drugged, but the event as it was recounted in the American newspapers was a Canadian national embarrassment. The American publications included details about the Order of the Midnight Sun. "Bold Conspirators Plan Revolt in the Klondike," read one headline. The article below the banner described the plan to overthrow the police and government officials. It said the conspirators would have a period of six months when they would be insulated from outside intervention by isolation and harsh winter weather, and in that time they would solidify their control. The paper made the preposterous statement that most of the conspirators were Canadian, including some members of the North-West Mounted Police who were ready to throw their fellow officers into jail.[395]

In February of 1902 Inspector Charles Constantine was dispatched from Ottawa to investigate the alleged conspiracy. His arrival ruffled the bureaucratic feathers of Superintendents Wood (in Dawson City) and Snyder (in Whitehorse), who felt their local authority was being challenged by head office. Constantine inspected the security measures being taken in Whitehorse, and then visited the Dalton Trail detachment and the nearby Porcupine community, reporting that he did not think "there is the slightest danger of any friction or lawlessness on the part of American citizens or miners in this part of the country." He said that if things were handled properly, there would be nothing to fear from the miners.[396] His report put the issue to rest, and although the Mounties maintained a heightened vigilance in the detachments for some time afterward, their daily round returned to normal.

INTERLUDE

Wheels on the Dalton Trail

I t was the summer of 2008, and the bikers were in town.

Not the Hell's Angels or the Harley Owners Group (The Hogs), but the healthy, energetic type with muscled thighs and enhanced lung capacity, filled with the urge to get out on the road: the type that rides bicycles. They were in Haines Junction participating in the Kluane–Chilkat International Bike Relay, an annual 150-mile cycling event in which the participants celebrate the virtues of liniment and ice packs. All were ready to undertake the challenge of endurance and speed, hoping to see their team be the first to pedal over the finish line in Haines a few hours later.

Only one hundred years ago, before the highway was built, travelling this same route took days, if not weeks. The smooth paved road that connects Haines Junction with the Alaskan coast obscures the reality of travel through this region for centuries. The hundreds of eager cyclists were probably oblivious to the significance of the improvement in the road. Few of them knew of the rich history of the area, nor of the vestiges left by previous generations that survive to testify to the past.

I was on this modern-day road to return to Neskatahéen, a historical point a few miles off the highway down a back road. On an earlier visit in 1977 I had been alone. Then in 2006 I accompanied a group of First Nation elders and youth who were participating in a summer culture camp. The elders introduced the young people to the fine art of gaffing salmon from the small stream that ran through the old village site. We took time to inspect the remains of the old village nearby.

I was startled by the changes that had taken place since my previous visit three decades before. Then, the remaining buildings at the site were still standing tall and proud; now, they looked decidedly sway-back. Before, the area was an open grassy space; now, the willows and poplar were taking over. There was once a good road leading to the site; now, the Tatshenshini River was cutting into the bank. The old road had washed away. Its replacement was a crude and bumpy track, suitable only for four-wheel drive, along an embankment skirting the encroaching waters.

During my earlier visit I had found some collapsed remains of the impressive longhouses that once stood in neat rows beside Village Creek. The finely smoothed planks still exhibited the axe marks that testified to their manufacture, but they were otherwise in sad shape, knocked down and pushed to the edge of the stream where they were exposed along the bank. In the 1960s a miner working in the area had bulldozed many of the old buildings and pushed them into the creek for no good reason. On that earlier visit I took photographs of what was left and then, startled by an ominous rustling in the brush beside the salmon-rich stream, I sprinted back to the safety of my truck in Olympic-record time and left, saddened by what I had seen. Nearby, I found that Dalton House exhibited even more clearly the results of the bulldozer blade: several buildings had been knocked down, the logs pushed up into piles of rubble. Again I took photos. This attempt to record the remains of the early days at Neskatahéen and Dalton House was one of my first efforts at historic preservation.

My consolation upon returning to the site in 2006 was that the group of young people were being taught the traditional practices of the Southern Tutchone people, and while the physical remains of olden days were slowly being swallowed up by the riverbank brush, the traditional practices themselves were being renewed, passed along by the Native elders.

Three decades before I had continued my journey, driving south along the Haines road to the Customs station at Pleasant Camp, looking for other remains of the past. On the Canadian side of the border, across the highway from the customs building, I had followed an overgrown path into the forest. The customs officers had warned me to watch out for bears, but I saw none that day. There, hidden away in dense overgrowth, I found the decaying and neglected remains of the abandoned Mounted Police post that once guarded entry to Canada. With the exception of one sod-roofed shed, the others had collapsed, leaving five or six courses of logs standing above ground. The logs were rotting away where the notched ends interlocked at the corners. The neat quadrangle of buildings and the open grassy field that once overlooked the Klehini River had given way to dense coastal rainforest.

A stone's throw away, on the opposite side of the boundary line that bisected the site, was the dilapidated Dalton Cache, once used by the famous American pathfinder. Then, it stood empty, with rusting sheet metal in patches on the roof. The breeze blew through the empty windows, rustling the waist-high brush that shielded it from the river. Today, however, Dalton Cache has been restored carefully by the United States government and interested travellers get the benefit of its interpretive presentation.

The modern Haines Highway hasn't erased all the history of the old road. It's still there if you look for it.

By the 1970s the old buildings from the Mounted Police post at Pleasant Camp had collapsed from decay and age. MICHAEL GATES COLLECTION

CHAPTER 10

The Decline and Fall of the Dalton Trail

As the frenzy of the Klondike gold rush abated, the usefulness of the Dalton Trail began to diminish. It had been and would remain a good route for bringing livestock into the Yukon interior by land, but the completion in 1900 of a rail and river network from Skagway to Whitehorse and Dawson eliminated the Dalton Trail as an economically viable option for hauling freight to the Yukon River. The Dalton Trail had never been the favourite choice of travellers going to Dawson by horse or by foot, and by the turn of the century there were few who followed its full length to the Yukon River. Most of the traffic on the trail became localized to the first fifty miles.

For Jack Dalton, there was little incentive to keep investing in the trail. By 1902 the improvements he and others had made a few years earlier were in disrepair, and the trail was in a terrible state. A final blow fell when many of the customers who had patronized his trading post at Dalton House in the interior migrated north to Champlain's Landing (by then its name had been altered to the more colourful name of Champagne), where Shorty Chambers had opened a trading post.[397] Dalton closed down his trade at Dalton House. Soon the toll traffic at the coast disappeared as well. By 1903 the Dalton Trail was virtually deserted from Pyramid Harbor to Porcupine, as travellers and freight haulers chose to avoid Dalton's charges and use a new trail on the opposite side of Chilkat Inlet.

The Klondike rush had been huge, and it had taught everybody in the north to dream of being a part of the next big one. Each new gold strike in the Yukon brought fresh hope, and as one prospect faded, another came along that promised to be better. So it was that new finds eclipsed the Porcupine. In 1901 when gold was discovered on Bear Creek, the *Douglas Island News* proclaimed that it would be bigger than the Porcupine.[398] The Mounted Police were getting reports of gold being discovered on Frasers Creek near Dalton House where some miners were said to be taking out fifteen dollars a day. "There seems no doubt," said Superintendent Snyder, "but that there will be a rush in there commencing in February next."[399] In early 1902 the Skagway *Daily Alaskan* described Mush Creek as the "New Eldorado" and an ideal poor man's district.[400] Rumours of big names associated with new prospects always heightened the speculative interest. News that The London Exploration Company had bonded Jack Dalton's Rainy Hollow copper property from Jack Dalton for $125,000 was appetizing to prospectors.[401] Soon it was reported that a railroad would be built to the site to transport the copper ore.

Each new mineral discovery attracted a crowd, and the expanding and contracting of the population in any given northern area in response to these finds was like the beating of a heart. When Felix Pedro discovered gold in the hills north of E.T. Barnette's trading post (soon to be named Fairbanks) on the Tanana River on July 22, 1902, word spread quickly. By April of 1903 a thousand miners had left Dawson City headed for the new find. Dawson merchants made a fortune selling supplies to the departing stampeders.[402] Even Jack Dalton and Henry Bratnober, who had gone off to the White River looking for copper again, got wind of the discovery on the Tanana. Their partnership dissolved when Dalton headed to the new bonanza at Fairbanks, while Bratnober didn't.[403]

A big event in the early summer of 1903 was a gold discovery in the southwest Yukon. In late June rumours started circulating that a rich strike had been made at or near Hutchi by Dawson (Tagish) Charley and Skookum Jim. Because of their involvement in the discovery of the Klondike, the names of Charley and Jim immediately gave credibility to the new find. The rumour mill in Whitehorse said Jim, Charley and Jim Boss from the Lake Laberge area were seen heading out of town, allegedly on a hunting trip, though it was noted that they carried only one rifle among them. They returned to the busy little transportation town of Whitehorse ten days later with a sample of nuggets and dust that went twenty-five cents to the pan. They filed a discovery claim and several other claims on Ruby Creek; in short order, every horse in Whitehorse was bought up and a stampede of five hundred prospectors headed to the southwest Yukon. A staking frenzy followed on Ruby, Fourth of July, Twelfth of July, Allie, Dixie, McMillan, Lamoureaux, McKinley Marshall and Granite creeks. Later in the summer a party of four miners from Porcupine (Altamose, Ater, Bones and Smith) staked Bullion Creek in the Kluane region and registered the claims on September 28. Soon, Sheep Creek, Burwash and Gladstone were the subject of interest. The four stakers on Bullion managed to recover forty-three ounces of gold in nine days before cold weather set in.

"Every day a few people can be met going to and coming from the creeks for the purpose of staking," wrote Superintendent Snyder, who was stationed in Whitehorse. "In my opinion there will be quite an influx of people into this region next spring and there will likely be quite a movement of supplies over the trail in the latter part of the winter preparatory to opening up of spring operation."[404]

The trail referred to by Superintendent Snyder was not the Dalton Trail, but a new trail from Whitehorse that led northwest to the Kluane district. Already, the Dalton Trail was almost an irrelevance. In the years since the Klondike rush the transportation dynamic in the southern Yukon had altered. First, the completion of the White Pass and Yukon Route railroad from Skagway to the new town of Whitehorse, just below the rapids of the same name, secured the Yukon corridor from its origin at Skagway to Dawson City as the main route of transport through the territory. In 1902 Whitehorse, though small in comparison to Dawson City, was emerging as the central community in the southern Yukon. In the summer, riverboats could leave Whitehorse with passengers and freight and make quick, relatively inexpensive delivery to Dawson City. During the summer of 1902 the White Pass Company, under contract to the territorial government, constructed a new winter trail with a twelve-foot clearance from Whitehorse to Dawson City, shortening the total distance by seventy miles.[405] From Braeburn to a point somewhere below Five Fingers, the new road followed the old Dalton Trail. A ferry was constructed to cross the

Takhini River and the new trail became a boon to passenger transporters and the freight haulers.[406]

"It has clearly been demonstrated," wrote Inspector McDonell, in charge of the Dalton trail detachment, "that this route [Dalton Trail] is not at all a practicable one to reach any diggings ... and also that the route via Whitehorse is the only feasible one."[407] Even Dalton, returning from his 1903 trip to Fairbanks, came up the Yukon River and out over the White Pass and Yukon Route railroad, rather than use his own trail. And while the number of miners working in the Kluane area would decline rapidly from between twelve hundred and fourteen hundred men in 1903 to fewer than one hundred in 1905 and only forty in 1906, the Kluane route had become firmly established as the alternative to the Dalton Trail. By 1903 there was also an alternate route running up the eastern side of Chilkat Inlet from Haines to Klukwan, built by the miners who refused to pay Dalton for the privilege of using his trail.[408] Even the Mounted Police had sent out patrols the previous summer to establish a more convenient route than Dalton's to get from Dalton House to the new trail from Whitehorse, and this would be the pattern henceforth. At the same time, the

The miners at Porcupine resented Dalton's monopoly of transportation and an alternative road was eventually built to the creek. ALASKA STATE LIBRARY, SHELDON MUSEUM, HAINES PHOTOGRAPH COLLECTION, P93-60

condition of the Dalton Trail was declining from lack of maintenance. The stretch from Dalton House to the Yukon River was in bad shape because of several bad bogs and fallen timber.[409]

In the summer of 1903 the Mounties in the Dalton Trail detachments had a new role: monitoring the expanding mining activity in the Kluane region. While fulfilling this task, the officers patrolling the area had a tragic experience. Inspector McDonell, accompanied by Constable Povoas and Special Constable Stick Sam, was returning from Ruby Creek and had camped the night of July 28 in the Kaskawulsh Pass, not too far from the place where Glave and Dalton had crossed the Dezadeash River twelve years before. The police officers rose early in the morning and proceeded to a point on the river where they could ford safely to the far side. McDonell went ahead, and thinking he had crossed the worst of the water, he signalled the other men to proceed. Special Constable Sam immediately found himself in deep water. According to McDonell:

> As soon as he struck swimming water he commenced tugging at the reins, until he pulled the horse over backwards, sinking him. The horse however came up again, struggled a little and turning on his side floated to shore about a mile down the river on the same side we had started in from.
>
> Sam took only a few strokes and then disappeared, not coming up again. By this time Constable Povoas had mounted again and had started to cross. This time his saddle cinch broke and the saddle floated away. He quit his horse and grabbed hold of the mule which was packed but which however swam quite high out of the water and got to shore that way. We then followed the stream down but see [sic] nothing of Sam, excepting his hat which landed a little above where the horse hung up.[410]

They dragged the river with grappling hooks and McDonell was confident of finding the body, but the grim outcome was that Special Constable Stick Sam left a wife and children practically destitute. Until further instructions were received, the saddened inspector continued to provide rations to the family.[411]

The mining bubble at Porcupine burst in the summer of 1902. While the newspapers still offered optimistic reports about the mineral potential of the region, the facts revealed a darker truth.[412] The Porcupine placers were not easy to work: the gold was buried deep beneath the surface and required costly equipment to extract it. As the previous mining season had demonstrated, the creeks of the Porcupine district were under an ever-present threat of flash flooding that could destroy the summer's work in a few hours. Dalton removed his sawmill from Porcupine at the end of 1902. By 1903 Porcupine was filled with abandoned cabins and only a few miners were left hand-working their claims. Dalton's store and the Lindsay Hotel remained open for business, but the other entrepreneurs had disappeared. In July, 1903, the Porcupine mining district was abolished and the records were transferred to Skagway; the US Commissioner's office also closed.[413]

Despite this shrinkage of population, the remaining miners put on a patriotic show for the Fourth of July. There were decorations, firecrackers, foot races, pie-eating competitions, greased pig wrestling, hurdles, horse pulling and a Mounted Police ride. It was the show by the Mounties that led to the most noteworthy incident of the day:

Jack Dalton (seated foreground) and other residents of Porcupine, c. 1900.
COURTESY OF M.J. KIRCHHOFF

Below discovery claim Number 1; the workings of the Porcupine Mining Company. ALASKA STATE LIBRARY, SHELDON MUSEUM, HAINES PHOTOGRAPH COLLECTION, P93-52

As the Mounties were finishing their performance, one of the horsemen detached himself from the group, rode furiously down the street, spurred his horse up the steps of the Lindsay Hotel, and right through a big window into the bar of the hotel. He then demanded a drink for himself and his horse. The stunned crowd ran over to the scene and rescued the trembling and bleeding horse. John Lindsay jerked the drunken rider from the saddle, cursing him profusely before having him escorted to the commanding officer. Just as all this was happening, the largest dog fight ever to break out in Porcupine got underway. Every dog owner rushed in to rescue his dog or dogs but the fury was too much—the pack would not respond to either the yelling or kicking. Only by throwing firecrackers into the melee was the fight broken up.[414]

A few miners "holed up" in Porcupine in the winter of 1903–04, and John Lindsay kept his hotel open until it was destroyed by fire in the spring.[415] There were hardly any people in the district in 1904. Only three prospectors were mining at Rainy Hollow. Forty-two men in the American and Canadian survey crews were busily demarcating the newly established boundary between the two nations. There was the detachment of Mounties at Pleasant Camp and one provincial constable manning the station at Wells. Jack Dalton had a crew of ten men working on the discovery claim on Porcupine Creek until the end of summer when they all departed, leaving one man to look after the store.[416] In 1904 and 1905 the gold production out of Porcupine was down to one-third of what it had been in the early years.

The Line is Drawn, and the Mounties Withdraw

After the *modus vivendi* had established a temporary international boundary in the Alaska Panhandle in 1899, the three nations involved—Canada, Britain and the United States—continued the laborious political process of negotiating the final line, with Canada in the role of intransigent junior partner. The real negotiations were between Britain, whose empire was waning, and the United States, the rising power. Britain always had interests to consider beyond the Canadian boundary, and President Theodore Roosevelt, in a blunt and direct fashion, threatened to take the decision into his own hands if the outcome of the negotiations did not favour the American position.

In eleventh-hour haggling, the British delegate to the Alaska Boundary Tribunal conceded that Canada would have no claim to the heads of the inlets, but would receive the Portland Canal and a "good mountain line." In the agreement, signed October 20, 1903, Canada got only two of the four islands at the mouth of the Portland Canal; the others went to the United States. The British delegate voted with the three American members of the tribunal, thus conceding a perceived strategic advantage to the States. In the end, with "Canadians sullenly refusing to discuss anything & announcing that they would not sign any part of the award," the United States won a symbolic victory, conveying to its citizens the appearance of a significant American triumph.[417] On the Dalton Trail, the boundary was withdrawn from the line established at Wells by the *modus vivendi* to one running delicately between the Mounted Police post at Pleasant Camp and Dalton's Cache, a stone's throw away.

The subsequent demise of the Mounted Police presence on the trail was plainly predictable. With Whitehorse becoming the patrol departure point to Pleasant Camp and steamer transportation displacing the hundreds of rafts and scows that went down the Yukon River during the gold rush, there was no longer any need to maintain the detachment at Five Fingers and it was shut down by 1903. On August 12, 1903, the detachment at Yukon Crossing, now an important stopping point on the newly constructed Whitehorse–Dawson wagon road, dismantled the buildings at Five Finger Rapid and salvaged what they could.

The Mounties continued to maintain detachments at Pleasant Camp and Dalton House, sixty miles to the interior, with the latter being operated by two constables under the command of Constable Stewart from the beginning of April to the beginning of October. The police kept all their Dalton Trail dogs there after the dogs finished hauling six months' worth of supplies up from Pleasant Camp in March, and the two Mounties were busy catching and curing 3,000 pounds of fish for dog feed.[418]

Again in 1903, there was very little traffic going in over the trail, with only $341.23 in duty being collected, while the government spent $31,000 to operate the detachment. When the boundary agreement was signed, Superintendent Snyder in Whitehorse was quick to seek instructions regarding the detachment at Wells, which was now clearly inside American territory, eighteen miles past the boundary on the way to the coast. The detachment vacated the site at the end of November, and the men spent the month of December making patrols from Pleasant Camp to Wells to relocate all the stores and "moveables" from the abandoned post.[419]

The inefficiency of maintaining the detachment of Mounties at Pleasant Camp was pointed out again in 1904. Clearly, the task of collecting customs duty could be better handled at Dalton House.[420] Dalton House opened again for the summer, with Constable Clayton in charge of the two-man detachment. Only eight prospectors went in over the Dalton Trail that summer, and again Inspector McDonell observed that the only practical route to the interior now was from Whitehorse. Until the boundary line was firmly established by survey, however, the post at Pleasant Camp was not to be shut down, but Superintendent Wood, with permission, was planning to reduce the number of men stationed on the trail. Only Sergeant Todd and two constables were to be left there for the winter. A further reduction in the men posted at Pleasant Camp was planned for 1905, and all stores were to be moved to Dalton House, which could be more easily supplied from Whitehorse than by the Dalton Trail.[421]

The governments were quick to respond to the boundary agreement. An American party under Major Richardson arrived from Haines on February 6, 1904, to find the exact location of Pleasant Camp. In June both Canadian and American survey parties arrived in the area to mark the precise line of the boundary, confirming that Pleasant Camp was in Canada—but just barely. When the parties left the region in the fall there were no miners left in the vicinity, and only a caretaker left at Porcupine to take care of the empty buildings.[422]

Once the line had been drawn, there wasn't much to do for the Mounted Police at Pleasant Camp. The detachment remained in place through the summer of 1905 under the command of Sergeant Todd, and the men made several patrols between there and Whitehorse, but in October the men withdrew to Dalton House, and the abandoned buildings were offered to the province of British Columbia. The attention of the NWMP was being redirected to the new road to the Kluane goldfields, and new detachments were established at "Champagne's Landing" and Kluane.[423]

The closure of Wells and Pleasant Camp brought to an end Jack Dalton's lucrative business of providing supplies to the Mounted Police. His business interests in Haines were profitable, but Dalton's trail was now history and the bustling business in Porcupine had dried up. Dalton and partners continued to operate the small launch *Chilkat* to transport supplies up Chilkat Inlet, but the focus of Dalton's business became the mine at the property on Porcupine Creek.

Dalton and company were optimistic about the gold mining potential for 1905 and they got off to an early start. By early June their bedrock flume was diverting water around the claim, allowing them to use hydraulics to wash away the overburden and reach bedrock. This was the richest ground they had ever worked on Porcupine Creek, and the sluice boxes were brimming with gold. Then an ice dam holding back a lake of water farther up the valley gave way in the summer warmth, unleashing a destructive wall of water. A flash flood surged down the valley and washed away their gold. All the spring's work was destroyed in minutes. [424]

Despite optimistic newspaper reports that he would make a good recovery after this flood, Jack Dalton had had enough. The search was on for a buyer and two years later, in 1907, Dalton and partners sold their interests in the Porcupine claims to a company headed by E.E. Harvey and J.H. Conrad for roughly forty thousand dollars each.[425] Dalton also sold Conrad his copper claims in the White River region.

The Last Cattle Drive

With so many of his businesses in decline on the Dalton Trail, Dalton went looking around for other opportunities, a search that took him to Cordova, Alaska. He was back in Haines in the spring of 1906, not to mine for gold on Porcupine Creek, but to take one final cattle drive over his trail. The plan was to supply meat to the burgeoning market at Fairbanks. Dalton planned this trip like a military manoeuvre: Ed Hanley, who was Dalton's partner in this venture, would handle two hundred cattle with help from seven cowpunchers hired outside. The cattle landed at Pyramid Harbor from the Steamers *The City of Seattle* and the *Humboldt* in mid-June, and the trail crew moved them successfully over the Chilkat Pass and on to Yukon Crossing. Meanwhile, Dalton shipped to Whitehorse some lumber and construction materials he had purchased in Seattle. Accompanied by one of his sisters, he took the train to Whitehorse, where he hired A.E. Henderson to construct three large scows, and then engaged SS *Dick* to tow the scows across Lake Laberge and down the river to Yukon Crossing. He got through Five Finger Rapid safely, although two other scows, loaded with cattle, sheep and horses belonging to S. Hielscher, were wrecked in the turbulent riffles.[426]

Dalton met Hanley and the cattle in mid-July at Yukon Crossing, where the crew loaded the beasts onto the scows and hauled them down the Yukon River to Dawson, towed by the steamer *Prospector*. The herd scows crossed into Alaska on August 4 and passed Rampart around the middle of the month.[427] The herders stopped each night so that the cattle could be taken ashore to feed. Arriving at Circle, they unloaded the cattle and herded them over the hills toward Fairbanks where they arrived on August 26. If they could find a buyer for the meat, Dalton and Hanley would leave as quickly as possible; otherwise, they would open a retail market in Fairbanks and another on the creeks. Fortune was on their side. A buyer by the name of Gardner took the entire herd off their hands.[428]

During the height of the Klondike gold rush thousands of cattle and sheep moved to market in Dawson over the Dalton Trail. With the completion of the White Pass and Yukon Route, livestock traffic for the Yukon interior shifted to the railroad, and while many of the animals were still off-loaded at Whitehorse and herded overland to avoid the lakes and rapids, the heyday of the Dalton Trail was past. In 1905, the year before Dalton took his last herd of two hundred steers over the trail, the White Pass and Yukon Route railway had shipped 1,488 cattle, 2,916 sheep and 223 hogs into the Yukon.[429] As fortunes changed, the Dalton Trail became a ghostly name for an empty trail, a pathway obscured by overgrowth and time.

INTERLUDE

Wings Over the Dalton Trail

The little Cessna taxied out onto the asphalt strip and Alkan Air pilot Ray Wilch requested the go-ahead for takeoff. He revved the engine and we sped down the runway, defying gravity and taking wing. It was the summer of 2008, and our aim was to follow the Dalton Trail from the air and determine its course. Earlier in the season, my foray with Ron Chambers into the country along the Dezadeash River had failed to produce the information I needed about the imprint of the ancient trail. We did not find evidence of the trail on the ground, so our hunting was inconclusive. What if we hadn't walked far enough away from the river? What if the signs of the trail were faint where we had put ashore?

After coming home I had consulted aerial photographs and I thought I detected in one the telltale line of a path snaking along the Dezadeash Valley south of Champagne. Was this the trail? Again, an answer was elusive; the line disappeared into the marshy land beside the river, and I couldn't find it in any other photos.

Fortunately, thanks to generous support from the Yukon Foundation and Alkan Air, I had enough money to charter a small airplane for a couple of hours to make another sortie—this time, from the air.

The plane banked to the southwest as it climbed and soon we had left behind the signs of civilization. With map in hand, we soared over the

"We soared over the rust-coloured rocky pinnacles to the west of Whitehorse. On one barren peak we saw three mountain sheep. Nowhere was there a sign of a human presence." MICHAEL GATES COLLECTION

rust-coloured rocky pinnacles to the west of Whitehorse. On one barren peak we saw three mountain sheep. Nowhere was there a sign of a human presence.

We descended when Kusawa Lake came into view. Through the haze and dull overcast, we could see Frederick Lake nestled in a valley between Kusawa and Dezadeash lakes. Here, in 1890, Jack Dalton and E.J. Glave, the first Europeans to visit this region, encountered a Native encampment.

Beyond Frederick Lake we banked to the left and with Dezadeash Lake to our right we winged south toward the Chilkat Pass summit into light rain. With darkening skies before us we turned north, came in low over Klukshu village and combed the right side of the shoreline along Klukshu Lake. The terrain beyond was irregular in character, with a number of small lakes and large tracts of beetle-killed spruce spreading out across our vista. At first we saw no signs of the trail.

We caught a glimpse of a road below us and circled. It was a tote road leading to someone's cabin. A couple of times we saw paths, but nothing that we could follow for any distance. Over the Dezadeash valley we were tantalized as tracks came into view on exposed treeless hillsides, but we would lose them again when the path entered grassland or forest. Circling over the area we could find no extension of these fragments of trail.

We soared over the site of Pennock's Post, the gold rush cabin that Ron

Chambers and I had located back in May. We could not see the decaying remains of the cabin from the air, but other details, which had been obstructed by brush when I was at ground level, stood out clearly from our eagle's perspective. On a good trail it would take two or three days to walk to this point from Klukshu. By air we covered the same ground in twenty minutes.

We continued our flight path down the Dezadeash River, criss-crossing the valley in search of the elusive trail, and emerged from between two mountains to fly over Champagne. North of the Alaska Highway we caught frequent glimpses of the trail. I could see the coarse irregularities of terraces, knobs and depressions in the valley which, without the guidance of a trail, would have been confusing and difficult to navigate.

Next we crossed over the site of Hutchi, the derelict Southern Tutchone village that was once home to two hundred people. Beyond Hutchi the Nordenskjold River meandered through a narrow valley. Again we picked up the trail. It seemed clear here and, in some places, it showed all-terrain vehicle tracks.

We flew over a plot of land that had been cleared recently, presumably for a homestead. A truck road leading from it disappeared into the hills to the east. Beyond Braeburn we banked sharply toward the south and made our return to Whitehorse.

The flight had been informative but, again, my hopes of locating a trail along this historic route were unfulfilled. I realized that a ground attack would be the only way to find segments of the trail. But the flight was not a wasted effort. Like switching lenses on a camera, flying over the terrain made it possible to view landscape as if with a wide-angle lens. Relationships between features of the land became more apparent and the bumps and irregularities of the trail, so obvious to me when hiking it, were softened and diminished.

If the view from a plane changed my visualization of the landscape, the same could be said for its impact on my sense of time. In ninety minutes we covered a linear route that would have taken ten days on foot, and we criss-crossed an area that could well have taken years to transect on the ground. From the air distances seem insignificant, compared with the way they feel during the plodding passage by foot. While the aerial view would give me a broad picture of the land, only the hard, grinding hike could provide the perspective experienced by travellers in the early days.

The flight certainly provided insights I could not have gained from the ground. But it didn't answer the questions I still was asking myself about the Dalton Trail.

From the air, looking north toward Hutchi. The trail is visible running across the lower half of the photograph. MICHAEL GATES COLLECTION

CHAPTER 11

Epilogue

With each passage of the land from summer into winter, more of the Dalton Trail disappears into the forests and mists of the north. Pyramid Harbor, once the trail's busy starting point, has been abandoned for years and only a few relics remain today, decaying on the shore of the Lynn Canal. The dense coastal rainforest has absorbed the remnants of the trail along the Chilkat Inlet. Many locations along the trail where buildings were captured in early photographs are recognizable today only by the contours of the mountains in the background. The Mounted Police post at Pleasant Camp is decomposing in the lush vegetation, although Dalton Cache, located behind the US Customs station nearby, has been restored and sits in a lovely park surrounded by a neatly kept lawn. It is the best-maintained vestige of the Dalton Trail.

Over the Chilkat Pass in the Yukon interior, some parts of the old trail survive as well-worn grooves in the forest, but most of the way stations have disappeared. Dalton Post is slowly crumbling and the remnants of the old longhouses at Neskatahéen are long gone. The frame buildings that survive there look more forlorn and sway-backed each year as the bush slowly encroaches on them. Pennock's Post, the cache at Champlain's Landing and Camp Storey are vanishing or already gone. Some relics of the past still mark the trail. Bones from the animals that perished on it during the gold rush still can be found, and the remains of butchered cattle herds still litter the banks of the Yukon River where cattlemen slaughtered them for the final voyage to market in Dawson.

The trail that was once so important to Native commerce and then to Jack Dalton's business ventures, has been superseded by more important roads, although the current highway from Haines on the Alaskan coast to Haines Junction in the Yukon follows the historical trail from the coast as far inland as Klukshu. Farther north at Champagne, the old trail intersects the Alaska Highway. On the Klondike Highway north of Whitehorse, somewhere between Braeburn and Montagu, the modern road takes up the same route followed by the trail to Carmack's old trading post on the banks of the mighty Yukon River. A grassy field where a photographer once captured one of Dalton's herds camped near the Montagu Roadhouse is now overgrown by willow and spruce. The last time I looked, the heavy rains of late summer had turned it into a marsh.

A few roadside signs remind visitors of where the trail passed by, but its stories are almost forgotten by those who narrate other old tales of the north. Unlike the Chilkoot Trail and the White Pass Trail, it has had no vocal champions to remind us of it. It has been overlooked in literature. It features in a couple of historical novels and is referred to briefly in passing by such chroniclers of the gold rush as Pierre Berton. Modern map makers, perhaps out of ignorance, omit this route from their depictions of historical trails to the Klondike. The Dalton Trail, and those who walked and rode upon it, deserve better remembrance.

Many of the people who feature in my account of the Dalton Trail went on to do other interesting things. Jack Dalton left the Haines area after he sold his mining interests there, but he continued to seek his fortune throughout southeast Alaska. In 1906 he led a survey party up the Copper River and confirmed that a railroad could be built from Cordova to the copper mine at Kennicott. He built a home in Cordova, developed his mining property and built a sawmill. It seems that prosperity did not make him a less pugnacious individual. He engaged frequently in litigation. In one famous case, he took on the Morgan–Guggenheim syndicate and emerged the victor.

During all his years in Alaska and the Yukon, Jack Dalton had an eye for the next good thing—not only in business, but also in love. In 1886 he had come back from a visit to Oregon with a wife, May Click. They worked together in Sitka on Dalton's scheme for a hot spring resort, but May died in 1888 while her husband was off at Yakutat prospecting for coal. The cause of her death was reported to be "excessive use of narcotics." A year later, back in Sitka, Dalton started a liaison with a Tlingit girl named Lizzie. Lizzie became pregnant, and descendants of her child still live today in coastal Alaska. Meanwhile, Dalton moved on, earning a reputation as a lady's man. His friends used to say, "Jack has a way with women and horses; he is always gentle on the bridle."[430] On May 10, 1892, Dalton married his second wife, Estella Richey, at Haines Mission. A year later in Juneau, Estella gave birth to a son, Jack Jr. Dalton also had a daughter, Margaret, with Estella. He was not a faithful husband. During his time in the Yukon interior, he formed a liaison with a Southern Tutchone woman. She bore him a daughter, but she and her child both died. Eventually Dalton's marriage to Estella failed, and they divorced in 1902.[431] He returned to Cordova, Alaska, from Outside in June of 1911 accompanied by Anna Krippaehne, whom he married on June 17. The marriage produced two offspring: a son, James, born in 1913, and a daughter, Josephine, born in 1916.

Dalton had become involved in political affairs. In 1910 he accompanied American conservationist Gifford Pinchot on his Alaska visit, acting as Pinchot's bodyguard. He attended the Republican Party national convention at Chicago in 1912 and in Alaska he supported the Republican candidate, James Wickersham, during his successful campaigns for a seat in Congress. Dalton continued to undertake major business ventures. In 1913 he was engaged by the US government to transport eight hundred tons of Alaska coal sixty-five miles from Chickaloon to Cook Inlet in the dead of winter for the US Navy.

Dalton left Alaska for good in 1916, and spent the next twenty-eight years living in the Pacific Northwest. In 1923, nearly seventy year old, he set off on one last adventure. On behalf of a group of Yakima investors, he travelled to the jungles of British Guiana to inspect a mining property. "The trip was a wonderful one," he reported upon his return to the United States, "but one that was about the hardest I ever took. Traveling in Alaska is a snap—compared to a trip through the bush in South America."[432]

Of all Dalton's marriages and romantic liaisons, the union with Anna endured the longest. It ended with Anna's suicide in 1929. Broken-hearted at the death of her mother and in ill-health herself, she tried to kill herself by drinking a flask of carbolic acid. In great agony, she finished the job with a bullet from Jack's gun. Dalton died in San Francisco on December 16, 1944. He was eighty-nine years old. He is buried beside Anna in Seaside Cemetery in Seattle.

Jack Dalton was a symbol of rugged individualism who came out of the Wild West in its last days and brought his skills as a great outdoorsman to the birth of a new American frontier in the north. He opened up many trails, including the trail over the Chilkat Pass, that were essential to the development of the Yukon and Alaska. Because he never engaged in the sensationalism and self-promotion typical of other iconic pioneers of the west, his story has not been popularized and distorted as have those of Billy the Kid, Kit Carson, Wild Bill Hickcock or Colonel George Custer. Dalton was simply the genuine article, a tough, able outdoorsman and pathfinder. He was violent, even murderous. He was loyal to his friends and business partners. He was inventive and resilient in a tight spot. He survived.

Although Jack Dalton's trail soon fell into relative obscurity, his name is remembered in the north on both sides of the international boundary. In Canada, a range of mountains in the Kluane region bears his name. The municipalities of Whitehorse, Yukon, and Haines, Alaska, have named streets after him.

Edward Glave returned to Africa where, between 1893 and 1895, he crossed the equatorial belt of the continent from east to west, documenting his travels. His writing exposed the brutality of colonial occupation of Africa. One of his accounts described a Captain Rom who was the Belgian commanding officer at Stanley Falls, deep in the Congo. After ordering the destruction of a village, Rom brought back twenty-one heads from those slaughtered at the village, and used them to line a flower bed in front of his house. This image electrified Glave's readers and ignited outrage at Belgian practices in the Congo. It is said that Captain Rom was the model for Kurtz, the ivory trader in Joseph Conrad's epic novel, *Heart of Darkness*. Glave never achieved the fame he sought. Sickened by fever he contracted during his demanding bisection of the continent, he died in Matadi, near the mouth of the Congo River, May 12, 1895. Glave was only thirty-two years old.

Like Dalton, some of the other travellers over the Dalton Trail went on to interesting exploits elsewhere. Joe Boyle, who led a party over the Dalton Trail in the fall of 1897, enjoyed a successful and colourful subsequent career as a mining entrepreneur. He helped organize the Canadian Klondyke Mining Company, which operated four gigantic gold dredges in the Klondike River valley. He is remembered in Dawson for his devotion to ice hockey. Trying to promote the sport in northern Canada, he took the Dawson City Nuggets hockey team on an epic journey to challenge the Ottawa Silver Seven for the Stanley Cup. Although the Stanley Cup is hockey's premier prize now, then it was a club challenge cup. Had the Dawson City Nuggets won their game, the cup might have languished on a shelf in the Dawson Amateur Athletic Association building, waiting for some team from the distant south to visit and try to win it back.

Boyle went on to distinguish himself during World War I. Several European nations honoured him with medals, and he became famous for saving the crown jewels of Romania. Boyle had an affair with the queen of Romania before returning to England, where he died in 1923 at the young age of fifty-six years. His remains were finally returned to his native Woodstock, Ontario, in 1983. The government of Canada has mounted a plaque in his honour on an enormous dredge bucket on Bonanza Creek, beside the largest dredge that ever worked in the Yukon.

"Swiftwater" Bill Gates, who travelled with Boyle that snowy October in 1897, had staked one of the richest claims on Eldorado Creek. From anonymity, he was thrust into fanciful notoriety, a position he seemed to relish. He became famous for his conspicuous displays of excess. He indulged his passion for gambling and he loved the ladies—many of them—with devotion. His pursuit of three of the Lamore sisters became the stuff of legend. He married at least five times. Wherever he went, Swiftwater seemed to find—and lose—one fortune after another until he moved to Peru around 1915, where he remained for the rest of his life. He died, a murder victim, in 1937.

Dalton's old partner, Henry Bratnober, became one of America's leading mining promoters and developers. After the Klondike he continued searching for copper until he developed the fabulous deposits of the Kennicott mine after Dalton had played a part in making them accessible. Bratnober made and lost a fortune and died in 1914. There is a mountain named after him along the Dalton Trail, not far from Champagne.

Arthur Newton Christian Treadgold, the British journalist who travelled over the trail in 1898, was instrumental in developing several mining ventures in the Klondike. He had consolidated all of the concerns in the Klondike into one big company by the mid-1920s; then, because of mismanagement, he lost control of the business and spent the remainder of his years in litigation.

J. B Tyrrell, the government geologist who examined the mining potential of the Yukon area in 1898, left the civil service after his northern explorations and in later years made a substantial fortune in mining ventures on the Canadian Shield in Ontario. He was honoured by the government of Canada for his accomplishments, and a plaque describing his distinguished career is mounted on a massive boulder beside the Commissioner's residence in Dawson City.

The Mysterious Thirty-Six might have been forgotten entirely had it not been for Arthur Thompson, who was a member of the party. Thompson took photographs of their journey and when he returned to Hartford, Connecticut, he gave illustrated lectures of his adventures in the Yukon and Alaska. He wrote a book, *Gold Seeking on the Dalton Trail*, that described in depth the travails of the mysterious prospecting party. A graduate of Yale, he had taken part in an expedition to Greenland before going to the Yukon during the gold rush. He never went north again. He worked in the insurance field until 1914, when he became the collector of taxes in West Hartford, a job he kept until he retired twenty-five years later. After his youthful adventures he settled down and became a leading citizen of West Hartford, being named the "Man of the Year" in 1954. Thompson died in 1960 at the age of eighty-seven.

As for the cattlemen, Charlie Thebo and Pat Burns became involved in the meat business in Dawson City in the years after the gold rush. So did the Waechter brothers. Burns opened stores in Mayo, Whitehorse and Atlin, but these were only a small part of his meat packing empire. He was one of four prominent cattlemen, known as the "Big Four," who sponsored the first Calgary Stampede. Billy Henry, who worked for Burns, headed north again with herds and supplies destined for the new gold fields of Atlin in British Columbia, but he never returned to the Yukon. He lived to the advanced age of 105, remaining alert and reliable as a source of information about the early days. George Tuxford and John Thomson returned to their farms at Moose Jaw, Saskatchewan. Tuxford went overseas during World War I, rising to the rank of brigadier general. The village of Tuxford, near Moose Jaw, bears the family name. It has fewer than one hundred inhabitants today.

Della Murray Banks went back to the United States after crossing the Dalton Trail, but a year later she joined her husband in Dawson City, where they stayed for thirteen months before going south to Los Angeles with a baby son. Her husband returned to the Yukon once more, and in 1901 she joined him in Skagway. Had the winter season not been so advanced, they would have continued to Dawson. That was her sixth and final trip to the north. Twenty years later she fell from a horse and was left paralyzed from the waist down. She was confined to a wheelchair for the remaining thirty years of her life. Her memories of the summer spent on the Dalton Trail were still vivid when she finally committed them to paper forty-five years after her adventure.

What of the Mounted Police? The permanent detachment on the trail was removed after the resolution of the Alaska–Canada boundary dispute, but members of the Dalton Trail detachment, including constables Pringle, Clayton and Hume, remained in the southwest Yukon after leaving the force. Pringle stayed on at Dalton Post, purchased the old Mounted Police buildings in 1912 and was still living there during World War II. His grave is located near the cabin in which he lived for nearly fifty years.

With the end of the gold rush the Dalton Trail was abandoned in favour of other routes between the Yukon and the Lynn Canal. Where once it had been considered the best choice for an overland road or railway to the Yukon River, it lost out to the White Pass, over which the White Pass and Yukon Route railway was constructed. (A highway over the White Pass did not open until the late 1970s). There were several reasons the Dalton Trail failed to become the major artery through the Yukon; these included Dalton's monopoly over the route, its entanglement in the boundary disputes and the Canadian government's preference for an all-Canadian route that avoided American territory. But in the end, the biggest reason the Dalton Trail lost out to the White Pass was because another venture was faster out of the starting gate, and its backers were more determined to construct a rail link to the Yukon River.

It is entertaining to consider how circumstances might have differed had a railroad been constructed along the Dalton Trail instead. Had there been no White Pass and Yukon Route, there would have been no Whitehorse. The settlement would have been nothing but a footnote in Yukon history. Instead, a community would have grown up on the Dalton Trail route around the rail terminus at Carmacks, Five Finger Rapid or Fort Selkirk. Imagine the community of Carmacks blossoming into the hub of Yukon commerce instead of Whitehorse!

When gold was discovered in the Kluane region, it was from Whitehorse, rather than Haines or Pyramid Harbor, that most of the prospectors stampeded and from which goods were supplied. Eventually the road out of Whitehorse became part of the famed Alaska Highway that was built in a hurry after the Japanese bombed Pearl Harbor in December of 1941. Although other highways run along sections of the trail blazed by Dalton, many travellers on these roads are unaware of their connection to the historic old pathway through the wilderness.

The initial influx of newcomers over the trail during the gold rush had direct and dramatic consequences for the First Nations of the Yukon, although its impact was felt less directly in the southwest portion than along the Yukon River and in the Dawson City area. In the country crossed by the Dalton Trail, waves of stampeders came over the old Native trade route in 1897, 1898 and 1899. Thousands of horses, cattle and sheep passed through the region, to the amazement of local inhabitants, and then disappeared, never to be seen again. During the trail's heyday, the Mounted Police patrolled the trail and applied a new set of rules for the original residents to follow. The police hired the Natives as special constables and, like many other newcomers, also employed them as guides. One young Native man, Jimmy Kane, is shown in an old photograph with a group of stampeders in 1898. In those years he worked for Jack Dalton on the cattle drives. He lived in the same area till his dying day.

As a result of the boundary negotiations conducted in nations far away, the homeland of the indigenous inhabitants of the north was carved up and segmented. Their patterns of relationship changed and their traditional trail from the coast fell into disuse. Hunting regulations varied from one jurisdiction to another. In some cases, local Natives were prohibited from following

First Nation people were employed by the North-West Mounted Police, and hired as guides. The young man in the centre of this group is believed to be Jimmy Kane, a resident of the area who worked for Jack Dalton on his cattle drives. ALASKA STATE LIBRARY, FRED HOVEY PHOTOGRAPH COLLECTION, P352-67

their traditional pursuits. When Jack Dalton sought permission from the United States government to charge a toll for travel on paths that the Native people had used for centuries, no one thought to consult them about it. Adding insult to injury, Dalton had the nerve to charge them a fee to use their own trail.

With the development of new corridors of access through the region, new stopping places were established. A trading post was built at Champlain's Landing (Champagne), while Dalton closed his post near Neskatahéen. The local people gravitated to Champagne from there as well as from Hutchi and Klukshu. Residents from Aishihik moved to Haines Junction and Canyon, which is on the Alaska Highway between the junction and Champagne.

Mining became an important pursuit for inhabitants of the area. Native prospectors started the Kluane gold rush; in the 1920s it was Paddy Duncan, a Southern Tutchone man, who discovered gold on Squaw Creek, south of Dalton House, and Native men mined many of the claims there.

Patterns of Native settlement changed because of new roads, and the entire dynamic of land use changed as well. With the construction of the Alaska Highway during World War II, a major road cut through the region skirting the St. Elias Mountains from southeast to northwest. After the highway was opened, the people living at Canyon and Aishihik became drawn to the new community rising at Haines Junction. At Haines Junction the new road connected with the Haines Highway, a road to the Alaskan coast that sliced through the mountains by following a traditional route and joining the track of the old Dalton Trail. Today the Haines Road is paved. As access to the area became easier, the governments of America and Canada set up adjoining nature preserves in the Kluane region. Eventually national parks were set aside on both sides of the boundary. A portion of that land is now a World Heritage Site.

After the Klondike gold rush, the influx of Europeans into the country of the Dalton Trail slowed to a trickle, but some still ventured into the southwest Yukon and northwest British Columbia: Mounted Police, missionaries, geologists, prospectors and the occasional big game hunter. They brought in alcohol, new diseases and residential schools, all of which took their toll on the resident population.

Land claims settlements have returned a degree of control to the First Nations that occupy the region. For more than thirty years, the First Nations of the Yukon negotiated with the Canadian government for a final settlement to their claims of land and compensation for what was taken away from them without due process. The resulting Final Agreements established traditional land use and other rights. Control over some of their land, known as settlement land, has been returned to the First Nations. During the land claims negotiations, several First Nations identified and mapped the network of trails that crossed their traditional territory. Many of the parcels of settlement land negotiated by the Champagne and Aishihik First Nations cover the route of the Dalton Trail. Thus, the control of the path that cuts through their traditional territory has returned to them. The Champagne and Aishihik First Nations have been active clearing sections of the trail on their settlement land for use as a hiking trail.

What can be said of the Dalton Trail today? Compared with other gold rush trails, almost nothing has been written about it. Pierre Berton, in his masterwork, *Klondike* (*Klondike Fever* in the United States), didn't even include the trail on his maps showing routes to the Klondike.

Other routes, over which relatively few stampeders successfully reached the Klondike, are described in detail, perhaps because of the tragedy and misadventure associated with them. The Chilkoot and White Pass routes facilitated the passage of the majority of gold seekers headed to the Klondike, while the long route up the Yukon River by steamer was also popular. There was the route out of Alberta down the Mackenzie River and over the divide from the present-day Northwest Territories, which extracted a brutal toll from its travellers. The all-Canadian route, over which the Yukon Field Force travelled, followed the vestiges of the old overland telegraph trail. Other travellers chose alternate routes, like Inspector Moodie of the Mounted Police who came overland from Edmonton in a year-long expedition via the Liard River in 1897–98. Some people came in over the massive glaciers of the Alaskan coast with tragic results. Only a handful ever made it to the gold fields this way, and those who did often suffered terribly from the experience. These routes, rich in drama, have all had their historians and bards.

Between 1897 and 1899 approximately fifteen hundred to two thousand travellers used the Dalton Trail. Perhaps ten thousand head of livestock were taken to Dawson City this way. The precise number will never be known. The 350 miles of travel did not permit the easy transport of the requisite ton of supplies mandated by the Mounted Police. Only a small number of men died on the trail; by comparison, the Chilkoot Trail was much more dangerous. The history of the Chilkoot includes tragic events such as the avalanche on April 3, 1898, at Sheep Camp, which took more than sixty lives at once. Today the Chilkoot Trail, on both the American and Canadian sides of the border, is notable for the number of graves that mark the passage of the stampeders.

The Chilkoot Trail had the golden stairs, its iconic image captured for future generations by photographer E.A. Hegg. The pictures of the thousands toiling over the steep slopes with heavy packs on their backs reinforce the memories of the crowd of men and women moving forward to the Klondike, each of whom had to repeat this climb two dozen times or more. The White Pass had the Dead Horse Gulch, into which countless horses fell from exhaustion, or flung themselves in despair. While the Dalton Trail also had a pass to climb and dead horses lay along it, fatalities of man and beast on the Dalton Trail were far fewer than those occurring on the other trails a few miles farther up the Lynn Canal.

If anything, the Dalton Trail was distinctive because there was no extraordinary loss of life, and because it lacked the profound obstacles that made travellers on the other trails seem like heroes. Aside from the heavy physical toll it demanded, the Dalton Trail did not evoke the passions or feed the obsessions of the gold rush as the other trails seemed to do. The most important role of the Dalton Trail during the gold rush was as the main route to bring cattle to the Klondike.

So why did I choose to chronicle this trail less travelled? The story is almost as long as my life. While travelling trails to remote places in the southwest Yukon and working there, I fell in love with the north. I craved the north with such intensity that I found a career as a curator for Parks Canada in Dawson City. I never left the north. I have no regrets.

As an aspiring young archeologist, I was struck by the needless vandalism that had been inflicted upon Dalton House and Neskatahéen and resolved, in my own way, to record the trails, bones, derelict buildings and artifacts that lay scattered thinly over the landscape.[433] More than that, though, the North, with its mountains, rivers, lakes and countless vistas, has a magnetic attraction. No matter where I have travelled, I always compare other places with the Yukon, where there is plenty of air to breathe and an abundance of uninterrupted sky to savour. Unlike Canada's densely populated southern fringe, the Yukon has no crowds. It is a fact that the thin scattering of people over this landscape accentuates the importance of the human presence.

I identified strongly with Edward Glave, the explorer who was a devoted student of local culture. After his first visit to the Yukon, he was determined to return to the region with hopes of finding fame or fortune. Not able to obtain formal support or funding, he forged ahead on his own, travelling "on the cheap," though his investment was not insignificant. The $4,000 he spent would amount to more than $100,000 today. Similarly, after my first trip to the Yukon, I kept returning at my own expense, to nurture my passion for the area. I learned to plan carefully and define my purpose clearly for these trips. Unlike Glave, I found not disappointment, but fulfillment. Each visit to Dalton Trail country strengthened my resolve to return—permanently.

There are some written accounts of Yukon history, both popular and academic, that lack a sense of place. Their authors suffer from an insufficient understanding of the geography. If they haven't been in the Yukon and felt the wind, rain and biting cold, or cursed the mosquitoes as they toiled along an isolated trail with a heavy pack, then their writing lacks authenticity.

When I write of the Dalton Trail, I have been there. I have stood on the shore of Dezadeash Lake and floated its waters. I have felt the rainforests of the coast, been hidden in the fog at the Chilkat summit and endured the dusty heat of the interior. I have carried my pack for days along the forgotten trail and travelled with packhorse over ground that Dalton himself once crossed. Reading the early accounts of the Dalton Trail and hiking it myself, I can visualize the Mysterious Thirty-Six toiling along the trail with their heavy loads; I can hear the hooves of the cattle as they slowly move north toward the Yukon River; I can imagine the faces of the stampeders etched by the weather and creased by determination.

Alone on the trail, I have felt how large the land is and how isolated a person can be in it without reference to GPS and satellite phone. The Dalton Trail has taught me how insulated we have become from our physical environment, and it has given me a different perspective on the world. Never have I felt so satisfied as when I have travelled to remote places as a history hunter. It is a great state of being. Perhaps you would like to experience it for yourself.

Acknowledgements

There are many agencies and people I must thank for making this book possible.

First, the Yukon Foundation and the Government of Yukon, Department of Tourism and Culture, provided financial support that made it possible for me to conduct research across the country and to take the time to write the draft. Equally important, their support also said that this project was worthwhile, something I myself questioned upon occasion.

In addition, there were several benefactors who encouraged me to continue: Steven Robertson and the *Yukon News*, Earl Bennett, Murdoch (Murd) Nicholson, Ron and Catherine Veale, Chris Sorg and Samson Hartland. These individuals share an admiration of the writer's craft and a love of collecting books about Yukon history.

The late Alan Innes Taylor played an important role in shaping my interest in writing about the Dalton Trail. His love of history influenced my career plans; because of him, I decided I wanted to spend my life recording, preserving and protecting the historic treasures scattered all over the territory.

Behind many a successful author is a loving partner. I pestered my wife Kathy constantly about the Dalton Trail for years. Using her excellent research skills, she provided me with a steady supply of references from numerous sources. She also served as a sounding board for my ideas, then as my editor and proofreader, and helped make my original drafts richer. Mark

Kirchhoff of Juneau wrote an excellent biography of Jack Dalton that complements my story of the Trail. If you like my account of the trail, you'll want to read his account of Dalton. Mark generously provided me with a volume of research notes that helped make my account more complete. He kindly reviewed the historical narrative and provided insightful editorial comments. Cynthia "CJ" Jones of Haines, Alaska, provided insight and understanding on the topic of Jack Dalton and the trail. If I sit down with Mark and CJ, we can talk about Dalton history all day. Ask Mark's wife Barb and Kathy if you don't believe me.

Writer and editor Patricia Robertson shared her insights and knowledge with me while I was formulating the manuscript. We discussed various approaches to combine my personal narrative with the history. She reviewed the manuscript at a critical phase in its development and made it a better product.

I owe special thanks to the staff at Harbour Publishing for having faith in this project, especially Anna Comfort O'Keeffe, the managing editor, who was always positive in her support, and to editor Elaine Park, who guided me through the manuscript chapter by chapter, turning the crude text into a smooth narrative. For a while during the editing of my work, the messages were flying back and forth like a tennis match. This was a very stimulating process at an important time in the formation of the story.

Various institutions provided important information, photographs, and sometimes patience for my many requests: Alaska State Historical Library, including Jim Simard, Gayle Goedde, Jacki Swearingen, Sandra Johnston, Anastasia Lynch and Connie Hamann; the Bancroft Library (Berkeley, California), especially Susan Snyder, Head of Public Services; the Alberta Provincial Archives (Edmonton) and the Archives of the Glenbow Museum (Calgary), especially Doug Cass; the BC Archives (Victoria); Bert Sheppard Library and Archives (Cochrane, Alberta), especially Janna Wilson and Val Jobson; EMR Library Government of Yukon, especially Pam Walden and Amy Ellis; Juneau–Douglas City Museum, notably Addison Field; Library and Archives Canada (Ottawa), especially Andrew Rodger; MacBride Museum (Whitehorse), especially Leighann Chalykoff, Don Watt, Tracey Anderson and Alex Hakonson; the National Map Collection (Ottawa), especially Jean Matheson; the Rasmusson Library, University of Alaska

(Fairbanks); the Saskatchewan Archives (Regina); the Sheldon Museum (Haines, Alaska), especially Nancy Nash, Karen Meisner, Jerrie Clarke and Blythe Carter; the Thomas Fisher Rare Book Library (Toronto); US National Archives and Records Administration, especially Bruce Parham; the Washington State Archives, notably Brigid Clift; Yukon Archives, especially Linda Johnson, Diane Chisholm, Ian Burnett, Peggy D'Orsay and Susan Twist, but including all the staff that I have pestered over the years.

There are many individuals I would like to thank for their contributions in so many ways to my efforts: David Ashley, Bruce Barrett, Earl Bennett, Geoff Bleakley, Carol Bookless, Jim Capra, Steve Cassidy, Ron Chambers, Bob Copithorne, Peggy Crook, Millicent Craig, Stuart Daniel, Bill Diment, Jane Gaffin, Karl Gurcke, Keith Halliday, Christine Hedgecock, Dan Henry, Doug Hitch, Loni Hotch, Marsha Hotch, Joe Hotch, Glenn Iceton, Mark Iceton, Linda Johnson, Tonya King, Alice Legat, Murray Lundberg, Gary Meier, David Neufeld, John Ritter, Rene Rivard, Sally Robinson, Steve Smith, Les Stephen, Candy Waugaman, John White, Paul White and Doug Whyte. Each of these people helped me personally in a variety of ways, by providing leads to useful sources of information, hiking the trail with me at one time or another, sharing information or photographs, engaging in lively and often thoughtful discussions and, in some cases, providing inspiration to keep going. If I tried to explain how each of them contributed to the making of this book, it would be twice as long. Over the years there have been others who spurred me on in one way or another. If, for any number of reasons, I forgot to note their help at the time and have thus not included their names, they know who they are, and will probably remind me of my lapses when we next meet. To them I extend my apologies in advance.

Bibliography

Newspapers

Alaska Journal
Alaska Mining Record
Alaska Miner
Alaska News
Alaska Searchlight
Alaska Weekly
Alaskan (Sitka)
Anchorage Daily News
Bessemer Herald, The
Bismarck Daily Tribune
Boston Evening Transcript, The
Brisbane Courier
Calgary Herald
Camden Democrat
Cedar Rapid Evening Gazette, The
Chicago Tribune
Daily Alaska Dispatch
Daily Colonist, The (Victoria)
Daily Gleaner, The (Fredericton)
Daily Herald, The (Delphos, Ohio)
Daily Iowa Capital
Daily Record-Miner (Juneau)
Dawson Daily News
Decatur Daily Review
Deseret News
Douglas Island News
Douglas Miner
Dubuque Daily Herald
Fairbanks Daily Times
Fort Wayne Sentinel, The
Fort Wrangell News
Fresno Weekly Republican
Juneau City Mining Record
Klondike News

Klondike Nugget
Los Angeles Daily Times
Macleod Gazette
Manufacturers and Farmers Journal
    (Providence)
Morning Olympian
Newark Daily Advocate
New York Sun
New York Times
New Zealand Evening Post
New Zealand Tablet
Oakland Tribune
Oregonian
Port Townsend Morning Leader
Reno Evening Gazette
Rio Grande Republican
San Francisco Call
San Francisco Chronicle
San Francisco Examiner
Saturday Budget
Seattle Post-Intelligencer
Skagway Alaskan
Skagway News
Spokane Daily Chronicle
Spokesman-Review, The (Spokane)
St. Louis Republic
St. Paul Globe
Syracuse Herald
Tacoma Daily Ledger
Twice-a-Week Spokesman-Review
    (Spokane)
Whitehorse Weekly Star
Winston Prospector, The
Worcester Daily Spy

Archival Sources
Cahoon, Charles P. n.d. "On the Dalton Trail and Mining in the Porcupine District."
    Unpublished typescript, Juneau and Douglas City Museum, Juneau.
Dalton Papers. n.d. Held by Mark Kirchhoff, Juneau.

Elizabeth Banks Nichols collection, MacBride Museum of Yukon History, Whitehorse.

Glave, Edward J. The E.J. Glave fonds, Yukon Archives, microfiche of Elmer E. Rasmuson Library (Archive M6/F5 1992-5897 folder 1-8; photographs microfiche 031-02, 031-03).

Gooderham, G.H.1967. "Notes made from memory after a visit by our old friend, Billy Henry."

D 920.H525, Glenbow Archives, Calgary Alberta.

Historical Records of the Office of the Magistrate. City of Skagway.

Lee, I.A. Letters. Yukon Archives, Coutts Collection, 78/69 pt. 1 Folder No. 1 MSS 091.

Library and Archives Canada. RG 13; RG 18; MG 27 D 1 (Clifford Sifton Papers); RG45.

Malony Papers, Alaska State Historical Society. MS 40-5-6.

Ogilvie, William. n.d. Blueprints and field books of William Ogilvie, Dominion Land Surveyor Energy, Mines and Resources Canada, Whitehorse, Yukon.

Redman, Earl. n.d. Untitled material. Porcupine file, Juneau and Douglas City Museum, Juneau.

Redmeyer, Hedley E. n.d. "With Reindeer in Alaska." Typescript account of Reindeer Relief Expedition of 1898, Sheldon Museum, Haines, Alaska.

Tuxford, Brig. General G.(eorge) S. n.d. "The Trail of the Midnight Sun." Volume 2, George S. Tuxford Memoirs Vol. 1–4. Saskatchewan Archives Board, University of Regina Microfilm R 2.247.

U.S. vs. Jack Dalton, court record, case 383, 1893. United States Federal Records Center, Seattle, Washington.

Wright Field Notes, Brooks Notebooks. United States Geological Survey, Anchorage.

Books and Articles

Adney, Tappen. 1900. *The Klondike Stampede*. New York: Harper Bros.

Alaska Boundary Tribunal. 1904. *Proceedings of the Alaska Boundary Tribunal,* Volume II. Government Printing Office, Washington, D.C.

Alberts, Laurie. 1977. "Petticoats and pickaxes." *The Alaska Journal* 7, no. 3: 146–59.

Alley, William. 2004. "But Few Obstacles to the Prospector: Alaska's Nunatak Glacier Route to the Klondike." *Columbia Magazine*. 18.3 (Fall 2004): 36–42. 1.26/2007 http://columbia.washingtonhistory.org/magazine/articles/2004/0304/0304-a4.aspx.

Archibald, Margaret. 1982. "A Substantial Expression of Confidence: The Northern Commercial Company Store, Dawson 1897–1951." Ottawa: Parks Canada, *Publications in History and Archeology* 63.

Arestad, Sverre. 1951. "Reindeer in Alaska." *Pacific Northwest Quarterly* 42: 211–223.

Banks, Della Murray. 1945. "Woman on the Dalton Trail" and "Rainbow's End." *Alaska Sportsman* Part 1, January: 1, 11, 25–33; Part 2, February: 14, 15, 21–27.

Bennett, Gordon. 1978. "Yukon Transportation: A History." Ottawa: National Historic Parks and Sites Branch, *Canadian Historic Sites: Occasional Papers in Archeology and History* 19.

Berton, Pierre. 1972. *Klondike: The Last Great Gold Rush 1896–97.* Toronto: McClelland and Stewart.

Bleakley, Geoffrey T. 1996. *A History of the Chisana Mining District, Alaska, 1890–1990.* Anchorage: Department of the Interior, National Park Service Resources Report NPS/AFARCR/CRR-96/29.

Brooks, Alfred H. 1900a. "A Reconnaissance from Pyramid Harbour to Eagle City, Alaska, Including a Description of the Copper Deposits of the Upper White and Tanana Rivers." Washington, D.C.: *21st Annual Report to the Secretary of the Interior, 1899–1900. U.S. Geological Survey. General Geology, Economic Geology, Alaska.* Part 2: 331–91.

Buteau, Frank. 1967. "My Experiences in the World." In *Sourdough Sagas,* edited by Herbert L. Heller, 85–92. Cleveland: World Publishing Company.

Cole, Terrence. 2008. "Klondike Literature." *Columbia* 22, no.2 (summer).

Constantine, Insp. Charles. 1895. "Report of Inspector Charles Constantine, 10th October, 1894." *Report of the Commissioner of the North-West Mounted Police Force, 1895.* Ottawa: Queen's Printer, 69–85.

Constantine, Insp. Charles. 1896a. "Report of Inspector Charles Constantine, 25th January,1896." *Report of the Commissioner of the North-West Mounted Police Force, 1895.* Ottawa: Queen's Printer, 7–12.

Constantine, Insp. Charles. 1896b. "Report of the Yukon Detachment, 20th November, 1896." *Report of the Commissioner of the North-West Mounted Police Force, 1896.* Ottawa: Queen's Printer, 232–39.

Cotton, Bruce. 1922. *An Adventure in Alaska During the Gold Excitement of 1897–1898.* Baltimore: The Sun Printing Office.

Crawford, Sally. 1962. "Yukon Cattle Drive." *Alaskan Sportsman* 28, no.1: 12–13.

Cruikshank, Julie. 1990. *Life Lived Like a Story.* Vancouver: University of British Columbia Press.

Cruikshank, Julie. 2005. *Do Glaciers Listen? Local Knowledge, Colonial Encounters and Social Imagination.* Vancouver: University of British Columbia Press.

Davidson, George. 1901. "Explanation of an Indian Map of the Rivers, Lakes, Trails and Mountains from the Chilkat to the Yukon, Drawn by the Chilkat Chief, Kohklux, in 1869." *Mazama* April: 75–82.

DeArmond, R.N. 1985. "Miners and Cattle Used Dalton's Trail." *Southeastern Log* January: B10-B11.

Demers, F. J. A. 1906. "Annual Report of Inspector F.J.A. Demers, Whitehorse." *Royal North-West Mounted Police Annual Report, 1905,* Part II, Yukon Territory, Appendix B: 37–50.

DeWindt, Harry. 1898. *Through the Gold Fields of Alaska to Bering Strait.* London: Chatto and Windus.

Dickinson, Christine Frances, and Diane Solie Smith. 1995. *Atlin: The Story of British Columbia's Last Gold Rush.* Atlin, BC: Atlin Historical Society.

Dietz, Arthur Arnold. 1914. *Mad Rush for Gold in the Frozen North*. Los Angeles: Times-Mirror Printing and Binding House.

Divine, Robert A., T.H. Breen, George M. Frederickson, and R. Hal Williams. 1984. *America Past and Present,* Vol. 2. Glenview, Illinois: Scott, Foresman and Company.

Dobrowolsky, Helene. 1995. *Law of the Yukon: A Pictorial History of the Mounted Police*. Whitehorse: Lost Moose Publishing.

Dunham, Sam C. 1983. *The Alaskan Gold Fields*. Anchorage: Alaska Northwest Publishing.

Faulknor, C.V. 1957. "That Long Trail North." *Canadian Cattlemen* November: 12–13, 19.

Fraser, S.M. 1900. "Annual Medical Report of Assistant Surgeon S.M. Fraser, Dalton Trail." *Northwest Mounted Police Report, 1900, Part III, Yukon Territory*. Appendix E:, 64–65. Gates, Michael. 1994. *Gold at Fortymile Creek: Early Days in the Yukon*. Vancouver: University of British Columbia Press.

Fraser, S.M. 1901. "Annual Report of Asst. Surgeon S.M. Fraser, Commanding Dalton Trail Detachment." *North-West Mounted Police Report, 1901*. Sessional Paper 28a Appendix C: 52–58.

Gates, Michael. 2010. *History Hunting in the Yukon*. Madeira Park, BC: Harbour Publishing.

Glave, E.J. 1890–91. "Our Alaska Expedition." *Frank Leslie's Illustrated Newspaper*; September 6/90: 86–87; November 15: 262; November 22: 286–287; November 29: 310; December 6: 332; December 13: 352; December 20: 376; December 27: 396–397; January 3/91: 414; January 10: 438.

Glave, E.J. 1892. "Pioneer Pack Horses in Alaska." *Century Illustrated Magazine* 22: 671–682; 869–881.

Government of the Yukon. n.d. "The Overland Trail: Whitehorse-Dawson City." Whitehorse: Department of Tourism, Heritage Branch, Whitehorse.

Green, Lewis. 1977. *The Gold Hustlers*. Anchorage: Alaska Northwest Publishing Company.

Hahnenberg, Frank. 1964. "Autobiography of Frank Hahnenberg." Typescript, on file with US National Parks Service, Skagway.

Hanley, Elizabeth Holiday. n.d. "The Dalton Trail." Typescript, in the possession of Mark Kirchhoff.

High River Pioneers' and Old Timers' Association. 1960. *Leaves from the Medicine Tree*. Lethbridge: *Lethbridge Herald*.

Hunt, William R. 1993. *Whiskey Peddler: Johnny Healy, North Frontier Trader*. Missoula: Mountain Press Publishing Company.

Jarvis, A.M. 1899. "Annual Report of Inspector A.M. Jarvis." *North-West Mounted Police Report, 1898*, Part III, Yukon Territory, Appendix H: 95–110.

Jarvis, A.M. 1900. "Report of Inspector A.M. Jarvis, Dalton Trail." *North-West Mounted Police Report 1900*, Part II, Appendix C: 56–63.

Jarvis, A.M. 1901. "Report of Inspector A.M. Jarvis, Dalton Trail." *North-West Mounted Police Report 1901*, Part II, Yukon Territory, Appendix E: 76–77.

Jarvis, A.M. 1902. "Annual Report of Inspector A.M. Jarvis, CMG, Dalton Trail." *North-West Mounted Police Report, 1902*, Part III, Yukon Territory, Appendix C: 67–77.

Johnson, Linda. 1984. "The Day the Sun Was Sick." *Yukon Indian News* Summer: 11–15.

Johnson, Linda. 2009. *The Kandik Map*. Fairbanks: University of Alaska Press.

Keithahn, Edward L. 1967. *Alaska . . . for the Curious*. Seattle: Superior Publishing Company.

Kirchhoff, M.J. 2007. *Jack Dalton, the Alaska Pathfinder*. Juneau: Alaska Cedar Press.

Kirchhoff, M.J. 2010. *Clondyke: The First Year of the Rush*. Juneau: Alaska Cedar Press.

Krause, Aurel, and Arthur Krause. 1993. *To the Chukchi Peninsula and to the Tlingit Indians, 1881/1882: Journals and Letters by Aurel and Arthur Krause*. Trans. Margot Krause McCaffrey. Fairbanks: University of Alaska Press.

Larsen, Dennis M. 2009. *Slick as a Mitten: Ezra Meeker's Klondike Enterprise*. Pullman: Washington State University Press.

Lee, Norman. 1960. *Klondike Cattle Drive*. Vancouver: Mitchell Press.

Leechman, Douglas. 1949. "Chief Jimmie Johnson." *Indian Summer*. Toronto: Ryerson Press.

Leechman, Douglas. 1962a. "Copper and Cats." *The Daily Colonist*, March 11: 12.

Leechman, Douglas. 1962b. "The Dalton Trail." *The Daily Colonist*, April 1: 2–3.

London, Jack. 1900. "The Economics of the Klondike." *The American Monthly Review of Reviews*, January: 70–74.

McArthur, J.J. 1898. "Exploration of the Overland Route to the Yukon by way of the Chilkat Pass." *Dominion Lands Surveys Report 20, Annual Report for the year 1897, Part 2*. Ottawa: Department of the Interior: 128–40.

MacBride, William D. n.d. "The Dalton Trail and the Mysterious 36." Newspaper clipping, Yukon Archives, Whitehorse.

McClellan, C. 1970. "Indian Stories About the First Whites in Northwestern North America." In *Ethnohistory in Southwestern Alaska and Southern Yukon*, edited by M. Lantis, 103–33. Lexington: University of Lexington Press.

McClellan, Catharine. 1975. "My Old People Say: An Ethnographic Survey of Southern Yukon Territory," Parts 1 and 2. *National Museums Publications in Ethnology* 6. Ottawa: National Museums of Canada.

McClellan, Catharine. 2007. "My Old People's Stories: A Legacy for Yukon First Nations, Part I: Southern Tutchone Narrators." *Occasional Papers in Yukon History* 5(1). Whitehorse: Yukon Tourism and Culture, Cultural Services Branch.

McDonell, A.E.C. 1904. "Annual Report of Inspector A.E.C. McDonell, Dalton Trail." In *Report of Commissioner A.B. Perry January 24, 1905*. Yukon Archives 351.740 62 NOR 1903: 69–74.

McDonell, A.E.C. 1905. "Annual Report of Inspector A.E.C. McDonell, Dalton Trail" In: *Royal North-West Mounted Police Report, 1904*, Part III. Yukon Territory, Appendix C: 58–62.

MacEwan, Grant. 1952. *Between the Red and the Rockies*. Toronto: University of Toronto Press,

MacEwan, Grant. 1979. *Pat Burns, Cattle King*. Saskatoon: Western Producer Prairie Books.

MacEwan, Grant. 2000. *Blazing the Old Cattle Trail*. Calgary: Fifth House Publishers.

Mann, Charles C. 2005. *1491: New Revelations of the Americas before Columbus*. New York: Knopf.

Martin, Archer. 1901. "Porcupine-Chilkat Districts: Report under the Porcupine District Commission Act, 1900." Victoria, BC: King's Printer.

Miller, Darlis. 1993. *Captain Jack Crawford: Buckskin Poet, Scout and Showman*. Albuquerque: University of New Mexico Press.

Morgan, Edward P., and Henry F. Woods. 1948. *God's Loaded Dice: Alaska 1897–1930*. Caldwell, Idaho: Caxton Printer.

Motherwell, Elizabeth. 1964. "Incidents in the Life and Times of Billy Henry." *Canadian Cattlemen* October: 23–26, 40–41, November 1963: 24, 25, 44–45, and January 1964: 10, 21–23.

Neufeld, David, and Frank Norris. 1996. *Chilkoot Trail: Heritage Route to the Klondike*. Whitehorse: Lost Moose Publishing.

North, Dick. 2006. *Sailor on Snowshoes: Tracking Jack London's Northern Trail*. Madeira Park, BC: Harbour Publishing.

Olson, Ronald L. 1936. "Some Trading Customs of the Chilkat Tlingit." In *Essays in Honor of A.L. Kroeber*, edited by R.H. Lowie, 211–214. Berkeley: University of California Press.

Penlington, Norman. 1972. *The Alaska Boundary Dispute: A Critical Reappraisal*. Toronto: McGraw-Hill Ryerson.

Porsild, Charlene. 1998. *Gamblers and Dreamers: Women, Men and Community in the Klondike*. Vancouver: University of British Columbia Press.

Rausch, V.R., and D.L. Baldwin (eds.). 2002. *The Yukon Relief Expedition and the Journal of Carl Johan Sakariassen*. Fairbanks: University of Alaska Press.

Rinaldo, Peter M. 1997. *The Great Reindeer Caper: The Missionary and the Miners*. New York: DorPete Press, Briarcliff Manor.

Robertson, Heather. 2007. *Measuring Mother Earth: How Joe the Kid Became Tyrrell of the North*. Toronto: McClelland and Stewart.

Rodney, Wm. 1974. *Joe Boyle, King of the Klondike*. Toronto: McGraw-Hill Ryerson.

Roppel, Patricia. 1975. "Porcupine." *The Alaska Journal*. 5, no. 1: 2–10.

Schwatka, Frederick. 1891. *A Summer in Alaska*. Philadelphia: John Y. Huber and Company.

Schwatka, Frederick. 1996. *Schwatka's Last Search: New-York Ledger Expedition Through Unknown Alaska and British America, Including the Journal of Charles Willard Hayes, 1891*. Fairbanks: University of Alaska Press. Introduction and annotation by Arland S. Harris.

Scidmore, Elizah Ruhamah. 1885. *The Sitkan Archipelago*. Boston: D. Lothrop and Company.

Scrimgeour, Gray. 1996. "Annotated Klondike Bibliography" In "Postal History Society of Canada Special CAPEX '96 Issue on the Klondike." *Postal History Society of Canada Journal* 85: 84–89.

Seton-Karr, H.W. 1891. *Bear-Hunting in the White Mountains*. London: Chapman and Hall.

Shape, William. 1998. *Faith of Fools*. Pullman: Washington State University Press.

Snyder, H.E. 1904. "Annual Report of Superintendant A.E. Snyder, Whitehorse." *Royal North-West Mounted Police Report, 1904*, Part III, Yukon Territory, Appendix A: 25–37.

Stewart, Robert Laird. 1908. *Sheldon Jackson*. New York: Fleming H. Revell.

Swanton, John R. 1909. *Tlingit Myths and Texts*. Bureau of American Ethnology Bulletin 39. Washington, D.C.: Smithsonian Institution.

"Suppliers of Beef to Dawson." 1940. *Canadian Cattlemen*: 373, 376.

Taylor, Leonard. 1983. *The Sourdough and the Queen*. Toronto: Methuen.

Thompson, Arthur R. 1900. *Gold-Seeking on the Dalton Trail*. Boston: Little, Brown and Company.

Thornton, Thomas. 2004. *Klondike Gold Rush National Historical Park Ethnographic Overview and Assessment*. US National Park Service NPS D-111.

Tyrell, J.B. 1899. "Yukon District (With Adjacent Parts of British Columbia)." *Geological Survey of Canada Report*, 1898. Vol 21: 36a–47a.

Walden, Arthur. 1931. *A Dog-Puncher on the Yukon*. Boston: Houghton Mifflin.

Wallace, Jim. 2000. *Forty Mile to Bonanza: The Northwest Mounted Police in the Klondike Gold Rush*. Calgary: Bunker to Bunker Publishing.

Weadick, Guy. 1949. "Billy Henry of the Open Range." *Canadian Cattlemen*, September: 22, 23, 26, 27.

Whymper, Frederick. 1869. *Travel and Adventure in the Territory of Alaska*. New York: Harper and Brothers.

Williams, Jay P. 1952. *Alaskan Adventure*. Harrisburg, Pennsylvania: The Telegraph Press.

Wood, Z.T. 1899. "Annual Report of Superintendent Z.T. Wood". *North-West Mounted Police Report 1898*, Part III, Yukon Territory, Appendix A: 32–56.

Wright, Charles W. 1904. "The Porcupine Placer District, Alaska." *United States Geological Survey Bulletin* no. 236.

Notes

1. Swanton, 1909 contains two versions of this story, 154–60 and 326–45 (Story 104). Cruikshank, 2005 provides a clear analysis and interpretation of the stories. In her version, the name of Qakē̓q!utê is rendered as Kaakex'wtí. According to Daniel Henry of Haines (personal communication), Chilkat elders Joe Hotch and Tom Jimmie Jr. tell another story about unknown people spotted by Klukwan villagers on Chilkat Pass. At first, they were so shy that locals called them *gunana*, or "strange people." Lured by salmon and eulachon oil left on rocks, the newcomers eventually established trading and family relationships with Chilkats who came to consider much of the southern Yukon as their economic realm.

2. Swanton, 1909: 160

3. Ibid.

4. Cruikshank, 1990: 271

5. Ibid.: 280

6. McClellan, 1975: 505

7. Olson, 1936: 211

8. Scidmore, 1885: 115

9. Johnson, 1984: 11

10. Davidson, 1901: 76

11. Ibid.

12. This wasn't the only map the Chilkat drew of this route. Some years before, a map showing the route over the mountains and down the Yukon River was drawn for Captain Dodd, commanding the British steamer, *Beaver*. The downstream journey took fifteen to twenty days, while the return trip took fifty. Whymper, 1869: 228–29.

13. Refer to chapter 3 for more information about this development.

14. Krause and Krause, 1993.

15. Glave, 1891: 875

16. The *Juneau City Mining Record,* May 3 and May 10, 1888. Seton-Karr, 1891: 94 states that the year was 1887.

17. Seton-Karr, 1891: 82; Note that the *Juneau City Mining Mining Record* for June 26, 1890, states the party left on their expedition to the interior on March 20, reaching the Alsek (Tatshenshini) River April 18.

18. Glave, 1890, August 9: 572.

19. Glave, 1890, November 6: 266.

20. Glave refers to the Tatshenshini River as the Alseck.

21. Glave, 1890, November 29: 310.

22. Ibid.

23. Glave consistently seems to overestimate the distances that they travelled.

24. Glave, 1890, December 6: 332.

25. Glave, 1890, December 13: 352.

26. Glave, 1890, December 20: 376.

27. Glave, 1891, January 3: 414.

28. Glave, 1890, November 22: 286.

29. Glave, 1890, November 22: 286–87.

30. Today Glave's four thousand dollars would be equivalent to more than one hundred thousand dollars.

31. *Deseret News,* August 17, 1897.

32. Glave, 1892: 672.

33. Glave, 1892: 677.

34. *New York Times,* July 22, 1892. At this time, the boundary between Alaska and Canada had not been formalized. In addition, Glave probably considered his American audience when lumping this region into Alaska.

35. Glave, 1892: 682.

36. Ibid.

37. Leechman, 1949: 39–40.

38. Cruikshank, 2005: 191; 281: footnote 51.

39. Leechman, 1949: 42–43. The author also was told this story on more than one occasion in the early 1970s, although in some versions of the story Dalton was replaced by the Hudson's Bay Company trader, Robert Campbell. The Southern Tutchone have always displayed a frank and often self-effacing sense of humour. McClellan (1970: 28) states that the interior people "have developed a comic genre of contact literature in which they themselves play the dupes."

40. In 1958 a team of six men, with the help of the Canadian Army and heavy equipment, spent five days to haul a slab of native copper weighing well over a ton out from the White River to the Alaska Highway. It is now mounted on display outside the MacBride Museum.

41. Schwatka, 1891.

42. Glave notebook, Thursday, August 13, 1891.

43. See Schwatka, 1996.

44. Glave,1892: 879.

45. Glave notebook, Thursday, August 17, 1891.

46. Glave,1892: 879.

47. University of Alaska Fairbanks, Elmer E. Rasmuson Library (Archive M6/F5 1992-5897 folder 1-8 entry for September 3, 1891).

48. Sitka *Alaskan,* November 21 and 28, 1891.

49. Victoria *Daily Colonist,* November 8, 1891.

50. *Brisbane Courier,* December 16, 1891.

51. *Worcester Daily Spy,* June 15, 1893.

52. *Juneau City Mining Record,* April 21 and May 26, 1892.

53. Kirchoff, 2007: 57.

54. Kirchoff, 2007: 56; see also report of the Alaska Boundary Tribunal, 1904: 411.

55. Kirchoff, 2007: 59.

56. *San Francisco Chronicle,* January 13, 1893; *Juneau City Mining Record,* February 9, 1893.

57. Neufeld and Norris, 1996: 39–47.

58. Thornton, 2004: 130.

59. Hunt, 1993: 113

60. Glave Notebook, entry for April 21, 1891, refers to fifty Chinese on board the steamer *Mexico*, which was en route to Pyramid Harbor.

61. The Sitka *Alaskan*, July 23, 1892.

62. Alaska Boundary Tribunal, 1904: 410, 412–13. Dalton was given high praise for his "efficiency and bravery," and it was recommended that he be placed on a retainer as a special deputy US Marshal.

63. The Sitka *Alaskan*, July 25, 1892.

64. United States Federal Records Center, Seattle, Washington: U.S. vs. Jack Dalton, court record, case 383, 1893. Testimony of Patrick Woods.

65. *Juneau City Mining Record,* July 13, 1893; *East Oregon Herald,* April 5, 1893.

66. *Alaska Journal*, May 13, 1893.

67. Sitka *Alaskan*, July 1, 1893. For a more detailed description of events, see Kirchhoff, 2007: 60–64.

68. *Anchorage Daily News,* September 25, 1898.

69. Jack Dalton married Estella Richey, the second of his three wives, May 10, 1892, in Haines. The marriage produced a son (Jack Junior) and a daughter (Margaret). The first marriage, to May Click, was childless; the third, to Anna Krippaehne, produced a son (James) and a daughter (Josephine). Dalton produced other offspring from extramarital liaisons in Alaska and the Yukon. See Kirchhoff, 2007.

70. Victoria *Daily Colonist,* January 13, 1894.

71. Constantine, 1895: 71 states: "Horses have been brought into the country by this route. I heard that four were coming in this fall in charge of a man by the name of Dalton."

72. DeArmond, 1985: B 10; *Alaska News*, October 18, 1894.

73. *Alaska News*, October 25, 1894; *Alaska Mining Record,* March 11, 1895 also now refers to this route as the Dalton Trail.

74. *Alaska News*, August 9, 1894.

75. *Alaska News*, January 24, 1895; *Alaska Mining Record*, March 11, 1895 states seventeen horses; *Alaska Searchlight*, March 11, 1895 states that he was bringing in seventeen horses and six hundred pieces of merchandise to Chilkat on the *Willipa*.

76. Alaska State Historical Society, Malony Papers, MS 40-5-6, Articles of partnership, March 9, 1895.

77. See DeArmond, 1985: B10; *Alaska News,* March 21, 1895; Constantine, 1896a: 13–14 also refers to smuggling of whiskey "by way of the Chilkat Pass and down the Takheena River." See also reference to the sale of liquor in the interior in *Alaska Mining Record,* July 8, 1895.

78. *New York Sun*, November 24, 1895.

79. *Alaska Searchlight,* May 27, 1895.

80. Leechman, 1962b: 2, says that this occurred in 1894; McArthur, 1898: 129–30 states that the event happened in 1895, but evidence places Dalton elsewhere in 1895. *Alaska Mining Record,* February 29, 1896; Kirchhoff, 2007: 68, place the event in 1896. *Alaska Mining Record,* December 28, 1898 refers to the mysterious

disappearances, but was this report merely part of the process of myth-making surrounding Jack Dalton?

81. For more information on the growth of placer mining in the Yukon valley during this period, refer to Gates, 1994.

82. Kirchhoff, 2007: 69–70.

83. Kirchhoff, 2007: 70.

84. As in many cases, the number of animals in a herd varies from one news account to the next. Kirchhoff, 2010: 31; personal communication; *Alaska Mining Record*, June 17, 1896; *Alaska Mining Record*, July 29, 1896; *Boston Evening Transcript*, October 11, 1896: 12; Tacoma *Statesman-Review*, August 17, 1896: 8.

85. Spokane *Spokesman-Review*, August 17, 1896.

86. *Douglas Miner*, September 23, 1896.

87. *St. Louis Republic*, October 17, 1897.

88. *Alaska Searchlight*, August 21, 1897. The Victoria *Daily Colonist*, October 12, 1897 states that the beef sold for thirteen thousand dollars. Newspaper accounts do not agree on the precise amount.

89. *Dubuque Daily Herald*, March 27 1897: 3, and April 1: 6. Also *Macleod Gazette*, March 26, 1897.

90. *Klondike News*, April 1, 1898: 4.

91. Kirchhoff, 2010: 18–19, 26.

92. Library and Archives Canada (hereafter cited as LAC), RG 18, Vol. 148, File 165: Letter from Constantine to Officer Commanding, Regina August 29, 1896.

93. Constantine, 1896b: 236; also Ogilvie field notes 1896: 11–25.

94. Glave, 1891: 871.

95. Mann, 2005: 284.

96. Berton, 1972: 47.

97. Joe Ladue interview, *Camden Democrat*, August 28, 1897: 1.

98. Archibald, 1982: 11–12 notes that the Alaska Commercial Company constructed two warehouses, followed by the store, which was complete by October 1, 1897.

99. *Alaska Mining Record*, February 10, 1897.

100. *Dubuque Daily Herald*, March 27, 1897: 3, and April 1: 6. Also *Macleod Gazette*, March 26, 1897.

101. MacEwan, 2000: 163. Fearon was well established in his Saskatchewan community. He was born in England in 1858 and served in the military, then the North-West Mounted Police for two years. During the rebellion of 1885, he served in Colonel Otter's Scouts, for which he was awarded a medal for bravery. He was subsequently a teacher, and then served in the legislative Assembly of the Northwest Territories when he was elected to the position October 31, 1894.

102. According to different sources, the herd was reported to be eighty head (MacEwan, 1979: 94) and sixty-eight head (*Calgary Herald*, July 29, 1897); MacEwan, 2000: 162–64.

103. MacEwan, 2000: 167–68.

104. *Alaska Searchlight*, February 27, 1897.

105. Crawford, 1962: 12.

106. *Cedar Rapid Evening Gazette*: 1. The article incorrectly names Bratnober as "Battlehouser, an agent of the exploration company."

107. Ibid.; See also: *Chicago Tribune,* July 20, 1897: 7. The interview with Charles M. Goodall of Goodall, Perkins and Co. states that Dalton was taking a herd of their cattle over his trail to the Klondike.

108. McArthur, 1898: 133.

109. McClellan, 2007: 130.

110. Ibid.: 12, 13.

111. McArthur, 1898: 134.

112. Crawford, 1962: 13.

113. According to Dunham, 1983: 22 there were sixty-four head of Dalton's herd along with a second herd of sixty head at Fort Selkirk on September 15, where the cattlemen were waiting for cold weather so that they could butcher the animals.

114. *Cedar Rapid Evening Gazette,* September 6, 1897.

115. McArthur, 1898: 136. Dunham, 1983: 22 estimates that by mid-September the number had swollen to 2,400.

116. LAC RG 18, Vol. 171, File 415, Letter from Z.T. Wood, Inspector, to Comptroller, NWM Police, Ottawa January 30, 1898.

117. *Cedar Rapid Evening Gazette,* September 6, 1897; see also *Rio Grande Republican,* November 19, 1897.

118. Buteau, 1967: 118.

119. See Gates, 1994: 44–45 for a description of the early prospector's diet.

120. Walden, 1931: 85.

121. Divine, et. al. 1984: 588.

122. *New York Times,* July 27, 1897.

123. *New York Times,* November 29, 1897.

124. Adney, 1900: 188.

125. Adney, 1900: 187.

126. Berton, 1972: 161.

127. Rinaldo, 1997: 33–34

128. *New York Times,* November 29, 1897.

129. Ibid.

130. Ibid.

131. *Alaska Searchlight,* August 21, 1897.

132. *New York Times,* November 29, 1898.

133. *New York Times,* October 3, 1897. Louis Long is quoted as stating that between two hundred and three hundred men would travel over the Dalton Trail in the next few weeks.

134. McArthur, 1898: 137.

135. *New Zealand Tablet,* issue 41 February 11, 1898: 9, See also Shape, 1998: 19.

136. *Newark Daily Advocate,* January 14, 1898, *New York Times,* November 29, 1897.

137. *New York Times,* October 3, 1897, *Syracuse Evening Herald,* October 6, 1897.

138. *New Zealand Evening Post,* February 26, 1898: 1.

139. *New Zealand Evening Post,* February 26, 1898: 1; Taylor, 1983: 42–43; *Dawson News,* Midsummer Edition, 1899; *Seattle Post-Intelligencer,* November 17, 1897, November 29, 1897; Rodney, 1974: 24–25; *Seattle Post-Intelligencer,* November 29, 1897.

140. *Seattle Post-Intelligencer,* November 30, 1897, *Dawson Daily News,* Midsummer Number, September 1899: 28.

141. *Los Angeles Times,* November 29, 1897.

142. Ibid.

143. *Seattle Post-Intelligencer,* November 29, 1897: 3; *The Twice-a-Week Spokesman-Review,* Monday, December 6, 1897: 7.

144. *Manufacturers and Farmers Journal,* December 9, 1897: 1.

145. *New York Times,* November 30, 1897; Martinsen 1974: 214–218; A variation of the *New York Times* account is found in the *Manufacturers and Farmers Journal,* December 9, 1897: 1.

146. *San Francisco Call,* October 5, 1897 Henry Bratnober reported that sixteen hundred sheep and four hundred head of cattle would have reached Dawson by freeze-up; *Fresno Weekly Republican,* October 8, 1897 McArthur is quoted as stating that the numbers were two thousand sheep and four hundred head of cattle.

147. Crawford, 1962: 13.

148. Ibid.

149. North, 2006: 96, quoting London (1981: 73) While Jack London wrote fiction, many of his stories are based upon things he saw and heard during his Klondike odyssey and can be corroborated by other historical sources.

150. *The Saturday Budget,* October 23, 1897: 1.

151. Thebo is also referred to as Thibo and Thibault in some newspaper reports.

152. *Alaska Searchlight,* July 10, 1897.

153. *Calgary Weekly Herald,* December 30: 1.

154. Adney, 1900: 168–169, Dunham, 1983: 59; MacEwan, 1979: 94.

155. According to a report in the *Saturday Budget* of October 23, 1897, the number was forty-nine, plus thirty-six horses.

156. *Oakland Tribune,* October 11, 1897: 2. When Clark and Brown encountered them near the summit, they had already lost fifteen pack horses.

157. According to the *Spokane Spokesman-Review,* October 26, 1897: 1, eighty-four horses were lost. This estimate may be overstated.

158. *Seattle Post-Intelligencer,* November 20, 1897; *Skagway News,* December 31, 1897 states that the herd was returned to Haines, where it was sold; *Klondike News,* April 1, 1898; Shape, 1998: 19 states that Thorp had a herd of two hundred cattle and sixty horses, but it is noted in the *Seattle Post-Intelligencer* for November 20, 1897 that Thomas Morgan, with a herd of forty and several smaller parties joined with Thorp for the trip, explaining the larger size of herd described by Shape; *The Spokane Spokesman-Review,* October 26, 1897: 1 states that Thorp lost eighty-four

of ninety-four horses and twenty-four of one hundred head of cattle before turning back. The remaining cattle were to be rerouted to Bennett to be slaughtered, frozen and hauled downriver on the ice over the winter. The animals were very thin so were almost worthless. The *New York Times* for September 13, 1897 states that Thorp was across from (Haines) Mission and expected to take thirty-five days to herd eighty head of cattle to the Yukon River.

159. *New York Times,* October 3, 1897; Rodney, 1974: 24; *Seattle Post-Intelligencer,* November 20, 1897.

160. *Seattle Post-Intelligencer,* November 20, 1897.

161. NWMP report, John Pratt Collection, MS 84/7, Yukon Archives calls it the Humboldt Co. of Boston; Kirchhoff, 2007: 80.

162. The *Spokane Chronicle,* November 4, 1897: 8. Note the name Holman Steuber conflicts with another newspaper (*The Winston Prospector*, January 6, 1898: 1) account in which his name is Herman Steuber. Given the German background of Waechter and Steuber, I surmise that Herman is the accurate name.

163. Heartland: http://www.newsminer.com/heartland/hland72698/pioneer.html. Also: MacEwan, 1979: 93.

164. Faulknor, 1957: 12; Note that in another article, Chris Bartsch is quoted as saying that the meat sold for one dollar per pound; "Suppliers of Beef to Dawson City," 1940: 373.

165. *Dubuque Daily Herald*, October 6, 1897.

166. Bennett, 1978: 24.

167. *Chicago Tribune,* October 3, 1897: 3, and October 10, 1897: 2.

168. *San Francisco Call,* October 27, 1897.

169. *New York Times,* December 3, 1897.

170. *Rio Grande Republican*, November 19, 1897, *San Francisco Chronicle,* April 5, 1898: 3.

171. *Newark Daily Advocate,* October 12, 1897.

172. *New York Times,* December 27, 1897.

173. Yukon Archives, Coutts Collection, 78/69 pt. 1 Folder No. 1 MSS 091.

174. Ibid.

175. *Seattle Post-Intelligencer,* September 16, 1897; *Alaska Mining Record*, September 29, 1897.

176. *San Francisco Chronicle*, January 15, 1898; *New York Times*, January 15, 1898.

177. The quantities of horses and cattle and the amount of equipment landed vary considerably from one newspaper account to another. All, however, convey the general impression that this was a well-financed and -equipped undertaking. *Seattle Post-Intelligencer,* October 5, 1897; *The Oregonian*, November 30, 1897; *New York Times*, November 14 and December 27, 1897 and January 22, 1898; *San Francisco Examiner*, November 14, November 21 and December 27, 1897.

178. *Seattle Post-Intelligencer,* November 29, 1897: 3; *Seattle Post-Intelligencer*, *New York Times*, January 22, 1897.

179. As early as November 30, 1897, the *Tacoma Daily Ledger* reports that the

party would not be able to cross the Dalton Trail during the winter. See also *San Francisco Examiner,* January 28, 1898.

180. *Alaska Miner,* July 29, 1899.

181. *Tacoma Daily Ledger,* December 4 and December 28, 1897; *Alaska Mining Record,* December 8, 1897.

182. *New York Times,* January 11, 1898; *Fort Wayne Sentinel,* January 11, 1898: 2.

183. *Tacoma Daily Ledger,* February 26, 1898.

184. *Seattle Post-Intelligencer,* March 5, 1898; *Fort Wayne Sentinel,* March 5, 1898: 1; *New York Times,* March 6, 1898.

185. Thompson, 1900: 51.

186. *New York Times,* September 22, 1897.

187. *Tacoma Daily Ledger,* January 23, 1898.

188. Delphos, Ohio, *Daily Herald,* October 5, 1897; *New York Times,* December 14, 1897; *Oakland Tribune,* January 27, 1898: 5; *Syracuse Herald,* February 13, 1898: 20.

189. *New York Times,* February 23, 1898.

190. Wood, 1899: 48.

191. Stewart, 1908: 387.

192. *Seattle Post-Intelligencer,* October 20, 1897.

193. *New York Times,* October 23, 1897.

194. *New York Times,* December 1, 1897.

195. Ibid.

196. *New York Times,* December 9, 1897; December 25, 1897.

197. *New York Times,* December 14, 1897.

198. Ibid.

199. Rinaldo, 1997: 107–8.

200. *New York Times,* December 20, 1897; *Decatur Daily Review,* December 21, 1897. He seems to have had a change of heart about the subject of starvation in Dawson. In the *Seattle Post-Intelligencer* for November 29, 1897, he stated, "Provisions are scarce, but I doubt if there will be starvation." Perhaps the possibility of landing a government contract to provide relief to the miners changed his opinion on the matter.

201. *New York Times,* December 31, 1897.

202. Ibid.

203. *New York Times,* January 1, 1898.

204. Miller, 1993: 210–213.

205. Rausch and Baldwin, 2002: 97.

206. Redmeyer, n.d.: 5.

207. Arestad, 1951.

208. See Johnson, 2009.

209. Davidson, 1901; Yukon Historical and Museums Assoc., 1995; Glave, 1892; Thompson, 1900, and McArthur, 1898

210. See Berton, 1972, for an excellent description of all of the trails of '98, except the Dalton Trail.

211. Berton, 1972: 197–200.

212. Gates, 1994: 33–35.

213. *San Francisco Examiner,* February 21, 1898.

214. DeArmond, 1985: B11; Kirchhoff, 2007: 87.

215. *Seattle Post-Intelligencer,* May 5, 1898; LAC Clifford Sifton Papers, MG 27 II D 15, Letter to Minister of the Interior Sifton June 14, 1898: James Walsh, first Commissioner of the Yukon, sent out a report to his superior in Ottawa via the Dalton Trail June 15, 1898; Jarvis, 1899: 105 states that the number of horses was two hundred and fifty, while DeArmond, likely quoting the *Settle Post-Intelligencer* article, states five hundred; Adney, 1900: 389–92 states the number to be three hundred and fifty. He also states that the fare from Dawson City to Pyramid Harbor was $250. It is not known what the incoming fare, which included easier downriver travel, cost.

216. LAC RG 18, Memo AM Jarvis to Comptroller of the NWMP, July 2, 1898.

217. Alaska State Historical Library (hereafter cited as ASHL), John F. Malony Papers MS 40, File 17.

218. Kirchhoff, 2007: 86–87.

219. Kirchhoff, 2007: 224, note 44.

220. *Alaska Mining Journal*, June 10, 1898.

221. Victoria *Daily Colonist,* July 16, 1898.

222. *Klondike Nugget,* July 9, 1898.

223. *Klondike Nugget*, June 16, 1898.

224. Scrimgeour, 1996: 53; Jarvis, 1899: 109.

225. Adney, 1900: 389–92.

226. There are other accounts of attempts by the Chilkat to kill Jack Dalton: Williams, 1952: 48–49; Hanley, n.d: 5. See also: *Fort Wrangell News*, June 29, 1898.

227. Kirchhoff, 2007: 90–91; *Seattle Post-Intelligencer,* June 26, 1898; Victoria *Daily Colonist*, June 28, 1898; *Fort Wrangell News*, June 29, 1898; *Skagway News*, July 1, 1898 reports that the man's name was Charley.

228. ASHL Microfilm AR 45, Letter, R.T. Yeatman, Captain 14th Infantry Commanding, Dyea, Alaska, to Adjutant General, 4 July 1898. Microfilm AR 45.

229. ASHL Microfilm AR 45, Letter Capt. R.T. Yeatman to Governor John Brady, July 8, 1898.

230. ASHL Microfilm AR 45, Letter R.T. Yeatman to Alaska Governor John Brady, July 8, 1898.

231. Banks, 1945: 31.

232. Weadick, 1949: 26.

233. Jarvis, 1898: 99.

234. *Alaska Mining Record*, January 11, 1899.

235. LAC RG 18, Vol. 148, File 165 November 4, 1897. Letter J.J. McArthur to Commissioner Walsh.

236. LAC RG 18, Report AM Jarvis to AB Perry, April 20, 1898.

237. *Douglas Island News*, August 14, 1901.

238. McArthur, 1898: 130; Banks, 1945: 29–30.

239. Thompson, 1900: 116.

240. Wood, 1898: 41.

241. Glave, 1890, November 22: 286.

242. LAC RG 10, Vol. 4037, f. 317050. In a letter written by Chief Jim Boss to the Superintendent of Indian Affairs January 13, 1902, Boss places the population of Hutchi at two hundred.

243. Arestad, 1951: 218.

244. The information provided here regarding the boundary between Canada and the US comes from Penlington, 1972.

245. Penlington, 1972: 34.

246. *New York Times,* January 24, 1898.

247. LAC RG 18, Memo A.B. Perry to Fred White, Comptroller of the NWMP, February 5, 1898; Ibid., White to Perry, March 11, 1898; Ibid., White to Perry, March 22, 1898.

248. LAC RG 18, Memo Comptroller to Z.T. Wood, February 17, 1898, Telegram to L.W. Herchmer, Commissioner of the NWMP, February 24, 1898.

249. LAC RG 18, Telegrams Comptroller White to A.B. Perry, March 23, 1898; Telegram Perry to White, March 29, 1898.

250. LAC RG 18, Memorandum of instruction from Superintendent A.B. Perry to Inspector Jarvis, April 6, 1898.

251. LAC RG 18, Report A.M. Jarvis to A.B. Perry, April 20, 1898.

252. LAC RG 18, Memo A.M. Jarvis to A.B. Perry, May 1, 1898.

253. LAC RG 18, Memo A.M. Jarvis to A.B. Perry, May 18, 1898.

254. LAC RG 18, Memo J.B. Tyrrell, to A.M. Jarvis, June 17, 1898. Tyrrell, a Canadian government geologist, later confirmed the location to be well within Canadian territory.

255. Jarvis, 1899.

256. Banks, 1945: 31.

257. LAC RG 18, Vol. 155, File 484–98, Letter from Inspector A.M Jarvis, August 16, 1898.

258. Jarvis, 1899: 107.

259. Jarvis, 1899: 110.

260. LAC RG 18, Monthly report, October 20.

261. LAC RG 18, Letter A.M. Jarvis to A.B. Perry, April 20, 1898. The Last Chance mining district was located along the eastern flank of the St. Elias Mountains in what is now the eastern boundary of Kluane National Park.

262. There are several newspaper accounts of the parties leaving the Yukon over the Dalton Trail: *San Francisco Call,* July 19, 1898: 3; Ibid., July 23, 1898: 12; July 26: 4; July 30, 1898. J.B. Tyrell field notebook, LAC RG 45, Vol. 174, September 23, 1898.

263. Larsen, 2009: 38–9.

264. Kirchhoff, 2007: 93.

265. Jarvis, 1899: 102–103. In his account Jarvis says that forty passengers who refused to go any further on the leaky vessel got off at Haines.

266. Hahnenberg, 1964. Hahnenberg's memories of the dates and events are jumbled, and he remembers meeting Robert Service camped on the Chilkoot Trail, writing his book *The Trail of Ninety Eight*. Service didn't arrive in the Yukon until 1906. Cahoon, however (Cahoon, n.d.: 3–4) recounts his voyage on the *Blanchard* and search for gold in the same area.

267. London, 1900.

268. Sitka *Alaskan*, quoted in Alley, 2004.

269. Sitka *Alaskan*, September 11, 1897, quoted in Alley, 2004.

270. Brooks 1900a: 338 reports in 1899 meeting prospectors D.D. Garvey and J.J. Haney, who made their way to the Kaskawulsh River from Yakutat.

271. Jarvis, 1900: 62; Fraser, 1900: 65.

272. Alley, 2004; Dietz, 1914; Note that Cole, 2008, questions the accuracy of the information from Dietz's book. Various inconsistencies of fact are found in this volume. Nevertheless, like many fictionalized accounts from the era, they seem to be based upon first-hand participation in the events.

273. Cotton, 1922: 107.

274. *Reno Evening Gazette,* April 18, 1898, attributes the discovery to Shorty Bigelow; *Skagway Alaskan,* July 15, 1898, reports the same; Thompson, 1900: 130, states that the discovery claim at the confluence of Alder and Union creeks was staked by J. Barry.

275. According to information from the file in the Elizabeth Banks Nichols Collection at the MacBride Museum, Whitehorse, there were ten from Massachusetts, six from California, four from Vermont, six from Connecticut, one from Victoria, one from London, England, and the remainder from other states.

276. Thompson, 1900: 62.

277. Champlain is mentioned in Thompson, 1900: 256–57, and by J.B. Tyrrell, *Alaska Weekly,* October 8, 1943.

278. Banks, 1945: 30.

279. E.g.: Thompson, 1900: 309, 322.

280. Thompson, 1900: 308; Jarvis, 1899: 101.

281. Banks, 1945: 28, 32.

282. The *Chicago Tribune* of September 14, 1898, reported that sixteen members of the party arrived in Port Townsend aboard the *Farallon* the day before. They were returning home to spend the winter, but the syndicate never returned.

283. Yukon Archives Placer Mining Series DOV 347, Shorty Creek.

284. Tyrrell, 1899: 40A; Robertson, 2007: 242–244. For a detailed account of Treadgold's career in Klondike mining, refer to Green, 1977.

285. LAC RG 18, Vol. 155, File 484–98: Extract from Report of Insp. A.M. Jarvis, August 31, 1898.

286. *Seattle Post-Intelligencer*, September 19, 1905.

287. Alberts, 1977.

288. Porsild, 1998: 208, for example, cited statistics from the 1898 NWMP census that only 1,195 of 14,342 or 8 percent of those enumerated were women.

289. *St. Paul Globe*, October 21, 1897; also Victoria *Daily Colonist*, October 12, 1897: 2.

290. *Chicago Daily Tribune*, October 10, 1897: 2. While Mrs. Bounds and Mrs. Galvin were coming out from Dawson over the Dalton Trail, two other women, Mrs. Waechter and Mrs. Steuber, accompanied their husbands and a herd of cattle in from the coast. Starting out too late in the season, they were driven back to the coast by winter storms, and redirected their efforts by taking their herd to Bennett BC, where they were to be butchered. The *Morning Olympian*, November 5, 1897.

291. Thompson, 1900: 72, 228, 323–24.

292. Robertson, 2007: 228–29.

293. Motherwell, 1964 (January): 10.

294. Ibid.

295. Ibid.

296. Banks, 1945, Part 1: 28.

297. Banks, 1945, Part I: 33; Jarvis, 1899: 106 stated that "One of Charlie Thebo's cattlemen en route to Five Fingers was taken ill, possibly with appendicitis and died near Hoochi, he was buried along the side of the trail." Tuxford, n.d.: 63, recorded the same burial, but cites a date of July 28, 1898.

298. Jarvis, 1899: 106; Wood, 1899: 56.

299. John Kill reported being robbed of $9,000 at Pelly on his way out after delivering a herd of cattle to Dawson. Another man named Collins lost three hundred head of sheep due to his own negligence.

300. Jarvis, 1899: 106; The *Tacoma Daily Ledger*, October 23, 1898 states that in an interview with Jack Dalton, Martin's death was confirmed and that the amount of money lost was $2,000. The *San Francisco Call*, September 26, 1898 states that he was found with his throat cut and $4,000 missing.

301. *Seattle Post-Intelligencer*, November 29, 1897.

302. *Spokane Daily Chronicle*, November 4, 1897: 8.

303. *Spokane Spokesman-Review*, October 26, 1897: 1.

304. Banks, 1945, Part 1: 31.

305. Shape, 1998: 83–91.

306. MacEwan, 1952: 142. MacEwan occasionally seems confused about the geography of the Yukon. He appears to confuse the Chilkoot Trail, which was virtually impassable to livestock, with the White Pass, which provided a steady grade and lower elevation at its summit.

307. MacEwan, 1952: 142; *San Francisco Call*, October 15, 1898: 2.

308. For more information on the challenges of this route, read Lee, 1960.

309. One photo collection from the Bancroft Library (BANC PIC 1961.016—ALB) shows horses and cattle swimming across the Yukon River at Carmacks. Tantalus Butte is clearly visible in the background.

310. *Seattle Post-Intelligencer*, October 30, 1897; *San Francisco Chronicle*, October 30, 1897.

311. *Dubuque Daily Herald*, October 6, 1897; *New York Times*, October 6, 1897.

312. *Klondike News*, April 1, 1898: 21. Klondike "King" Pat Galvin was reported

as having bought twelve hundred head of cattle. It was his plan to use vessels from his transportation company to meet the herd at the end of the trail and haul them to Dawson.

313. MacEwan, 2000: 177; High River, *et al.*, 1960: 188; photo, Bancroft Library: BANC PIC 1961.016—ALB; *San Francisco Call,* June 6, 1898: 3 states that the number was to be 1,300 head.

314. Colonel F.O. Sissons from Medicine Hat had a herd on the trail, as did MacDonald and Dunbarton, who brought in a herd of sixty-five animals, Weadick, 1949: 26; Charlie Dunbarton from Seattle was the tall cattleman who brought his new bride with him, Motherwell, 1964, January: 10; Jack Dalton (or his partner Ed Hanley) was reported to be driving a herd of seven hundred head of cattle to Dawson City, *The Bessemer Herald,* May 7, 1898. There is no evidence that Dalton actually herded any livestock over the trail the summer of 1898 unless it was handled by one of his partners, as he was occupied guiding Henry Bratnober on a copper prospecting expedition into the White River region, Bleakley, 95–96; Also Sitka *Alaskan,* December 10, 1898; Brooks, 1900: 380; Other herds of unspecified size were being moved overland by H. "Cow" Miller of Seattle, and Zelnick and "Dutch" Dick also from Seattle. Two partners named Rudio and Kaufman from Walla Walla, Washington, were also on the move, as was a man named Braden from Brandon, Manitoba, "Suppliers of Beef to Dawson," 1940: 343; MacEwan, 2000: 179, quoting from George Tuxford's journal, refers to "Rudion's" outfit.

315. Jarvis, 1899: 106; Tyrrell field notebook, RG 45, Vol. 174, September 23, 1898. Jarvis states that two thousand cattle and a similar number of horses came in, but he lost his field book and could not provide an accurate count, Jarvis, 1899: 106, 109. Tyrrell copied the information before the book was lost. The *Alaska Mining Record,* August 17, 1898 stated at least three thousand head of beef cattle were brought in, a count that corresponds to the number provided by Private Wakefield of the Yukon Field Force, stationed at Fort Selkirk, Fredericton *Daily Gleaner*, October 20, 1898: 3.

316. LAC RG 18, Vol. 155, File 484–98; Letter, Inspector Jarvis to Supt. Z.T. Wood August 20, 1898, and August 6, 1898; also Jarvis 1899: 106; name also reported as Ekjor and Elker.

317. MacEwan, 1952: 145; Weadick, 1949: 26; High River *et al.* 1960: 187.

318. High River Pioneers *et al.* 1960: 187; Weadick, 1949: 26.

319. The complete account of this cattle drive can be found in Tuxford, n.d.

320. MacEwan, 2000: 175–81.

321. Tuxford, n.d.: 67.

322. High River Pioneers *et al.* 1960: 188; Weadick, 1949: 26.

323. *Klondike Nugget,* October 22, 1898: 3.

324. Ibid.

325. Lee, 1960: 36.

326. Weadick, 1949: 26.

327. High River Pioneers et al., 1960: 187.

328. "Suppliers of Beef to Dawson," 1940: 376.

329. Weadick, 1949: 26; Gooderham, 1967: 3.

330. MacEwan, 2000: 181.

331. *Klondike Nugget,* November 2, 1898: 1.

332. "Suppliers of Beef to Dawson," 1940: 376.

333. Jarvis, 1899: 103. See also Wood, 1898: 56, which states that the discovery was made September 24, 1898.

334. LAC RG 18, Memo from A.M. Jarvis to Officer Commanding, Bennett Lake.

335. LAC RG 18, Memo from Inspector Jarvis to Z.T. Wood, September 1, 1898; Wood 1899: 40.

336. LAC RG 18, Memo from Inspector Jarvis to Z.T. Wood, September 1, 1898.

337. Redman, n.d.: 192.

338. *Alaska Mining Record,* December 28, 1898.

339. *Alaska Mining Record,* December 28, 1898; in the *Alaska Mining Record,* November 9, 1898, $165 rather than $185 is stated.

340. *Alaska Mining Record,* November 8, 1898; LAC RG 18, monthly report of Assistant Surgeon S.M. Fraser, Dalton trail, to the Comptroller, NWMP, Ottawa, November 30, 1898. *Alaska Miner,* December 24, 1898: It is possible that this partner was Jack Dalton, because by October 22, Dalton was a partner with Wiley, Fenley and Mix on the discovery claim.

341. Roppel, 1975: 2; *Alaska Miner,* December 24, 1898.

342. Untitled Articles, Earl Redman: 1–2; 195–96.

343. Roppel, 1975: 3; *Alaska Miner,* November 19, 1898.

344. *Seattle Post-Intelligencer,* November 2, 1898.

345. *Seattle Post-Intelligencer,* November 1, 1898.

346. *Seattle Post-Intelligencer,* November 26, 1898.

347. Dickinson and Smith, 1995: 25–29. Gold was found in the Atlin area by Fritz Miller and Kenny McLaren in March 25 of 1898, and claim of discovery was filed at Tagish post on July 27.

348. *Skagway Alaskan,* December 28, 1898.

349. *Alaska Mining Record,* October 18, 1898, November 8, 1898.

350. *Skagway Alaskan,* May 24, 1899.

351. *Alaska Mining Record,* February 1, 1899.

352. *Seattle Post-Intelligencer,* February 10; Kirchhoff, 2007: 103; Wright 1904: 12; Roppel, 1975: 6; Sitka *Alaskan,* March 17, 1899.

353. Roppel, 1975: 6; Kirchhoff, 2007: 108.

354. Roppel, 1975: 3.

355. Roppel,1975: 6–7.

356. Brooks, 1900: 390.

357. The *Alaska Miner,* July 15, 1899; correspondence with Cynthia Jones, June 29, 2011.

358. Skagway *Daily Alaskan,* September 15, 1900.

359. Kirchhoff, 2007: 111.

360. *Alaska Mining Record,* January 25, February 1, 1899; *Seattle Post-Intelligencer,* April 9, 1899.

361. US Geological Survey, Anchorage, Brooks Notebooks, May 27, 1899; Brooks, 1900a: 390 also mentions it and says that there were a couple of miners at work here.

362. Brooks, 1900a: 390; US Geological Survey, Anchorage, Brooks Field Notebook, entry May 1899.

363. *Seattle Post-Intelligencer,* April 9, 1899.

364. Jarvis, 1900: 62.

365. Penlington, 1972: 45.

366. *Bismarck Daily Tribune,* March 18, 1899: 1; *Daily Iowa Capital*, March 17, 1899.

367. LAC RG 18, Vol. 190, File 1900-406, Memo Wood to Commanding Officer, Yukon Territory, March 3, 1900.

368. *New York Times,* March 21, 1899.

369. Penlington, 1972: 45, 51.

370. Fraser, 1901: 57.

371. Jarvis, 1900: 60–61.

372. LAC RG 18, Vol. 168, File RCMP 1899-230.

373. See Martin, 1901.

374. Fraser, 1901: 53–54.

375. *Douglas Island News*, April 25, 1900; *Skagway News*, April 13, 1900.

376. *Skagway News*, September 30, 1900; *Daily Alaska Dispatch*, October 7, 1900; Skagway *Daily Alaskan,* Special Edition November 19, 1900; *Douglas Island News*, December 5, 1900.

377. *Alaska Mining Record*, December 22, 1900.

378. *Douglas Island News*, April 4, 1900; Kirchhoff 2007: 103, refers to Dalton's application to the government to formalize his collection of tolls for use of his road.

379. Jarvis, 1901: 55; Wright, 1904: 30. The alternate road was called the "Throp Trail," presumably a misspelling of Thorp, after the route used by Willis Thorp a few years earlier.

380. Skagway *Daily Alaskan*, May 18, 1900; June 14, 1901.

381. Morgan and Woods, 1948: 174–75.

382. *Douglas Island News*, May 15, 1901; Kirchhoff, 2007: 116.

383. Kirchhoff, 2007: 116–17; LAC RG 13 Vol. 212, File 355, Monthly report of Inspector Snyder for October, 1901; *Douglas Island News*, August 14, 1901; Jarvis, 1902: 70.

384. Skagway *Daily Alaskan*, December 5, 1901.

385. Jarvis, 1902: 69.

386. Jarvis, 1902: 70.

387. *Seattle Post-Intelligencer*, February 8, 1901. See also Skagway *Daily Alaskan*, February 16, 1901; *Alaska Record-Miner*, March 1, 1901; *Douglas Island News*, November 14, 1900; Skagway *Daily Alaskan*, October 31, 1900.

388. *Alaska Mining Record*, March 1, 1901.

389. Skagway *Daily Alaskan*, July 10 and 16, 1901.

390. This is probably the same Dickinson referred to as a trader elsewhere in this account.

391. Jarvis, 1902: 70; *Skagway Daily News*, July 10, 1901.

392. Skagway *Daily Alaskan*, July 28, 1904; *Port Townsend Morning Leader*, July 29, 1904: 2; *Douglas Island News*, August 3, 1904.

393. Kirchhoff, 2007, quoting Hanley, n.d., 49–53.

394. LAC RG 18, Vol. 207, File RCMP 1901-204, memo Supt. Primrose to Comptroller of the NWMP, September 10, 1901.

395. *San Francisco Call*, November 17, 1901: 21–22.

396. Wallace, 2000: 195–206 provides a detailed account of the event. See also Dobrowolsky, 1995: 100–101.

397. Kirchhoff, 2007: 119.

398. *Douglas Island News*, October 2, 1901.

399. LAC RG 13, Vol. 212, File 335, Monthly report of Superintendent Snyder for December, 1901, January 2, 1902.

400. Skagway *Daily Alaskan*, April 4, 1902.

401. *Skagway Daily News*, April 4, 1902.

402. *Douglas Island News*, April 1, 1903.

403. Kirchhoff, 2007: 122; Skagway *Daily Alaskan*, June 6, 1903.

404. Snyder, 1904: 29–30; LAC RG 18, Vol. 251, File 262, Monthly report of Superintendent Snyder for June, 1903; Skagway *Daily Alaskan*, October 28, 1903; LAC RG 18, Vol. 251, File 262, Monthly report of Superintendent Snyder for August, 1903.

405. Government of Yukon, n.d., 3–4.

406. LAC RG 18, Vol. 251, file 262, Monthly report of Supt. Snyder for the month of September, 1903.

407. McDonell, 1904: 73.

408. US Geological Survey, Anchorage, Wright Field Notes.

409. Jarvis, 1902: 71.

410. LAC RG 18, Vol. 251, file 262, Monthy report of Supt. Snyder for the month of July, 1903.

411. LAC RG 18, Vol. 272, file RCMP 1904-286.

412. Skagway *Daily Alaskan*, March 20, 1903 states that John Lindsay is planning to increase the size of his hotel, and Porcupine was ready for a busy season; the Sitka *Alaskan*, November 9, 1902, reports new potential for gold in the flats in Porcupine City, and refers to the excellent timber and the agricultural potential.

413. Roppel, 1975: 6

414. Kirchhoff, 2007: 122; LAC RG 18, Vol. 251, file 262, Monthy report of Supt. Snyder for the month of July 1903 indicates that Const. J.J. Joyal was fined twenty dollars by Inspector McDonell and confined to barracks for twenty-eight days for being drunk when returning from patrol. He had gone into Porcupine without permission.

415. Kirchhoff, 2007: 125; Skagway *Daily Alaskan*, May 6, 1904.

416. LAC RG 18, Vol. 229, File 448, Inspector A.E.C. McDonell to Officer Commanding, Whitehorse, June 24, 1904; Ibid., Letter Z.T. Wood to Comptroller NWMP, September 12, 1904.

417. Penlington, 1973: 82–102.

418. McDonell, 1904: 71; LAC RG 18, Vol. 212, File 355-01, Monthly report of Superintendent Snyder for October, 1903.

419. LAC RG 18, Vol. 299, File 1905-448, Letter AE Snyder to Z.T. Wood, October 26, 1903 and other correspondence; McDonell, 1905: 58; LAC RG 18, Vol. 212, File 355-01, Monthly Report of Superintendent Snyder for December 1903.

420. LAC RG 18, Vol. 299, File 1905-448, Letter Z.T. Wood to Comptroller, NWMP June 5, 1904.

421. LAC RG 18, Vol. 299, File 488: Letter Comptroller NWMP to ZT Wood August 18, 1904, and ZT Wood to Comptroller September 12, 1904; McDonell, 1905: 61; The *Daily Alaska Dispatch* for August 27, 1904, suggests that the posts are to be discontinued on September 1.

422. McDonell, 1905: 58–59.

423. By the turn of the century the origin of the place name "Champlain's Landing" seems to have been forgotten. References in text and on maps now start corrupting the original name to "Champagne Landing," and eventually to "Champagne."

424. Kirchhoff, 2007: 132; Roppel, 1975: 7; *Skagway Alaskan*, June 30, 1905.

425. Kirchhoff, 2007: 126–32; *Skagway Alaskan*, March 14, 1907; Historical Records of the office of the Magistrate, City of Skagway, Vol. 42, Miscellaneous No. 1—Porcupine, Book 2, 1901–1910, pages 158 and 160, DNR Recorders Office, Juneau February 4, 1907; agreement between Jack Dalton et al. and E.E. Harvey, February 4, 1907.

426. *Whitehorse Weekly Star,* July 27, 1906.

427. Dalton Papers, held by Mark Kirchhoff.

428. *Fairbanks Daily Times*, August 26, 1906; *Daily Alaska Dispatch*, September 26, 1906.

429. Demers, 1906: 43.

430. Kirchhoff, 2007: 114, quoting Elizabeth Hanley. Kirchhoff documents other possible romantic liaisons of Dalton

431. Cruikshank, 1990: 203. Members of the community also have provided comments about this relationship.

432. *Dawson Daily News,* June 19, 1923.

433. Gates, 2010: 11, "How I Became a History Hunter."

Index

Photographs indicated in **bold**